SHIFTING
THE SCENE

SHIFTING THE SCENE

Shakespeare in European Culture

Edited by
Ladina Bezzola Lambert
and Balz Engler

Newark: University of Delaware Press

© 2004 by Rosemont Publishing & Printing Corp.

All rights reserved. Authorization to photocopy items for internal or personal use, or the internal or personal use of specific clients, is granted by the copyright owner, provided that a base fee of $10.00, plus eight cents per page, per copy is paid directly to the Copyright Clearance Center, 222 Rosewood Drive, Danvers, Massachusetts 01923. [0-87413-860-4/04 $10.00 + 8¢ pp, pc.]

Other than as indicated in the foregoing, this book may not be reproduced, in whole or in part, in any form (except as permitted by Sections 107 and 108 of the U.S. Copyright Law, and except for brief quotes appearing in reviews in the public press).

Associated University Presses
2010 Eastpark Boulevard
Cranbury, NJ 08512

The paper used in this publication meets the requirements of the American National Standard for Permanence of Paper for Printed Library Materials
Z39.48-1984.

Library of Congress Cataloging-in-Publication Data

Shifting the scene : Shakespeare in European culture / edited by Ladina Bezzola Lambert and Balz Engler.
    p. cm.
  Includes bibliographical references and index.
  ISBN 0-87413-860-4 (alk. paper)
  1. Shakespeare, William, 1564–1616—Appreciation—Europe.
2. Shakespeare, William, 1564–1616—Stage history—Europe.
3. Shakespeare, William, 1564–1616—Translations—History and criticism.
4. Shakespeare, William, 1564–1616—Influence.
5. Theater—Europe—History. I. Lambert, Ladina Bezzola.
II. Engler, Balz.
PR2971.E85 S54 2004
822.3'3—dc22   2003020073

Contents

Acknowledgments	7
Introduction	11
LADINA BEZZOLA LAMBERT and BALZ ENGLER	

Part I: Emerging

Staging Europe in Shakespeare	21
PETER HOLLAND	
"In states unborn and accents yet unknown": Shakespeare and the European Canon	41
MANFRED PFISTER	

Part II: Applying

The Translator's Visibility: The Debate over a "Royal Translation" of *Hamlet*	67
HELENA AGAREZ MEDEIROS	
Shakespeare and Cervantes in 1916: The Politics of Language	78
CLARA CALVO	
Camel, Weasel, Whale: The Cloud-Scene in *Hamlet* as a Hungarian Parable	95
PÉTER DÁVIDHÁZI	

Part III: Staging

The British Personality of the Millennium: British Shakespeares, Amateur and Professional, in the New Century	113
MICHAEL DOBSON	
Accommodating Shakespeare to Ballet: John Cranko's *Romeo and Juliet* (Venice, 1958)	129
NANCY ISENBERG	
Jocza Savits: Organic Shakespeare for the Folk	140
RUSSELL JACKSON	

Unstopping Our Mouths: Shakespeare in Swiss-
German *Mundart*   152
  Sylvia Zysset

Part IV: Instilling

National Identity and the Teaching of Shakespeare   167
  Ruth Freifrau von Ledebur
Undoing Nationalist Leanings in Teaching Shakespeare: Shakespeare and Eminescu   182
  Madalina Nicolaescu
Children's Hours: Shakespeare, the Lambs, and French Education   193
  Ruth Morse
Teaching Shakespeare: Indoctrination or Creativity?   205
  Ros King

Part V: Rendering

Sexual Morality and Critical Traditions   219
  Lloyd Davis
King Lear: Kozintsev's Social Translation   230
  David Margolies
The Shakespearean Sound in Translation   239
  Alexander Shurbanov
Translation and Performance   258
  Alessandro Serpieri

Bibliography   282
Notes on Contributors   297
Index   302

Acknowledgments

THE EDITORS WOULD LIKE TO THANK ALL THOSE WHO MADE THIS collection possible: the participants of the conference on "Shakespeare in European Culture" at Basel University, Switzerland, in November 2001, who offered such rich and varied fare as to make selection difficult; those who were involved, in various functions, in organizing the conference, especially Werner Brönnimann, Ruth Züllig, and the team of the research project "Shakespeare in Europe"; and those who helped in preparing the selected papers for publication, especially Sonja Grieder and Sabina Horber.

SHIFTING
THE SCENE

Introduction

Ladina Bezzola Lambert and Balz Engler

WHAT DO SHAKESPEARE'S WORKS MEAN? CRITICS HAVE BEEN working on this question for centuries, not surprisingly without ever arriving at a single, persuasive answer. Yet the rhetoric of their work is usually based on the assumption that one may be given. Looking at the way Shakespeare has been understood over the centuries and in different places the only possible answer can be: Shakespeare has meant different things to different people.

But if we make this concession, which opens exciting perspectives, we still tend to take something else for granted that needs examination: that "Shakespeare" is something stable, an unchanging essence that because of its richness or its openness may have been perceived differently by various people at different times and in different places. This is a view that is spelled out in the very notion of "reception."[1] It is probably the stability of the text, especially the printed text, that tempts us to ascribe stable meaning to it. In the case of Shakespeare we do not even have a single text of many of his works, not to speak of manuscripts, to which we can try to ascribe ultimate authority. Margareta de Grazia (1991) has described how the canon of Shakespeare's texts gradually evolved toward the end of the eighteenth century, and we are experiencing how this canon is dissolving again, with new plays being included, with various editions existing beside each other (for distinct scholarly or marketing reasons), with single editions printing several texts of the same play (the two *King Lear*s in the Oxford edition, the three in the Norton edition, or the three *Hamlet*s in Arden 3).

Moreover, we have learned to acknowledge other authorities besides the text, most prominently that of theatrical production and its traditions in performance criticism, where the text figures as just one factor, albeit an important one;

other institutions like education and the visual arts likewise may have considerable authority. Instead of speaking of the *reception* of Shakespeare's texts we should then rather speak of the *construction* and *reconstruction* of his works.

Hence the title of this collection, which adapts words of the Chorus at the beginning of *Henry V*, act 2. Its essays try, without denying authority to the text and the theater, to widen the area of inquiry to include other institutions, and to juxtapose the constructions of Shakespeare and his works that have been produced by them. However, as in *Henry V*, where the scene shifts to Southampton and eventually to France, there is also a geographical dimension. The collection goes beyond England and the English-speaking world and focuses on Europe (including Britain), where, especially due to early constructions since the eighteenth century, we find a particularly rich patchwork of different views and uses of Shakespeare.[2]

It cannot be denied that widening the area of inquiry in the two directions mentioned has also its political implications. In the case of the various institutional constructions, it concerns academic politics. It tries to widen the scope of what is considered "Shakespeare" beyond the study of literature and the theater.

It may be argued that, apart from the limitations of space, there is no reason why the geographical area should be limited to Europe, especially as Shakespeare seems to have become, with the spread of Western culture, the one global author. However, the collection posits, perhaps contentiously, that Europe should be viewed as one cultural area. Whereas traditionally *classical culture* is taken to provide Europe with a common heritage, Shakespeare may be the prime example of a *modern* author who can play a similar role. We need not go as far as Harold Bloom, who claims that Shakespeare "invented us" (Bloom 1999, xvii), to accept such a claim. Shakespeare's importance for European culture is documented by the role he has played, since the late eighteenth century, for national literatures, by the many translations and adaptations made, and especially by the frequency of Shakespeare productions on the European stage.

Shakespeare highlights differences as well as a shared heritage. There is no other author whose works offer as rich material for comparative study. Since Shakespeare's time, the concept and geographical space of Europe has been determined by lines of division, channels that demarcate borders—whether political, ideological, linguistic, or cultural—separating the areas they circumscribe from what lies outside them, but also conveying a sense of unity to what lies within. In a Shakespearean context, one such channel is, first of all, *the* channel (the English Channel, *la Manche*). In his essay in this collection, Peter Holland shows how, in *Cymbeline*, Shakespeare uses the word "Europe" to distinguish British culture from a continental European one; it is the otherness of Europe that defines Britain. At the same time, such geographical distinctions often remain ambiguous. Europe as a geographical space in Shakespeare's drama remains fluid so that places oscillate between here and there, then and now.

In a contemporary context, the definition of local and regional versus European identities carries particular resonance in the vision of a united Europe and the hopes and anxieties it evokes: the shifting of centers and margins between East and West, North and South; being at the heart of Europe and outside it, as in the case of Switzerland. Yet however unified it may present itself, Europe remains a composite of distinct languages, dialects, histories, and cultural practices; it remains the result of wars, different political regimes and economies as well as different acts of self-definition. It may appear as something of a paradox, then, that such acts of self-definition should often be performed through the figure of Shakespeare. Shakespeare is a border crosser (Engler 1996) who has often served to legitimate definitions of national identities within the larger European context.

Issues like the following are of particular interest: How does Shakespeare appear in various cultures and at different times; what does his figure stand for? How have Shakespeare's works been adapted in different genres? What notions of translation have been applied to Shakespeare? How has Shakespeare been adapted to serve various regional/local, political, and emotional needs? Are there European/national traditions of studying Shakespeare? What has Shakespeare's role been in shaping the academic traditions of various countries? What role has Shakespeare played in the schools of different countries? Which plays (if any) have been read? In the students' mother tongue or in English? What has the discussion of the plays focused on?

Clearly, a great deal of work remains to be done, work that tells us something about both Shakespeare and those who are involved in constructing and reconstructing his work. This collection offers a small selection of papers from a conference on "Shakespeare in European Culture" that was held in Basel (in the heart of Europe, yet outside its Union) in November 2001. The criterion of their selection has been the extent to which they are representative of the general project outlined above, as the sections in which they have been grouped indicate: *Emerging, Applying, Staging, Instilling,* and *Rendering*. As such the collection is a contribution to a growing field of research,[3] but it also takes work a step forward by including issues of education and Shakespeare as a cultural icon.

Why always Shakespeare? What are the reasons for the unflagging popularity of his work? Manfred Pfister sees one reason behind Shakespeare's towering position in the European canon in the fact that his work refers to so many different places on the European map and thus opens itself up to various cultures. To find one's country on Shakespeare's map is ennobling and confers political legitimacy. This mechanism has become particularly important in Eastern Europe with the disintegration of the Soviet Union and former Yugoslavia into a growing number of independent states. As Sylvia Zysset shows in her study of Shakespeare performances in Swiss German, the translations of Shakespeare into Swiss German regional dialects have ennobled their language in the eyes of actors and members of the audience alike. Quite likely more so than Claudius's tardy Switzers.

Beside the integrative and legitimating power of Shakespeare's work, its apartness in relation to a local culture appears to be equally decisive for the role conferred on it. Shakespeare's role both in support of the regimes and as a subversive tool against them is well documented.[4] The gradual liberalization of the political system saw the introduction of English into school curricula as an alternative to Russian, which up to that point had been a mandatory subject at all levels of education. This made Shakespeare's plays accessible to students in the original Elizabethan English. Apart from serving as a tool for or against the regime, Shakespeare's world thus also offered a utopian space that was detached from contemporary history and uncontaminated by local squabbles. The remoteness of Shakespeare's language possibly furthered this effect in as much as Shakespearean English remained distinct from American culture and American hegemony.

Shakespeare's role in the process of establishing national identities in late- and postcommunist Eastern Europe continues an older European tradition. Germany's appropriation of Shakespeare as the father of its national drama is a frequent point of reference in the history of the dramatist's work. In her essay on the tercentenary in 1916 of Shakespeare's and Cervantes's births, Clara Calvo shows how, in Britain, the debates on how this event should be celebrated were marked by the urge to reclaim one's national poet from what was seen as German usurpation. Three other contributions on the question of Shakespeare's role in Britain and Germany today make the success of this enterprise questionable: Michael Dobson points out that, with the exception of the productions of the Royal Shakespeare Company, Shakespeare has virtually disappeared from the professional stage in Britain; on the other hand, his continuing strong position in amateur dramatics wins, at best, an embarrassed smile from critics and scholars alike. (This, one may add, stands in marked contrast to the German-speaking countries, where Shakespeare remains a towering presence on the professional stage and has almost supplanted classical German drama.) The compulsory presence of Shakespeare in the English national curriculum launched in 1990 has not improved the situation, but has rather come close to relegating the teaching of Shakespearean drama to multiple-choice exams. Ros King has tried to remedy the situation by devising new ways of teaching Shakespeare's plays to children younger than the target group set by the curriculum. Ruth Freifrau von Ledebur's history of Shakespeare in East and West German school curricula during and after the separation sets an interesting contrast to the British scene: her history gives evidence of the dramatist's strong position in German education, albeit in quite different ways in the two parts of the country.

Both King's and von Ledebur's contributions expose the common tendency in school curricula to make Shakespeare's plays serviceable to ideological purposes. In her work on French school adaptations of Charles and Mary Lamb's *Tales from Shakespeare*, themselves an adaptation,

Ruth Morse reveals similar tendencies in a remoter period in the history of education. Her essay also illustrates the great differences in the construction of the *Tales* in Britain and France. According to Morse, such cultural differences "shed light on what anglophone readers and critics take for granted; French Shakespeares offer alternative approaches to problems grown over-familiar and can offer correctives to current, insular, critical preoccupations" (194). David Margolies's study of Grigori Kozintsev's translation of *King Lear* into the medium of film draws similar conclusions in showing how a Russian rereading of Shakespeare's tragedy achieves a welcome break away from the standard English reductionist reading of the play as a private family drama and reactivates a social reading of the tragedy "that had in effect been expunged from English Shakespeare" (237). In this way, Shakespeare's translation into different ideologies and cultural settings offers new insights into his texts.

How radically Shakespeare's reception may change between different cultural settings becomes evident in Péter Dávidházi's resetting of the cloud scene in *Hamlet* into the context of Hungarian history: the exchange between Hamlet and Polonius, which in Western Europe is habitually understood as yet another clumsy attempt by the old courtier to manipulate Hamlet, suddenly appears with reversed roles. From a Hungarian perspective, the scene is about negotiations of power and the inescapable interplay between power and interpretation. To avoid having "this taken from this," Polonius has no choice but to acknowledge Hamlet's social superiority by submitting to his manipulations. In her discussion of John Cranko's choreography of *Romeo and Juliet*, Nancy Isenberg offers an instance of a cultural translation that moves in the opposite direction. Cranko's translation of the play text into the language of ballet also involves a translation from the Kirov production of the late 1930s, on which his choreography was based, into an Italian postwar setting with the radical social changes that marked this period.

The work of these three contributors reveals the potential inherent in the kind of cultural and geographical shifts of scene on which this volume focuses, and shows how foreign (re)visions and (re)constructions of Shakespeare have been instrumental in transcending the limits of regional perspectives. Lloyd Davis's discussion of critical responses to Shakespeare in seventeenth- through nineteenth-century Europe emphasizes this point by means of a counterexample: he illustrates how prominent writers in England, France, Germany, and Russia joined in the creation of a celebratory naturalized image of Shakespearean love, which rather than exemplifying a universal human trait, directly reflects contemporary moral values. Besides showing how their discourse of human love is culturally determined, Davis's argument also gives evidence of a widely shared ideological culture among European intellectuals in that period, a culture that the First World War brought to an end. Against this, Madalina Nicolaescu draws our attention to the fact that a fruitful transfer of critical positions into a different cultural context requires adaptation. Her discussion of Shakespeare's role in the academic world of contemporary Romania reveals a strong tendency to transcendentalize rather than historicize Shakespeare, resulting in strongly nationalist appropriations of his work. "The tradition of resistance against the intrusion of 'ideology and politics' [into the study of literature] has lingered on" (188) and has led to the rejection of anything that smacks of Marxism in the academic environment, including the kind of approaches feminists and cultural materialists have developed in the West. Nicolaescu therefore emphasizes the need to adapt new theories to the postsocialist context of Eastern European countries.

She also draws attention to another divide that characterizes the construction of Shakespeare in Romania as much as elsewhere: the diverging cultures of theater and scholarship. In Romania, the theater is much more dynamic and politically involved than the academic environment (a situation hardly unique to that country). This may have to do with the fact that Shakespeare in the theater reaches a much wider, less professional audience than Shakespeare scholarship, which causes it to be more alive and linked to present concerns. For this reason, Shakespeare on the stage cannot but be politicized.

Russell Jackson's essay relates an episode in German performance history of Shakespeare's plays that reflects a different trend: Impatient with the methods of realistic illusion practiced in the theaters all over Germany at the time, Jocza Savits devised a "Shakespeare Stage" with which he aimed at nothing less than showing his German contemporaries the "original" Elizabethan Shakespeare on stage.

We have referred repeatedly to divides of all sorts—

institutional, ideological, national—but have so far neglected the one perhaps most obvious: the linguistic divide that necessitates translation in order for Shakespeare's plays to be read and performed in countries with languages other than English. Translating Shakespeare is a notoriously difficult task, not least because a good translation of his plays needs to make them accessible both to private readers and to theatrical audiences. Alessandro Serpieri's contribution focuses on the translator's task to take into account the nonlinguistic codes embedded in dramatic language and to consider the performative aspect of speech so as to convey the hybridity of Shakespeare's language. Another difficulty for the translator lies in capturing Shakespeare's distinctive sounds in translation and establishing a delicate balance between excessive estrangement from the target language and total appropriation. Alexander Shurbanov analyzes this problem with reference to different Bulgarian translations of the dramatist's works, showing how some of these translations have brought about radical changes in the conception of what is to be seen as legitimate poetic practice. Helena Agarez Medeiros discusses the heated debates surrounding the appearance of the first Portuguese translation of *Hamlet* by a very distinguished translator, the king himself. They show that questions regarding Shakespeare's translatability may not only refer to how his works are best translated, but also to when and where this is done and, not least, to who translates. To return to the prologues of *Henry V*: It matters when princes act and contribute to the swelling scene.

Notes

1. Marvin Rosenberg, in his impressive studies of Shakespeare's tragedies (Rosenberg 1961; Rosenberg 1972; Rosenberg 1978; Rosenberg 1992), has tried to distill such a dramatic essence by studying productions of his plays from different periods and different countries.

2. Jonathan Bate, in a number of publications (Bate 1986; Bate 1989; Bate 1992), has discussed Shakespeare in a European context during the age of the Romantics.

3. Work of the kind outlined here has been restricted almost entirely to theater studies. Important publications include Kennedy 1993a; Hattaway et al. 1994. There is now also *Four Hundred Years of Shakespeare in Europe* (Pujante and Hoenselaars 2003).

4. For example in Hattaway *et al.* (1994).

I
Emerging

Staging Europe in Shakespeare
Peter Holland

I BEGIN WITH A QUIZ QUESTION: WHO AM I DESCRIBING? SHE WEARS "a gown of *Crymson* taffety, on her head an imperiall crowne conferred on her by the other three as *Empresse* of the *earth*, and holding in her hand a cluster of grapes, to signifie her full swolne plenty" (Squire 1620, A2v). The answer is, of course, Europe or, more accurately Europa, at least according to John Squire, the author of the description of *Tes Irenes Trophæa or The Triumphs of Peace*, an entertainment performed in 1620 to mark the inauguration of Sir Francis Jones as Lord Mayor of London, probably created by Francis Tipley. The celebration was paid for by the "right worshipful and ancient Society of the Haberdashers" of which Tipley was a member and we can therefore quite reasonably assume that the costume was splendidly ornamented. The "other three" who had "conferred" the crown on Europa were the continents Asia, Africa, and America, but all four were placed on small islands at the corners of the ship that bore the chariot of Oceanus. Since this was a city pageant, you will not be surprised to learn that each of the continents gestured "inuiting their trade vnto their coasts" (Squire 1620, A2v).

The mayoral pageant with its image of the world as competing trade-fair, with continents seeking the global market, was one of only two occasions on which Europe herself seems to have appeared on stage in the early modern period. The other was Thomas Campion's masque, usually known as *The Masque of Squires*, written for the celebration of the ill-fated marriage of the Earl of Somerset to the notorious Lady Frances Howard on 26 December 1613. The antimasque was controlled by four enchanters—Error, Rumor, Curiosity and Credulity—and consisted of three dances, each by a group of four representing, in sequence, the four winds, the four elements, and the four continents. Europe on this occasion was, as six years later, "in the habit of an Empresse, with an Emperiall Crowne on her head" (Campion 1909, 152). After each group had "daunced together in a strange kind of confusion," they "past away, by foure and foure." After which Eternity appeared, followed by the three "Destinies" and Harmony.

The plays of the early modern period are packed with individuals representing the nations of Europe. There is no shortage of individual characters or groups; there are armies, merchants, aristocrats, monarchs, doctors, and lawyers who are identified as French, Germans, Swiss, Italians, Spaniards, Belgians, Flemish, Dutch, Portuguese, Hungarians, Poles, Muscovites, Russians, Albanians, Greeks, and assorted other nationalities, including English, Welsh, Scots, and Irish. But there were no Europeans on stage; only these two appearances of Europe.

The first citation in the *Oxford English Dictionary* for the word "European" itself is as late as 1603 in Richard Knolles's *The Generall Historie of the Turkes*, a work that Shakespeare read and used when writing *Othello*. Its use in plays of the period is remarkably infrequent; my database search found only four. Massinger, intriguingly, uses it in 1632 in his play *The Maid of Honour*, when a Spanish courtier speaks of "*England*, / The Empresse of the European Isles," an explicit definition of a new English imperial status, here seen by Massinger as directly consequent on the failure of the Armada and hence on England's naval authority, for Spain "yeelds precedence [to England]; / When did she flourish so, as when she was / The Mistresse of the Ocean" (Massinger 1976, 1:128). As Europe is the empress of the continents in the masque and the civic pageant, so England is the empress of Europe in the play. The hierarchies and ranks of world governance are always clear. Ben Jonson uses "European" in a description of the antimasque for *Love's Triumph Through Callipolis* (1630), where twelve danced "a distracted *comœdy* of *Loue*, expressing their confus'd affections, in the Scenicall persons, and habits, of the foure prime *European* Nations" (Jonson 1925–52, 7:736). Neither Herford and Simpson nor Stephen Orgel glosses the last phrase, for Jonson does not indicate which are the "foure prime *European* Nations"; I leave the choice to others. Nonetheless, the word is suggesting a cartographic and imaginative space within which individual countries belong, a geographic unity, but one that has little further significance. The freshness of the word—as well as its comparative unimportance and infrequency of use—is striking. Right in the middle of Shakespeare's career, then, a word starts to be used to describe or create a concept of an adjectival Europe, but none of the four examples in plays performed before 1642 identifies an individual, someone who, as it were, belongs to the continent, a citizen of a broader concept than the nation-state.

Whatever Europe looked like when she appeared on the stage, it is the conceptualization of an entity called Europe in the early modern period that is my first concern today. At the start of his brilliant book *Shakespeare and the Geography of Difference,* John Gillies defines his concern as an investigation of the early modern concept of the extra-European, the others who lurked dramatically or cartographically beyond the borders of the civilized European world, in order to answer the question "What do they tell us, either about Shakespeare's construction of 'Europe,' or about his construction of its exterior?" (Gillies 1994, 2). But Gillies's strategy, the discovery of Europe through the examination of what it is not, does not really consider what Europe *is* in relation to another state of otherness. Put at its simplest, the crucial question seems to me not what is not-Europe but whether early modern England saw any means of defining an answer to a question that still seems to bother the English and their politicians now: Is England a part of Europe or not? Does the concept of Europe place England inside or outside, harmoniously combined with or in opposition to, incorporated or explicitly separated? Not the least important part of the answer will be dependent on reformulations of that word "England" and the understanding of which people and which nations might be comprised within it. Shakespeare is concerned at different stages of his career both with England and with Britain and the shifts between them redefine a concept of Europe and Shakespeare's nation's relation to it.

The England/Europe link is a conundrum with which Shakespeare complexly and imaginatively toys and I shall come back to that later. But when Europe and the other continents appeared in the company of the winds and the elements in Campion's 1613 masque, Campion was reinforcing an association of these three groups that was common on maps of the period. Visscher's world map, printed in Amsterdam around 1617, shows the four continents, seasons, and elements as well as the twelve months, four conquerors, and seven acts of charity, all of which take up far more space than the map itself. The trope of imperial Europe that I have described being staged was also a common visual image: Plancius's map of 1594 shows her crowned, seated with an overflowing cornucopia (a sign both of a natural plenty and a trading advantage), astrolabe, lute, caduceus, and musket placed beside her, the signs of learning, music, medicine, and war. These symbols of European-ness, power and intelligence, the arts and healing, all enable Europe to occupy as of right its imperial status, though it is armed force that actually underpins its authority. The 1620 mayoral pageant suggests some kind of meeting of the continents at which a vote is taken to agree to "confer" the crown on Europe, but this is merely a striking version of the consensual myth of colonialism, the notion that the colonized world freely and happily agrees to be dominated in this way.

It is conventional for the continents to be gendered as female but in the context of European politics the imaging takes on complex overtones. Ton Hoenselaars, in his fine article "Mapping Shakespeare's Europe," mentions that the concept as a geomorphic anatomy begins in Joannes Bucius's 1537 map. Hoenselaars has helpfully reprinted Sebastian Muenster's image of Europa Regina, the map of Europe turned into the image of a woman regnant as a celebration of Charles V's power (Hoenselaars 1994, 243). Incidentally, Hoenselaars mentions that it accompanied a chapter advising how the map might be used to travel from Basel, where Muenster's *Cosmographica* was printed, to Spain. This image, turning the map through ninety degrees so that Spain is at the head and Italy is Europe's right arm, maps Charles's imperial world by feminizing the expression of his European authority. The gender of the figured map is dissociated from the monarch. But, in the 1598 Dutch image of Queen Elizabeth as the defender of Europe against Catholicism, the conventional gendering of the region is re-formed on the body of the monarch: Europe is female because it is the Queen's body that figures it. The image of English power is also the image of the continent and the perfect consonance of the two creates an icon of natural authority.

Europe was also female because of Europa. Though the name of the woman carried on the back of Jove disguised as a bull to Crete may just as easily be the product as the cause of the name for the continent, there were examples of seeing the narrative as the convenient originating myth. Valerio, in act 5 of George Chapman's play *All Fools* (1605), in his long speech in praise of the horn, quotes Europa as one of his authorities:

> Europa when she was carried through the sea by the Saturnian bull, was said (for fear of falling) to have held by the horn, and what is this but a plain showing to us, that all Europe, which took name from that Europa, should likewise hold by the horn. So that I say it is universal over the face of the world, general over the face of Europe, and common over the face of this country. (Chapman 1968, 90–91)

But Europa was not the only myth for the formation of the continent. Its status as a pagan or classical narrative was balanced by a Christianized or at least biblical narrative, here articulated by Anthony Munday in the preface to his Lord Mayor's pageant of 1605 for Sir Leonard Holliday, *The Triumphes of Re-United Britania*:

> Most Writers do agree, that after the Deluge, *Noah* was the sole Monarch of all the World, and that hee deuided the dominion of the whole earth to his three sonnes: all *Europe* with the Isles therto belonging (wherein this our Isle of *Brytaine* was one among the rest) fell to the lot and possession of *Iaphet* his third sonne. (Munday 1605, A2r)

It is, incidentally, striking that Munday, remarkably close to the time Shakespeare would begin writing *King Lear*, describes the monarch of the world dividing his kingdom among his three children.

However Europe emerged as a conceptual entity with its myth of origin, its most frequent invocation in the period's drama is as a place of absolute comparison. Again and again it is seen as the limit of a field. The Duke in the anonymous play *Two Merry Milkmaids* tells the humble heroine, with a fine sense of decorum, "Hadst thou Birth equall vnto Wit and Beautie, / Thou wert a Wife for any Prince in Europe" (Cumber 1979, 39), just as Lewis of France announces in *The Troublesome Raigne of King John* (1591) that "A louely Damsell is the Ladie *Blanche*, / Worthie the heir of *Europe* for her pheere" (*The Troublesome Raigne* 1591, D2a). Ben Jonson is particularly fond of this kind of phrase. In *Cynthia's Revels*, he mocks those who would swear that *The Spanish Tragedy* is "the onely best, and iudiciously pend play of Europe" (Jonson 1925–52, 4:42). Sir Epicure Mammon in *The Alchemist* tells Doll that "Here, by your side, / Doth stand, this houre, the happiest man, in *Europe*" (Jonson 1925–52, 5:363). Wellbred tells Young Knowell that Justice Clement is "a citie-magistrate, a Iustice here, an excellent good Lawyer, and a great scholler: but the onely mad, merrie, old fellow in *Europe!*" (Jonson 1925–52, 3:354). The form is so familiar that it almost passes unnoticed. Europe is an imaginative space within which the crucial determinant of value can be made. It really does not matter if a woman is the most beautiful in the world: the only husband worth having would be any prince in Europe. Where else would one want to find merry madmen than across Europe? African, Asian, or American examples would hardly be worth considering.

There are times, of course, when Europe is only a conceptual comparative space on the way to a larger vision. Simon Eyre, Dekker's shoemaker, sees "the Gentle trade" as "a liuing for a man through Europe, through the world" (Dekker 1953–68, 1:56). Richard III, facing the final battle in the anonymous *The True Tragedy of Richard III* (1594), announces bravely or boastingly "ioyne England against mee with England, Ioyne Europe with Europe, come Christendome, and with Christendome the whole world, and yet I will neuer yeeld but by death onely" (*The True Tragedy* 1594, H2v). It is a linguistic form that can be comically inverted like Marston's bawd, Mary Faugh, in *The Dutch Courtesan* (1605), who praises "honest flatte-cappes, wealthy flat-caps, that pay for their pleasure the / best of any men in Europe, nay, which is more in *London*" (Marston 1968, 37–38).

The examples I have been using might suggest that the form "the best something in Europe" can only be a weak cliché and mostly used comically but when Bosola looks at the dying Duchess of Malfi something of great pain appears in the linguistic turn: "What would I doe, wete this to doe againe? / I would not change my peace of conscience / For all the wealth of Europe" (Webster 1995, 1:550).

I have been tracing this form of the word for two reasons. The first is that spoken language is also a form of staging. Europe is effectively staged every time it is mentioned. Unseen it appears in the play's determined space. The other is because Shakespeare's own use of the word seems to have gone effectively unnoticed. I will, of course, be moving on to other moments and other ways in which Shakespeare stages Europe but his use of the word is intriguing. Excuse the pedantry of working through the facts. Shakespeare uses "Europe" ten times and "Europa" three. It is not a vast number, but as a proportion of the fewer than two hundred occurrences of either word in English drama up to 1620 it seems to me an interestingly high figure. Once Europa slides into Europe as Claudio teases Benedick so dangerously close to the end of *Much Ado*:

> Tush, fear not, man, we'll tip thy horns with gold,
> And all Europa shall rejoice at thee
> As once Europa did at lusty Jove
> When he would play the noble beast in love.
>   (5.4.44–47)

The same transformation occurs to Falstaff's mind as he waits by Herne's Oak in Windsor Forest: "Remember, Jove, thou wast a bull for thy Europa!" (5.5.3). But the word and its variants seem to have been on Shakespeare's mind at this point in his career. Falstaff complains to Bardolph that "the sack thou hast drunk me would have brought me lights as good cheap at the dearest chandler's in Europe" (*1H4*, 3.3.42–44). Falstaff is fond of the word: he signs himself in his letter to Prince Henry "Jack Falstaff with my familiars, John with my brothers and sisters, and Sir John with all Europe." (*2H4*, 2.2.123–25) and tells Coleville that "An I had but a belly of any indifferency, I were simply the most active fellow in Europe." (4.2.20–22). By the time of *Henry V* the word comes to be linked to the French: Exeter warns the Dauphin that King Henry will "make your Paris Louvre shake for it, / Were it the mistress court of mighty Europe" (2.4.132–33), while Orleans's horse "is the best horse of Europe" (3.7.5).

What interests me here is the way in which the word seems particularly to appear in Shakespeare's writing consequent on his return to English histories. He had used it in *Henry VI Parts 1* and *3*: if act 1 of *1 Henry VI* is indeed by Shakespeare then it marks his clearest separation of England from Europe; as Bedford leaves to take an army to protect England's possessions in France, he announces, "Ten thousand soldiers with me I will take, / Whose bloody deeds shall make all Europe quake." "All Europe" but not presumably England, which has no reason to quake at Bedford's army's deeds. In *Part 3*, Edward, lamenting the killing of his father, Richard Duke of York, laments that "Clifford, boist'rous Clifford—thou hast slain / The flower of Europe for his chivalry." It seems as if, as Shakespeare explores the concept of nation for England, so the comparison with Europe becomes visible. There is, crucially, not a single occurrence of "Europe" in any of Shakespeare's tragedies nor, apart from the use of "Europa" that I have referred to, in any comedy. Only with the last plays does he return to the word, in *The Tempest*, where Alonso "would bless our Europe with your daughter," with *The Winter's Tale* where Paulina, apostrophizing Hermione, proclaims, "Good Lady, / No court in Europe is too good for thee," and *Cymbeline*, where Imogen did not want to lose her jewel "for a revenue / Of any king's in Europe!"

I shall return to *Cymbeline* later and at length, but I am also intrigued by the physicalization of nation on stage. On an effectively scenery-less stage, place is of course determined in spoken language and in costume. There are armies representing a series of nations and doctors from France, England, and Scotland, aristocrats from much of Europe and so on. When the lords in *Love's Labor's Lost* disguise themselves as "Muscovites, or Russians"—and Boyet's phrase indicates that he perceives a distinction between them—their entrance must somehow have visually identified their assumed nationality. But there is also the process by which characters quite literally embody nation. When kings identify themselves as countries their body becomes, with its complex interaction with the doctrine of the King's two bodies, nation itself. In *King John*, for instance, in which the word "England" is spoken so frequently (more than forty times in the play), two people are England: John himself is England. When Chatillon is asked to say "What England says" (2.1.53), King Philip wants to know what the King of England is saying. It is there too in the inquiry from the Citizen: "Who is it that hath warned us to the walls?" Philip: " 'Tis France for England." John: "England for itself." In a scene with a character called Austria the effect of a meeting not only of rulers but of nations is strong. But when Hubert picks up the dead body of Arthur on the Bastard's line, "How easy dost thou take all England up!" the corpse itself is invested with the name both of nation and of sovereignty. There are of course similar effects in *Hamlet*, which has offstage characters called Norway and England and three onstage figures who have a right to the title Denmark: Old Hamlet, who is "the majesty of buried Demark"; Claudius who asks Hamlet to "look like a friend on Denmark" and whose cannon sounds when "Denmark drinks"; and Hamlet himself, who might have become Denmark and is "Hamlet the Dane." The country's name oscillates between nation and individual monarch in a way that is unsettling and often indeterminate: which sense is it that operates when the ghost tells Hamlet "Let not the royal bed of Denmark be / A couch for luxury and damnèd incest"? And the nation can be strangely imaged as a single body with its monstrous ear: "So the whole ear of Denmark / Is by a forgèd process of my death / Rankly abused." Shakespeare stages nations simply by the entrance of a single character.

There are two occasions in Shakespeare when the range of European nations is especially manifest. The first is in *The Merchant of Venice*. Nerissa's account of Portia's suitors in 1.2—a comic set-piece, an ancient comedian's routine—explores national stereotyping for Naples, the Rhine Palatinate, France, England, Scotland, and Saxony. The young men who represent their nations so emphatically, who are evoked into the sound-world of the play to stage the gathering of European nations at Belmont in the quest for Portia, are also doubly absent. They are absent because invisible, but also because they are named and listed, considered, and evaluated only in order to be doubly dismissed, dismissed by Portia as potential suitors and by the narrative because Nerissa indicates their irrelevance: "They have acquainted me with their determinations, which is indeed to return to their home and to trouble you with no more suit" (85–87). They will trouble neither Portia nor the play. The nations of Europe recede to be replaced by the exotic otherness of Morocco and the different difference of Aragon before the arrival at Belmont of "a Venetian, a scholar and a soldier," Bassanio, who is first identified to Portia through his link to yet another place: "that came hither in company of the Marquis of Montferrat" (1.2.94–96). I find the lengthy irrelevance of Nerissa's list a fascinating piece of dramaturgy: easily cuttable but rarely cut, the comic routine stages not the glories of Europe but the gathering of its young fools, a group in which Bassanio might well be numbered. Of course, Dromio's wonderful analysis in *The Comedy of Errors* of Nell's body as world-map includes a cartographic charting of Europe by country but this is physical geography (in both senses: the world and her body) as much as a politics of nation-state.

But it is in *Cymbeline* that Shakespeare stages Europe most completely and he does it precisely because he is staging a particular version or even vision of England. It will take time to reveal what is occurring here. At the beginning of 1.4 of *Cymbeline* five characters come onto the stage, none of whom the audience has ever seen before: "Enter Philario, Giacomo, a Frenchman, a Dutchman and a Spaniard." If the members of the audience have been paying proper attention in the first scene, they may remember that Posthumus, as he left his Imogen for exile, told her that "My residence in Rome at one Philario's, / Who to my father was a friend, to me / Known but by letter." It is the only time Philario is ever named in the play's dialogue and I will return to his name in a moment.

When Philario enters in scene 4, there needs to be some way in which the audience can identify him, since we will not hear his name. There are many ways that, in performance, the group of men, clearly talking about Posthumus before his entry twenty lines into the scene, could indicate that one of their number is Posthumus's host and therefore the once-named Philario. It is Philario's function as the man with whom Posthumus is staying that matters; his name matters far less. Only at the very end of the scene, when Philario tells the Frenchman "Signor Giacomo will not from it," is Giacomo's name identified for the audience; for the rest of the scene thus far he has been as nameless as the Frenchman, Dutchman, and Spaniard remain.

I am pursuing these acts of naming—and I shall pursue them a little further—because they are part of a particular and largely unanalyzed process in the performance of Shakespeare and indeed all drama, the means by which certain kinds of information are given to the audience. Lacking programs, the early modern spectators at the Globe or the Blackfriars needed to learn about characters and location from onstage events in action and dialogue, costume, and such scenery as may have been used. Nothing in this scene tells us explicitly exactly where the action is set; only by a process of memory and extrapolation can we in some sense know that we are watching a scene in Rome at Philario's house. The complex means of an audience's absorption of information are problematic and yet largely unconsidered. How this place is determined is complex. The traditional view of how place functions and when it is referred to is enshrined in a statement like this, taken from Sylvan Barnet's general introduction to the Signet Shakespeare editions, written in the early 1960s:

> Actors would ... establish (if necessary) the new locale by a few properties and by words and gestures. Here are some samples of Shakespeare's scene painting:
> This is Illyria, lady.
> Well, this is the Forest of Arden. (Shakespeare 1963, xvi)

I shall return to Illyria and Arden at the end of this paper. In case such an elderly example appears unfair, Andrew Gurr, perhaps the current greatest authority on early modern staging, states that "Usually any special location would be signaled in the first words of a new scene" in his essay on "The Shakespearean Stage" in the Norton Shakespeare of 1997 (Shakespeare 1997, 3295).

Since the work of Bernard Beckerman in *Shakespeare at the Globe 1599–1609*, published in 1962, we have grown used to the concept of three kinds of scene: localized, unlocalized, and general. Scenes range, that is, from tight specificity like Gertrude's closet, to indeterminacy: Lennox is somewhere when he talks in *Macbeth* to an unnamed lord about the state of things in Scotland but nothing states where. But most scenes, by Beckerman's count some 209 of the 342 scenes in Shakespeare's plays written for the Globe in those ten years, are somewhere vaguely in between. The rioting citizens of the first scene of *Coriolanus* are somewhere in Rome but no one knows—or really cares—exactly where. As Beckerman argues,

> Without a doubt we know when the scene is Rome and when Egypt in *Antony and Cleopatra*. Dramatically that is all we need to know. To endeavour to isolate the whereabouts of Octavius' meeting with Antony ... would reduce the stature of that meeting. (Beckerman 1962, 66)

But how do we know where we are "without a doubt"? How does place become identified and performed? How do *we* answer Viola's question "What country, friends, is this?" There is another kind of article that I could be writing, one that belongs in a long tradition of analysis of the meaning of geographical references in Shakespeare. If you take the excellent volume edited by Michele Marrapodi and others on *Shakespeare's Italy*, the subtitle defines the purpose of the essays: "Functions of Italian Locations in Renaissance Drama." But few of the writers consider how that location is created, the specificity of referentiality, the mechanisms of dramaturgy. I feel as though my task for the next few paragraphs is a riskily dull one, to uncover a process of theatricality, to reconsider the transfer of information, to make explicit the dynamics of the theater sign-systems that reveal place within the early modern theater. How, precisely, are we told that it is Europe that is being staged? Is it, indeed, Europe at all?

Let me first return to the question of character identification. A printed version of this scene in *Cymbeline* written by George Bernard Shaw—who, after all, provided *Cymbeline* with a new ending in that much underrated play *Cymbeline Refinished*—would identify Giacomo simply as "The Italian" throughout since his name is unspoken until the last lines of the scene, after his exit. We might see this scene then as an encounter between Posthumus, who is an ancient Briton, since throughout the play Shakespeare identifies Cymbeline's nation as Britain and never as England, with Philario and four people who represent four countries of early modern Europe: France, Holland, Spain, and Italy, nations and nationalities that have no link with the early modern conception of an early history, ancient Britain, within which Posthumus and Imogen live. If Imogen's name was chosen by Shakespeare as an echo of the name of the wife of Brut or Brutus, the descendant of Aeneas and the founder of Britain, her name alludes to an inaugurating past, a moment of naming of nation as potent as the narrative of Europa and the bull. Cymbeline, as Shakespeare's audience might just have remembered from the chronicles, was king of Britain at the time of the birth of Christ, a temporal moment that constitutes another crucial mark of origin: the origins of Britain now connect directly with Christ's birth, linked also with the accession of James and the creation of his new empire. This is a play that recapitulates the whole of British and English history in its temporal stratifications, layerings that are inscribed in the namings of the landscape.

Certainly the argument between Cymbeline's Britain and Rome is with an ancient Rome, where Augustus is emperor. The problem for the setting of the scene at Philario's house is then not only *where* it is but, even more significantly, *when* it is. It must be in Rome but is it a classical Rome or an early modern one? Which one it is matters substantially to the action of the play, for *Cymbeline* dramatizes its complex interlacing of temporal levels in a remarkable creation of synchronicity; if its allusions, as in Imogen's name or in that of her husband Posthumus, which probably alludes to the grandfather of Brut, stretching the play's time frame even further back, begin in the prehistory of Britain itself, its dramatized time scales range from the moment of the birth of Christ through to King James's establishment of a new Augustanism, an inauguration of an empire that would be a "Great Britain," the precise label for the nation whose king he was proclaimed as being in October 1604, where Cymbeline had ruled over a Britain not yet able to bear the weight of "Great," to carry its crucial adjective of scale and power. It is, I want to suggest in passing, not only reference to place that dramatizes place. The drama of Britain, of British history, in *Cymbeline* is a carefully created bypassing of England and of English history in search of a larger concept of the geography of the islands. Though Simon Forman, the play's first spectator whose comments have survived, annoyingly and mistakenly headed his notes on the play "Of Cymbeline, King of *England*," the country where the action of *Cymbeline* takes place is emphatically not England. "England" is a word entirely absent from the play while, of Shakespeare's sixty-five uses of "Britain" and its cognates in the whole canon of his works, all but eighteen appear in this play. Indeed most of the other references to Britain are to an entirely different country, for the word is also used as an early modern form for Brittany, Bretagne, so that, for instance, the four references in *King John* to Arthur of Britain are to his French dukedom, not to his identification with a pre-English state. *King Lear* is similarly set in an ancient, prehistoric Britain, where Edgar as Poor Tom smells the "blood of a *British* man" while a messenger tells Cordelia that "The *British* powers are marching hitherward" while Oswald advises Edgar to seek out "Upon the British party." It is not simply that the same geographical area named Britain becomes England and then in turn Great Britain, but that the labels define differing expanses, other mappings, as King of Great Britain James had, through his own genealogy and political will, linked Scotland to England and Wales.

To speak of Britain is to perform place and history. But place in *Cymbeline* and elsewhere is also crucially enunciated through acts of naming of characters, their names functioning as identifiers of a spatial as much as historical schema. And a single name may itself traverse some of these possibilities. Imogen's husband, Posthumus Leonatus, has, as I have already suggested, a name that allusively precedes Britain itself. But the first gentleman begins his account of Posthumus's ancestry, his answer to the Second Gentleman's question "What's his name and birth?" with the potent statement, "I cannot delve him to the root." Delving into the roots of the name reveals more for the name also carries another allusion to place and time, for Scots born after James's accession to the English throne in 1603 were called *post nati*, those "born after" the Union, and the labeling of a precise moment of historical and geographical transition is made palpable in the beginning and end of the name, *post*humus leo*natus*, an effect even more clearly heard since "th" was probably pronounced as two sounds "t-h" rather than as one, "post-humus" rather than "posthumus." The character, whose name has been given him by Cymbeline himself, traverses histories and geographies, Rome and the creation of Britain, British prehistory and the most immediate contemporaneity, the name surrounded by the future of the geographical entity of Great Britain.

And Philario's name is also part of the problem of this temporal slippage. Throughout the scenes in which the character appears, his name is spelled with an initial "ph." Though we cannot hear the difference in performance, it makes the name look classical, like the name of the Roman soothsayer who solves the riddle of the play's oracle in act 5: Philharmonus. We hear in the name the Greek root of "loving," "friendly" so that this person who is Posthumus's friend as he had once been his father's. But on that single occasion when the name is spoken it appears in F1 as "Filorio," spelled with an initial "f," making the name look and sound rather close to Shakespeare's contemporary John Florio, the translator of Montaigne. As Roger Warren, *Cymbeline*'s most recent editor, notes, "'Filorio' might be an attempt to suggest a Renaissance Italian name rather than a classical one"

(Shakespeare 1998, 269). The name spoken might then harmonize with Iachimo, which is, I take it, Giacomo, a modern Italian form and with the Frenchman, the Dutchman, and the Spaniard.

These three, the anonymous representatives of place, are the next part of the problem. The Frenchman's speech identifies him as someone who has at least been in France: "I have seen him [i.e., Posthumus] in France" he tells Philario while he greets Posthumus with "Sir, we have known together in Orléans." There is nothing in his speech to represent French pronunciation, a kind of Frenchified English that, as I will come back to later, Shakespeare reserves for forms of parody. His voicing of place may be sufficient identifier: not just that I happened to see him in France as I was passing through on my way from somewhere else, but that I saw him in my own country when I was resident in Orléans. But it is his dress that must work most precisely to create national identification. There is an enormous quantity of information and comment in the period on contemporary national fashions in dress and these must also operate to identify the Dutchman and the Spaniard, for nothing else will. If we are to see visibly on stage in this scene some kind of mini–European Union, what Roger Warren refers to as "the impression of a cosmopolitan gathering" (Shakespeare 1998, 34), then that can only be achieved by the costumes' performing place, making apparent a gathering of gentlemen from a variety of visually defined, emphatically early modern nations. We can therefore reasonably argue that the gathering at Philario's represents a group of contemporaries, not ancient nations (for what, after all would, for an early modern audience, an ancient Frenchman, Dutchman, Spaniard, or Italian have looked like?). For the play to develop its argument about the contrast between Roman virtue and Italian vice, and between British virtue and European corruption, that is, between classical values and modern valuelessness, and between the value systems appropriate to a remade and renamed Great Britain and those of the continent (a kind of Tory Euro-skepticism), Giacomo needs to be placed in his time frame, in the place when, rather than the place where, something that is in part achieved by his explicitly modern Italian name, contrasting with the names of the play's Romans like Caius Lucius.

Shakespeare almost certainly borrowed this detail of the

gathering of nationalities from one of his sources, a prose tale called *Frederick of Jennen*, that is, of Genoa, available in translations printed in England in 1520 and 1560. In Boccaccio the merchants are all Italian. But strikingly Shakespeare did not keep to the nations represented in *Frederick of Jennen*, where they come from France, Spain, Florence, and Genoa. There is no one from Holland and there are two from Italy; indeed the wager there is between the Florentine and the Genoese. Shakespeare's deliberate change creates an expansion across the geographical spread of Europe, not simply something centered on the Mediterranean; in effect his choice of nationalities redraws the map of the drama, moving into Northern Europe, bringing the groupings closer to England or to newly Great Britain. *Cymbeline* stages its very particular version of Europe, the fullest Shakespeare achieves, precisely because the play is concerned to map the most complete political history of the new Great Britain. Without its Europe it can have no Britain. The otherness of continental Europe, that which lies beyond the sea that bounds Britain, is as complete as the othernesses that Gillies charts as lying beyond Europe. Europe is a staging-post on the way to finding not the other but the immediate, the political realities in their geographical mappings, that are James I's new empire.

As *Cymbeline* maps its Europes, setting a modern set of national boundaries against their previous absorption within the Roman Empire, charting the movement of the center of empire westward (the so-called *translatio imperii*) toward its new home in James's Britain (just as Cymbeline's Britain represents the westward margin of Roman control), there is one country whose status as part of this structuring of the European map is, to say the least, vexed. As has often been pointed out, most eloquently by Terence Hawkes, though from act 3, scene 3 onward the play is almost entirely set in Wales not a single Welshman or woman appears. There are Welsh names (Morgan and Cadwal), but these are assumed names. For a play much of whose climactic action takes place in or near Milford Haven (a place given its English, not Welsh, name rather in the way that Brian Friel's brilliant play *Translations* [1981] sees the renaming of place as the performance of imperialism), the potency of the place is partly to do with landscape (its natural harbor being a convenient site for the invasion by the Roman army), but primarily to do with history, for its true impact on the play is not, of course, the Roman invasion but a later one, the landing of Henry Richmond with an army to defeat Richard III, the landing that leads to the crowning of Richmond as Henry VII and the inauguration of another dynasty intersecting with the play, the Tudors. Richmond and his army, incidentally, are repeatedly identified in Shakespeare's *Richard III* as Britains in the sense of Bretons, that is, French not English, foreigners not native. Wales is effectively suppressed, erased from the play's mapping. Indeed, while Milford Haven is mentioned thirteen times by name, the word "Wales" is only heard once, when Imogen wonders "how Wales was made so happy as / T'inherit such a haven" as Milford. Wales becomes, in effect, almost unperformed, lost in the play's performances of its histories and geographies, a place whose identity has no potent meaning other than within the English history of annexation and suppression. The geographic entity is emphasized precisely in proportion to its political eradication. If there are no Welsh, how can there be Wales? The topographical fixity is set against the political fluidity.

There is a risk, along the line I have been following, that we assume that the more we are told of a place in Shakespeare the less fixed it becomes. The multiplying ramifications of place in *Cymbeline* are anxieties of history as well as geography, of the temporal nature of place and the topography of time. Place in Shakespeare is never as opulently excessive in its immediacy as it is in Jonson or Middleton, and it leads toward a kind of indeterminacy that is imaginatively potent. Though Jonathan Bate has recently argued (in a lecture at the World Shakespeare Congress) for the political significance of spaces in *The Winter's Tale*, spaces that seem as vaguely and potently imaginary as it is possible to be, I doubt if anyone can quite do the same for *Twelfth Night*'s Illyria, which seems to be named largely for the sake of Viola's pun in reply "And what should I do in Illyria? / My brother, he is in Elysium." Though Illyria is the same as the modern former Yugoslavia, I do not think there is much to be learned about the play by looking at what was happening there in and around 1600. Shakespeare and his audience thought of it as a dangerous area of piracy (as the play refers to) and as a group of city-states, rather than a nation, currently under the rule of Venice and that may explain what an Orsino or an Olivia are doing there but it says nothing of the presence of

Sir Toby Belch or Sir Andrew Aguecheek, who have clearly somehow been displaced from England. Their names key a spatial ambiguity signified by the inhabitants of such Shakespearean countries, a process as confusingly present in the Verona of *Romeo and Juliet*, where there are servants called Peter and Gregory, rather than Pietro and Gregorio, not to mention Abraham, Samson, and a count called Paris. As Stephen Orgel has brilliantly reminded us (in another recent lecture at the World Shakespeare Congress), the name of the character we see as central in *The Merchant of Venice*, Shylock, is also not an Italian name nor a Jewish one. Shylock, Orgel argues,

> is an English name—this was first pointed out by M. A. Lower, in 1849, who found a power of attorney granted to a Sir Richard Shylok of Hoo, Sussex, in 1435. The surname Shylock appears in the hundreds rolls, and the name had been, since Saxon times, a native one. It means white haired, and is the same name as its more common English equivalents Whitlock and Whitehead, which are still in use. It is not some form of a biblical name; in Shakespeare's time it was clearly and unambiguously English.

If a name performs place then the play's villain is not a Venetian Jew but a member of an ancient English family. The signifiers of place here become dizzyingly a kind of mobility, a movement powerfully toward the audience rather than away from it. And we might recall the way that both *Hamlet* and *Macbeth*, at the same point in their action (roughly, as it were, three-quarters of the way through), move toward England, in *Hamlet* for one of the travelers never to arrive while the other two, Rosencrantz and Guildenstern, fatally do, while in *Macbeth* England becomes an emblematic place of the saintly king and source of a restoratively invading army.

Gary Taylor's recent—and remarkably convincing—claim that *Measure for Measure* (in yet another lecture at the World Shakespeare Congress) was never set in Vienna by Shakespeare at all and that it was Middleton's revision of the play that relocated a play originally set, as in some of the sources, in Ferrara, speaks eloquently of the unimportance of place in many Shakespeare plays. It does not seem to me that the result of Taylor's argument is to make any difference to our perception of the play, only to how Vienna comes to mean in one part of the play's argument, a discussion of the King of

Hungary that, as John Jowett has shown, depends on events in 1621 so that topicality is a function of Middletonian revision where Shakespeare's play underlying it is neither explicitly topical nor concerned with topography. Setting *Measure* in Ferrara or Vienna makes little difference. Place is only obscurely and irrelevantly generated in a play whose characters are ambiguously from Italy or London.

It may be time then to revisit Shakespeare's geographical errors—the seacoast of Bohemia or the waterways from Verona to Milan—for the mistakes in Europe exclude England. Shakespeare never adjusts or is in error about British geography and an English audience is largely unaware of the other problems. I have to admit that, so bad is my geography, I had no idea that the link of either Bohemia or Milan to water were errors until I read a footnote. Shakespeare's Europe, as a dramatic space, has the same kind of geographical fluidity as Shakespeare's treatment of events in English history, a fluidity that allows spaces to move. But some of the movement is a complex simultaneity of there and not there, here and not here.

Of the two conventional examples of scene location I quoted earlier, one, "This is Illyria, lady," proves a sign of a space largely emptied of meaning. It is the other, "Well, this is the Forest of Arden," with which, briefly, I want to close. For Arden proves to be both there and here, now and then, subject to the shifting geographies and the disruptive histories of place that I have been exploring throughout. There is nothing new in the ambiguity I am charting. Scholars and critics have long shown that Shakespeare bases *As You Like It* on Thomas Lodge's romance *Rosalynde,* which is set in the Forest of Ardenne (which stretched across what is now much of northern France, Belgium, and Luxembourg). Oliver tells Charles that his brother Orlando (an Italian name from Ariosto's *Orlando Furioso*) is "the stubbornest young fellow of France" and the family name of the three brothers is de Bois, another of the play's onomastic penetrations of its woodland setting. With Amiens and Le Beau and two characters called Jacques, the play's Frenchness is certainly there. But so too is its Englishness: its location in that massive and potent historical forest not of Ardennes but of Arden that stretched across much of the English midlands but that was diminishing rapidly in Shakespeare's time and that had its farms and harsh masters, its enclosures and agricultural unrest, the immediate and contemporary and geographically familiar and local world with which the play deals, a forest that had given its name to Shakespeare's mother's family, the family of Mary Arden. The lords who flock to Duke Senior in the forest live "like the old Robin Hood of England" and the forest's priest is Sir Oliver Martext. We know far too little about early modern pronunciation of French or quasi-French to be sure but the names of *As You Like It* pose a problem: de Bois ("bwah") or de Boys, "Jakewez/Jakes" or Jacques ("Jark"), Arden or Ardenne. The names become potentially disambiguated by speech as if theater resists the ambiguity of place with which the play so insistently toys. The more French the more romance, the more unreal; the more English, the more contemporary, the more realist and crucially therefore the more politicized, subversive, dangerous. Which place and therefore which time was it that an early modern audience watched? Here and now, there and then? The one slides irrevocably but never irreversibly into the other, like Gombrich's rabbit/duck paradox, we can see each in turn but not both at once. The Arden/Ardenne paradox becomes an elision of Europe into England, England into Europe, a transitory, troubling performance of two places at once, a layering of one mapping onto another in a way that denies Euro-skepticism and binds romance Europe and contemporary England together. Tony Blair might wish to take note.

"In states unborn and accents yet unknown": Shakespeare and the European Canon

Manfred Pfister

1

CANONICAL WORKS ARE MONUMENTS ERECTED AND KEPT IN constant repair by the culture that defines itself, its own identity, through them. They are important points of reference within a cultural memory sustained by institutions and rituals.[1] Thus it does not come as a surprise that actual monuments or sculptures—the exclamation marks of cultural memory, as it were—commemorate their authors in public spaces, honoring them and at the same time claiming their greatness for the society that honors them. Let me, therefore, begin with one of the many monuments dedicated to Shakespeare (see illustration, page 42).

This is certainly not one of the great Shakespeare monuments: it is not the one set up in the Holy Trinity Church in Stratford-upon-Avon early in the seventeenth century; it is not the one in Westminster Abbey that has honored Shakespeare as the great national Bard ever since 1741, nor has it stood since 1758 in David Garrick's "Temple of Shakespeare"; it is not the "Gower Monument" erected in the park at the Avon in 1888 nor the one in Weimar's "Ilm Auen," the first Shakespeare monument in Germany and the second on the Continent, unveiled in 1904. As—at least to my knowledge—there is no book or catalogue tracing the spread of Shakespeare monuments in England, in Europe or worldwide, I will not put you to the rack any longer and will tell you right away where it is: the bust stands in the bustling middle of Berlin—although few Berliners have noticed so far—and it has been standing there since 1987 at a place not

Shakespeare monument. Photograph by Elke Kossmann.

surprisingly called "Shakespeare Platz," although, again, few of the many people who pass by or cross this little square daily seem to have noticed. The photograph documenting its inauguration on 27 August 1987 shows Shakespeare's bust framed by the mayors of London and Berlin accompanied by their first ladies and the sculptress Pamela Taylor, (see illustration, page 43).

And where exactly is this—to say the least—unobtrusive monument on its unobtrusive square? Those of you who have

Inauguration celebration for the Shakespeare monument. Private archives of Kuno Schuhmann.

conscientiously explored Berlin as culture-conscious tourists may well ask. Well, the situation is not some hidden corner at all, but actually quite prominent and distinguished. Shakespeare's bust and square are right across Bismarck Strasse from the Deutsche Oper, literally a stone's throw from where Verdi's Shakespeare operas are frequently performed. But how did they get there?—or, how did *he* get there? Well, when Professor Kuno Schuhmann of the Technical University, Berlin, prepared the World Shakespeare Congress of 1986, he was struck by the fact that there was not a single street or square in either part of the then still divided city commemorating the great English and European dramatist. After all, there are Shakespearean street names all over Germany; why then should Berlin, the city with its rich theater and Shakespeare traditions, be and remain without one? He therefore wrote a friendly letter to the mayor, who— the mere name of Shakespeare working miracles once again—reacted promptly and positively and, by doing so, triggered a chain reaction that would honor any Shakespearean farce, comedy, or tragicomedy. Thus, for instance, the superintendent of works for the district of Charlottenburg suggested the following worthy site (I quote verbatim, translation mine):

> Adjacent to the area where many of the employees of the British tutelary powers live, there is an unnamed space framed by Tharauer Allee, Schirwindter Allee and the tracks of the inner-city railroad. It would be easily possible to call it "Shakespeare Platz," as nobody lives there and therefore no problems of renaming and renumbering would arise.

An uninhabited indentation of an inhospitable street in front of the abandoned station of a shut-down railway line as a worthy site to honor the great man of the theater—no wonder, our colleague protested! And he was successful, and after much further ado the present site near the West Berlin opera was found, the little square at the corner of busy Bismarck Strasse and tranquil Krumme Strasse in the heart of Charlottenburg (and thus the heart of what was then still the British sector of West Berlin), complete with a design of flower beds and paths that discreetly suggests the Union Jack and the Shakespeare bust donated by the City of London. Of course, this monument came too late for the ritual, the World Shakespeare Congress. Moreover, it was not to everyone's satisfaction. It actually proved highly controversial. I quote from the *Spandauer Volksblatt* of 15 August 1987, in these preunification days still a radically left-wing paper:

> After 750 years of city history and after twenty years of a more short-range history a new square is inaugurated in Berlin. At the very place where twenty years ago the student Benno Ohnesorg was shot during a demonstration against the Shah's visit to Berlin [the seminal event that triggered the students' revolution of 1968], this afternoon a site in front of the Deutsche Oper will be rebaptised "Shakespeare Platz" and a bust of the great English dramatist will further adorn it. ... The memory of Benno Ohnesorg has been successfully repressed.

Two cultures clash here and contest each other's claims to appropriate a particular site and dedicate it to the commemoration of their own version of history—a left-wing political culture needing to mark its own identity by ritualizing the memory of its own canonized martyrs, and a bourgeois culture oriented toward the great European canon of art and poetry and defining itself in terms of this canon by exhibiting and celebrating it. What this albeit tragicomic showdown demonstrates is that canons, and the cultivation of canons, are always political—even if they are not always aware of this.

2.

Shakespeare knew what a canon is. At least, he knew the word "canon" and used it and the verb derived from it, "to canonize," more than a dozen times in his plays (Spevack 1973, 179). And he could obviously take it for granted that his audience—or, at least, the more educated part—knew it. The word, after all, had been with the English language ever since King Alfred's translation of Bede's *Ecclesiastical History*.

Let us look at what is perhaps its most famous occurrence in the works of Shakespeare. We find it in Hamlet's first soliloquy:

> O that this too too solid flesh would melt,
> Thaw, and resolve itself into dew,
> Or that the Everlasting had not fixed
> His canon 'gainst self-slaughter!
>
> (1.2.129–32)[2]

Obviously, Shakespeare does not use the word here—nor anywhere else—in the sense in which I have used it so far, not as referring to the sum total of all the works and texts that count as particularly significant, meaningful, valuable, authoritative, or binding in a culture, but in the much narrower sense of laws and injunctions or collections of such laws and injunctions, in particular those of "canonical" or ecclesiastical law. And when he or his contemporaries referred to the process of "canonization," what they had in mind was not the promotion of a particular work or author into the "top league" of aesthetic perfection and time-transcending significance but the official acknowledgment of a person's sainthood, his or her adoption into the rank of those whom the church declares to be patterns of saintliness to be imitated, and appealed to for their intercession—to be "canonized and worshipped as a saint," as Cardinal Pandolf has it in *King John* (3.1.104). What our modern usage of "canon" and "canonization" shares with the original meanings of the word is the notion of a normative guideline or pattern to be followed, be that a law or a body of laws, the exemplary life of a saint, or, since the late eighteenth century, when the term "canon" found its new application, an exemplary author or work.

Even if Shakespeare did not have the modern concept of a literary canon at his disposal, he was aware of the dimensions that we now associate with the word, namely the time-transcending authority of masterworks and its continued affirmation in the homage due and paid to them. This awareness articulates itself particularly in references to his own works and characterizes him as a Renaissance artist representative of his epoch and culture, which had rediscovered the classical models and soon began to measure its own achievements against such founding texts of a European canon. In a poetics of *imitatio, variatio,* and *emulatio* it had rediscovered the value of time-enduring models transcending national particular cultures, of working with them and trying to compete with their glory, eventually claiming for their own works the same representative and exemplary rank.

Such claims to classical or canonical status have inscribed themselves into Shakespeare's texts, although, paradoxically, these are *not* written in genres that would in themselves aspire to timeless public relevance: his emphatically private sonnets, which circulated in manuscript among his friends and patrons and whose publication he does not appear to have actively urged, and his plays written for the public, yet evanescent and ephemeral medium of the theater.

In the *Sonnets*, the gestures anticipating their own future canonization are one of the leitmotifs of the whole cycle. The repeated promise to immortalize his friend in these poems, to erect a poetic monument to the eternal memory of his beauty, presupposes proudly and boldly that the sonnets themselves will survive beyond the vicissitudes of history and live on into the distant future. The famous eighteenth sonnet already strikes this note emphatically, celebrating its own immortalizing powers and canonicity:

> So long as men can breathe or eyes can see,
> So long lives this, this gives life to thee.

This idea will appear in ever new inflections throughout the cycle and sonnet 55, also a famous anthology piece, is entirely dedicated to it. The high astounding terms and the self-assured confidence with which it speaks of its own powerful presence in this world until the end of history are astounding indeed:

> Not marble nor the gilded monuments
> Of princes shall outlive this powerful rhyme
> . . . .
> So, till the judgement that yourself arise,
> You live in this, and dwell in lovers' eyes.

What the poet says here is, of course, nothing new. Others have said it before him, and he says it fully aware he is citing a well-known topos here. Others—that is, for instance Horace, who, with "Exegi monumentum aere perennius" [I have erected a monument more durable than ore], refers to his odes at the end of the third book (3.30.1), or Ovid looking back at his *Metamorphoses* and celebrating them in the same terms. By having his poet cite and recycle the *Verewigungstopos* (topos of eternisation) (Curtius 1961, 469–70), Shakespeare recalls his classical predecessors and underwrites their confident trust in the future of their verse. With this, he also inscribes himself into the European canon and anticipates at the same time his own canonization.

The "canon" is a performative concept here: it is constituted both in the *performativity* of the texts themselves, their potential power to move readers across the ages, and in and through *performances*, that is, the acts of reception, of reading and staging, of interpretation or homage, of imitation, adaptation, parody, or other forms of creative rewriting. It is in such private or public, individual or institutional performances that their performative potential is again and again enacted and confirmed.[3] Poems do not live on in a transcendental order of existence *beyond* time and history, but by continuing to be read and used *in* time and history, and they become, and remain, canonical only to the extent that they continue to be read. Indeed, Shakespeare's sonnets again and again anticipate their being read by future readers and even thematize the future eyes and ears that will receive, and the future tongues that will recite, them. As, for instance, in the last quartet of sonnet 81:

> Your monument shall be my gentle verse,
> Which eyes not yet created shall o'er-read,
> And tongues to be your being shall rehearse
> When all the breathers of this world are dead.

There is one word I would like to draw particular attention to here, the verb "rehearse": "And tongues to be your being shall rehearse." The word refers us to the medium of the theater, which in its rehearsals and performances stages and reenacts the past and thus keeps it alive. And we, who today read the sonnet, rehearse and perform it too: our own eyes are "the eyes not yet created" and our own tongues are "the tongues to be" of which it speaks. Our rehearsal, our performance fulfills once again what the sonnet promises and is an instance and confirmation of what it speaks about, that is, its canonicity.

Under such performative auspices it is hardly surprising that Shakespeare stages the anticipation of his own canonization in the theater as well, the medium of performance par excellence. One example must suffice again. In his *Julius Caesar*, he adopted a subject that belonged to the canonical core of European history in his own time and had already been "rehearsed" in countless textual, visual, and theatrical versions as an exemplary case in political philosophy. Shakespeare's staging of the subject includes the staging of his awareness of its European canonicity or canonical dignity, the awareness that his own performance is part of a long series of performances. In the central scene of the play, there is a moment in which he grants this awareness even to his characters, who realize that what they enact on the political stage will be reenacted again and again in countless theatrical performances:

> *Cassius:* How many ages hence
> Shall this our lofty scene be acted over,
> In states unborn and accents yet unknown!
> *Brutus*: How many times shall Caesar bleed in sport,
> That now in Pompey's basis lies along,
> No worthier than the dust.
>
> (3.1.112–17)

Implicitly, the play speaks about itself here: the characters' awareness of acting, in the double sense of the word, of actually killing Caesar and of performing like actors on a stage, and their prophecy that their performance will become exemplary and canonical in ever-new future reenactments found their fulfillment in each performance on the Elizabethan stage. And within the Elizabethan performance this acquires a further prophetic force that only we, living many centuries afterward, can fully realize at each new performance of Shakespeare's play: ours are the "states unborn and accents yet unknown" in which the canonization of Julius Caesar's rise and fall as a crucially significant event in European history and the canonization of Shakespeare's stage version renews itself with each performance. Shakespeare's play not only anticipates, but stages its own canonization: canon formation occurs right in front of our eyes and ears—indeed depends upon them for its continuance.

3

Shakespeare was right: his texts have indeed survived in the "states unborn and accents yet unknown" he addresses and they are constantly reedited, translated, and retranslated, read, staged, filmed, quoted, interpreted, taught, discussed, and re- or deconstructed and that not only in Europe but globally. Of course, this is not true of all his works to the same extent. *Julius Caesar*, for instance, has been popular with English audiences throughout the centuries and has been acknowledged as a masterwork fairly early all over Europe: it was, not by coincidence, the first Shakespearean play to be explicitly referred to in Italy (in Antonio Conti's preface to his own *Cesare* in 1726), the first to be translated into German (by Caspar Wilhelm von Borck in 1741), and among the two first in Russia (by Nikolaj Karamzin after Eschenburg's translation in 1787) and has remained at the core of the European Shakespearean canon ever since. The *Sonnets*, in contrast, had to wait two centuries before they came to be recognized—on the Continent earlier than in England itself—as a classic of English, European, even *Weltliteratur* and promoted to the canonical heights upon which we approach them today.

Of course, the selection and ranking of the plays in the Shakespearean canon have not been the same in the various European countries.[4] This has not been sufficiently explored yet, and such a comparative study of national canon formations and Shakespeare's role in them is still a desideratum to which we might dedicate one of our future symposia. For the time being, I shall therefore have to make do with a few scattered remarks. *Hamlet*, for instance, has not played everywhere in Europe the same crucial role that it played in Germany, Poland, and Russia: the role of epitomizing Shakespeare's achievement and of serving as a mirror in which the receiving nation discovers its own cultural identity. And for his history plays, so tied up with the "matter of England," it took a fairly long time before they effectively crossed the channel and became part of the European canon—or, to be more precise, part of a particular nation's version of the European canon. In Germany, this happened in the years before the *Reichsgründung*, inspired by an upsurge of patriotic sentiments. It was in the Shakespeare Jubilee year of 1864 that the whole cycle was first staged as part of the festivities inaugurating the new *Deutsche Shakespeare-Gesellschaft* at Weimar, and when Franz Dingelstedt in 1867 launched the new edition of the *Königsdramen*, he accompanied it with the appeal: "Pflegt das klassische, das historische, das nationale Drama!" [Cultivate the classical, the historical, the national drama!] (Schabert 2000, 653). A very similar appropriation of the history plays occurred at roughly the same period in Romania, where they were also adopted into the canon to enhance a new sense of national identity and stimulate the production of a new national historical drama.

Finally, there are crucial differences also in the speed and intensity with which Shakespeare was received into the various national literatures and into their particular adumbrations of a European canon. In countries like France and Spain, which in the seventeenth and eighteenth centuries already had their own national theater canon to draw upon, there was, and often still is, considerable resistance to the adoption of such an un-Catholic or flagrantly unneoclassical "changeling," whereas in Germany or Hungary, for instance, Shakespeare was avidly adopted and the "Cult of Shakespeare" (Dávidházi 1998) filled the lacuna left by the painful absence of national theater classics, and at the same time provided a model for a future national theater. None of the Continental nations, however, went as far as Germany: here he was not only promoted to the towering figure of the European canon, but appropriated, indeed "nostrified," as the "third German classic," flanked by Goethe and Schiller, in the nascent German national canon (Pfister 1992).

In spite of all these necessary differentiations between plays, genres, and receiving cultures, it remains an unquestionable fact in European cultural history that Shakespeare has—from the eighteenth century onward and in a series of leaps, of which Romanticism was the first—constantly gained in European canonical status. His works are still alive all over Europe—and that not only with an academic public. And it is a measure of his international canonical rank that even people who have never read a line of Shakespeare, and have never been to one of his plays, are aware of his cultural prestige and pay lip service to it; constantly encounter traces of, or allusions to, his works in the mass media; and are able to recognize them or even play with them. Shakespeare has, as behooves a canonical author, entered the "cultural unconscious" or the "collective memory" of Europe—and beyond—and his images, variously mediated and trivialized, have become free-floating signifiers beyond the control of hermeneutic institutions and scholastic authorities. Of course, the Shakespeare canonized in the various periods and cultures has by no means remained the same. Even the very process of canonization has changed his works and what we do with them or to them: what started as ephemeral and locally bounded playscripts of little cultural prestige has been processed into one of the most valuable treasures of Europe's cultural heritage and as such demands the highest respect or, conversely, provokes iconoclastic reactions.

In performative terms, the history of Shakespeare's canonization has to be seen as a continued process of processing, recycling, and "reinvention" (Taylor 1989). Currently, this history has reached a particularly interesting and exciting phase. On the one hand, Shakespeare's European rank and status seems to be safer than ever: his texts are centerpieces in the curricular canon of schools and universities from Greece to Iceland and the theaters of Europe—even in countries like France, Italy, Germany, Poland, or Russia, which have their own rich dramatic traditions to draw upon—would have to close were they forced to do without him.

This shows that Shakespeare does not only continue to be part of the European canon but continues to occupy an eminent rank within its hierarchical orders. Harold Bloom has recently confirmed this emphatically from beyond the Atlantic in his equally monumental and problematic *Western Canon* (Bloom 1994). Twenty-six authors from Dante to Beckett constitute his "Western" canon, which actually boils down to a *European* canon; one of them, however, towers above them all: "Shakespeare, Centre of the Canon." It is with him that Bloom's mighty tome begins and ends, and it is he who has created more than anyone else and he alone who has "invented" us all by initiating the specifically modern "depiction of self-change on the basis of self-overhearing" (48).

Shakespeare as the demiurge of the modern world!— Bloom's exaggerated claims made for his canonical role already give away the anxieties lurking behind them. He writes on the defensive, in defense of a Western canon threatened by an all-leveling postmodernist culture. His paean to the canon as that great "agon" between the solitary heroes of the mind and the imagination is the reverse side of his polemic against what he calls "the School of Resentment" (Bloom 1994, 25 and passim), an insidious and invidious movement undermining our educational and academic institutions and their traditional role as guarantors of canonical greatness. With that, I have reached the other aspect of the tense and contradictory situation in which the canon and Shakespeare's place within it find themselves. They are both under fire from various directions, and Shakespeare as the bastion of the European canon is frequently singled out for particularly heated attacks. The mere idea of a canon as a hierarchical order and time-transcendent guideline is regarded as out of tune with our democratic, pluralistic, and fast-changing times. And even worse: as part of the hegemonic culture the canonical works are either in a natural complicity with the ruling class or are made to serve its interests through its educational system. The strategies of inclusion and exclusion through which a canon is formed privilege the already privileged groups and marginalize or exclude marginalized groups altogether: women, homosexuals, ethnic minorities, the working class, non-European cultures...

This critique deserves to be taken seriously—more seriously than Bloom's trivialization of it as mere resentment takes it. What is surprising, however, is that the critique has not really done serious damage to Shakespeare and his canonical status. There is a paradox at work here: the widespread criticism of the canon has not only *not* eclipsed Shakespeare's visibility and presence within contemporary culture but has actually enhanced it. In short, it has proved counterproductive. Thus, the project of "Opening Up the Canon" (Fiedler and Baker 1979) to the products of the mass media and popular culture has led to an increased awareness of Shakespeare's presence in domains far from those of "high" culture, of the extent to which he has permeated film and television and popular music, comic strips, video, and advertising down to "Kiddie Culture" (Burt 1998; Hodgdon 1998).

A similar paradox has riddled the critical assault against the canon as an instrument of oppression and hegemonic power: instead of dethroning Shakespeare, it has actually contributed toward keeping him on the academic and cultural agenda. The project of revealing Shakespeare as the "patriarchal bard" (McLuskie 1985) has not only involved new and exciting close readings of his plays, meticulous reconstructions of the gender order of his times, and dramatic revisions of the history of his reception; it has fanned out into a large-scale research project that has made Shakespeare more interesting than ever—and that not only as an object of academic research—and has enriched our experience of the plays in ways which neoconservative canonizers of Shakespeare could only dream of, were they not blind to them.

The case with colonial and postcolonial studies is similar: they have not only successfully demonstrated to what extent the allegedly timeless genius of Shakespeare was imbricated in the colonialist views and visions of his own time and to what extent canonization as the great national Bard and the icon of English cultural strength has served imperialist purposes. They have, at the same time, discovered with what subtlety his plays negotiate the conflicting relationships between centers and margins, the Self and the Other. And, drawing attention to the new English literatures "writing back" and subversively rewriting canonical works of the colonialist culture, they have shown what liberating creativity some of Shakespeare's plays have stimulated and provoked in the colonies—against the intentions of those who imposed them upon the colonized as part and parcel of the imperial educational canon (Loomba and Orkin 1998). Which shows once again that it is the iconoclasts rather than the hagiographers of the canon who are the more efficient canonizers these days—a paradox that hardly surprises once one adopts a performative view of the canon.

This paradox is also at work with new historicism and cultural materialism. Both are anticanonical and iconoclastic—or "canoclastic," if you permit me so newfangled a neologism (Lecercle 1999, 90): the American variety, in that it levels down the great masterworks to a mere tube in a system of veins or channels in which the social energies circulate (Greenblatt 1988); the British variety in its attempt to prove that canonical rank is nothing but the effect of ideological machinations in the interest of hegemonic power. Yet in the final account they both serve the canon and Shakespeare's crucial role within it—because they have contributed so importantly toward making the academic study of Shakespeare interesting once again and thus safeguarding his central place in the institutions of Eng. Lit. It is, therefore, not surprising that Greenblatt with his team of new historicists has recently erected a monument to Shakespeare, the monumental *Norton Shakespeare* (1997), which, enshrining Shakespeare's greatness within his age, defies the current critique of the canon in resolute silence. And a similar core of silence riddles cultural materialists in England and on the Continent: persuasive and enlightening as their reconstructions of the processes of Shakespeare's canonization across the ages are, and of the crucial role that class, national, colonial, and imperial interests have played in them, they have demonstrated at the same time the "virulence," the creative and provocative potential of his plays in the most diverse historical situations. The richer the results of their research, the more the one question they tend to avoid becomes irrepressible: why Shakespeare? Why not Marlowe or Ben Jonson, Robert Greene, and John Peele? Why *Hamlet* and not *The Revenger's Tragedy*? Why *The Tempest* and not *Friar Bacon and Friar Bungay*? But also: Why Shakespeare and not, or to a considerably lower degree, Dante or Cervantes, Racine, or Goethe?

4

Let us face this question: why Shakespeare? What was it, what is it, that has qualified Shakespeare and his works—

and some of them more than others—to play such a central role not only in the national English canon, but also in the European canon, and by extension in that of *Weltliteratur*? Are there any qualities inherent in his works that have made him eligible for performing this role in ever-changing performances across the centuries and cultures, qualities that would account for Ben Jonson's prophecy having come so clamorously true:

> Triúmph, my *Britaine*, thou hast one to show,
>   To whom all Scenes of *Europe* homage owe.
> He was not of an age, but for all time!
>
> (Jonson [1916] 1946, 4)

Of course, there are often-rehearsed answers to this question: his greatness or his genius, his visionary or archetypal images, his dramatic skills and his mastery of language, his impartiality and wisdom, or the width and the profundity of his knowledge of the human soul. Such "idealist" answers are of little avail, however, as they raise more questions than they settle. We therefore will have to do without them and ask ourselves in a more modest and down-to-earth fashion what has made his works so particularly open and accessible for all kinds of aesthetic and nonaesthetic discourses and performances across the *longue durée* of half a millennium.

I will take as my point of departure the one play that has had the strongest impact in England and even more so across Europe: *Hamlet*. Is it by chance that this is, at the same time, Shakespeare's most European play? Any glance at its sources already opens up European horizons: the English play reworks the medieval Latin *Historia Danica* of the Danish historian Saxo Grammaticus in a recent French version, and its hero seems to be as familiar with Montaigne's *Essais* and Lutheran theology as with Juvenal's Roman satires. Its European dimensions have inscribed themselves even more visibly into the dramatic space it unfolds: although set throughout in and near the Danish royal palace at Elsinore, the events suggest a topography of emphatically European scope and reach out across the whole of Europe—to the German Wittenberg, from where Hamlet and his fellow-students Rosencrantz and Guildenstern are called back home; to Norway, where Cornelius and Voltemand are sent to settle Danish claims; to Paris, where Laertes is to acquire courtly polish; to the Danish capital, from where the players arrive, whose report on the theatrical setup there could not but remind a London audience of its own capital; to a strangely Italianate Vienna, scene of "The Mousetrap"; to Poland, against which Fortinbras marches; and finally to England, where Hamlet barely escapes his death and Rosencrantz and Guildenstern find theirs. There is a constant coming and going that positions Elsinore, guarded by Switzers,[5] at the center of a spider web of European dimensions—comparable in this respect only to the other Elizabethan tragedy that also projects a European topography and also belongs to the very core of the European canon, Marlowe's *Doctor Faustus*.

Of course, I am not suggesting that such a European map suffices in itself to qualify a particular work for promoting it into the "Champions' League" of the European canon. It does help, however, to open it up to the neighboring cultures and recommend it for canonical adoption. Just look at the Danish, German, or Polish contributions to *Hamlet* criticism, and you will see what an important role the references in the play to the receiving culture play. Or talk to professors, teachers, and students in the new Croatia about Shakespeare, and you will soon see how important it is to them to find their country on Shakespeare's map, dubious as such efforts may be, as in the case of Illyria in *Twelfth Night* or, even more so, of the "coast of Bohemia" in *The Winter's Tale*! The effect of this is a double one: to be on the map of a great canonical work from abroad nobilitates, as it were, one's own culture and this intercultural contact with the canonical work enhances at the same time its standing within the international canon.

Almost all of Shakespeare's works trigger such effects, as the European geography of *Hamlet* only epitomizes the general tendency of his oeuvre to open up and cross the borders to other European cultures. His comedies, with one exception, all take place in continental, frequently Mediterranean realms. Of his canonical four "Great Tragedies," only one is set in England—to say nothing of the Roman and Greek plays, which unfold a Mediterranean map including the coasts of the Middle East and North Africa. Even the history plays, by their very nature concerned with the growth of the English nation and the establishment of an English nation state under the Tudors, frequently convey their audience safe across the Channel and stage national history within a

European context (Helgerson 1992, chapter 5). And the plays' intellectual map is as international and European as their theatrical topography: with Seneca's tragedies, Plautus's comedies, or Plutarch's biographies Shakespeare aligns himself with the classical European canon, and his dialogues with Italian Petrarchism and *novellas*, the French essay or with the *colloquia* of Erasmus of Rotterdam inscribe a more recent international canon into his plays.

For a dramatist canonized by his own national culture as the figurehead of insular Englishness or Britishness and associated with a "Merry Old England" of "beer and beef," of Queen Bess, John Bull, and John Falstaff, this is not a bad performance in European cultural relations, indeed. After all, what is at stake here is not mere geography but a cultural topography, a semiotics of cultures. In *Hamlet*, the name "Wittenberg" not only denotes a small provincial town in the heart of Germany; it rather evokes its new university inspired by the spirit of the Renaissance and the place where Luther launched the Reformation—the two modernizing thrusts felt throughout Europe. And to choose Denmark and not—as the convention of the genre would have suggested—Spain or Italy as the setting of this revenge tragedy was not a mere geographical translocation: it replaces the extrovert and easily kindled passions associated with a Mediterranean culture with the introvert self-questioning (stereo)typical of the North of Europe. Where in previous revenge tragedies Machiavellian "policy" and Catholic ostentation, hypocrisy, and corruption provided the explanatory frame for a world of sophisticated depravity, amoralism, or moral ambiguity, now, in *Hamlet*, we find as thematic center the Protestant ethos of religious self-questioning and a troubled probing into the very foundations of the belief in a beyond, in a divine order of the cosmos and society and in the freedom or predestination of human action.

Thus a play like *Hamlet* not only reflects a European topography but concentrates and focalizes, as in a burning-mirror, the crucial processes of transformation within the European cultures of the early modern period. It projects both a European map and a European history—the Reformation and the New Science calling all in doubt; Humanism and Platonism, Montaigne and Machiavelli, the rise of the nation-states and the new complexities of personal and political interaction. The Shakespearean negotiations of a new national and cultural self-understanding here as in most of the other plays take place within wider European horizons, and these include the colonial projects in the new worlds beyond the seas as well. This opens up his plays to a European dialogue with and about them—a dialogue that will continue as long as the questions they raise are still our questions, or can be recognized and reformulated as ours. Here I would argue with and against Gadamer at the same time: what keeps canonical works canonical is, indeed, a hermeneutics of questions and answers.[6] What keeps Shakespeare, as any classical author, alive and in the canon are, however, less the answers he may proffer to new questions than the questions his texts raise and that, by our recognizing them as still ours, will provoke us to new answers. The provocative power of his questions as to the nature of subjectivity, the relationship between the subject and increasingly precarious metaphysical and ideological constructions, or the conflict between divergent social, ethnic, and gender orders has proved efficacious right down to our postmodern present—or particularly in our postmodern present, which begins to recognize its own immediate prehistory in early modern Europe, even more so than in previous periods. The one Shakespeare that ruled the canon in the eighteenth century, may no longer exist, but his pluralization into a rather heterogeneous host of "Shakespeares" is a sign of canonical strength rather than weakness.

Shakespeare's career within the European and the global canon was also fostered by the very medium he worked in— his language and the theater. By "language" I do not intend here the poetic excellence of his language in verse and prose; this is, after all, a quality that easily gets lost in translations, and some of the early translations—many of them translations of translations—were linguistically and poetically so poor that Shakespeare's canonization could be said to have occurred in these cases in spite, rather than because of, the language of the texts read or performed. What I rather intend is again something much more basic—the simple fact that Shakespeare wrote in English. In his own times, English was a rather marginal language in Europe. As John Florio (1969, 59) had it in the fifteenth Anglo-Italian dialogue of his *First Fruits*:

> what thinke you of this English tongue, tel me, I pray you? It is a language that wyl do you good in England, but passe Douer, it is woorth nothing.

> Is it not vsed in other countreyes?
> No sir...

To write in such a language is a liability rather than an asset on one's way to European canonization, and it was not before the position of English within the European polyphony changed that Shakespeare—his works and not just the distant reputation of his name—began to be adopted into the European canon. The first signs of change were felt already in the second half of the seventeenth century when Giovanni Torriano, one of Florio's successors as Italian teacher in London, wrote in the preface to his *Piazza Universale di Proverbi Italiani* in 1666:

> In somma la Lingua *Inglese* è hoggi giorno una Lingua copiosissima, fiorita, & concettosa, & degna che il Forastiero ci metta studio & applicatione ad impararla & possederla come si deve, quando non fosse per la parlata, almeno per intender & capire le loro Comedie & Tragedie stupendissime.[7]

The international success of Shakespeare's and his contemporaries' "Comedie & Tragedie stupendissime" in the eighteenth century was to a considerable extent due to an increased European interest in all things English—its trade and commerce, its liberal constitution, its self-confident middle class, its scientific advances, its philosophy and journalism, its humor and sentiment—that in turn stimulated an interest in the English language and literature all over the Continent. Shakespeare's language, in his own days barely known "passe Douer," challenged the position of French as the leading European language in the eighteenth century, was spoken within a worldwide empire in the nineteenth century, and has, in the twentieth century, become the global lingua franca of a world dominated by an earlier British colony and together with this Shakespeare became first a European, now a global player (Bode 2000, 39). Where Latin lost its function as lingua franca long ago, and where the classical languages in general have survived only in narrowly circumscribed niches; where French, Italian, Spanish, German, or Russian—in spite of all political lip service paid to a polyglot European Union—are, outside their own territories, understood by small elites only, Shakespeare by now has a potential readership and audience of more than a billion worldwide.

But, of course, Shakespeare's plays are more than just language; their texts script theatrical performances that rely only in part upon verbal means to communicate with the audience. They were written for a fairly new and "hot" medium, the public theater, which had become within a few decades the only mass medium in early modern England to rival the sermon in appealing in spoken language to audiences recruited from—almost—all levels of society and walks of life. To write successfully for such a medium, as Shakespeare did, meant to meet and satisfy widely divergent cultural and aesthetic expectations. The art required in this was, indeed, one of offering "caviare to the general," and that made for plays that were at the same time popular and sophisticated, excitingly spectacular and intellectually demanding, entertaining, and critically incisive. Drawing upon native popular traditions (Weimann 1967) as well as upon the canonized European cultural heritage, these products of a nascent early modern entertainment industry already anticipated what postmodern art often only dreams of, namely, to "Cross the Border—Close the Gap" between high and low, between popular and elitist culture (Greenblatt 1988). Encouraged by their very medium, the public theater, to straddle these borders and gaps, Shakespeare's plays have proved to be accessible to ever new audiences across the centuries and cultures. That this is also a factor that contributed importantly to Shakespeare's unprecedented canonical success all over Europe can easily be shown by way of contrast: a Petrarch or a Racine never ventured such feats and the very media they worked in and the very notions of art they adhered to would have ruled them out to begin with.

Equally important has proved to be the fact that plays, and Shakespeare's plays in particular, are not only "words, words, words," but flamboyantly engage nonverbal means—gesture and movement, action and interaction, music and stage effects—to convey their total meaning. Being beyond language, they have helped to carry Shakespeare's plays across language barriers. This process of "Europeanization" began already during Shakespeare's lifetime with the "English Comedians" performing drastically simplified adaptations of his or Marlowe's plays, first in English, then in maccaronic versions, along itineraries crisscrossing large parts of the Continent (Price 1953, chapter 2; Limon 1985). They proved effective and stageworthy quite independent of the name of the author, who did not even have a name outside England at that point, and also quite independent of the language, the particular poetic qualities of which got completely lost on the way. That Shakespeare's European canonization occurred not because, but rather in spite of, the poetic richness and density of his language, was further instanced in the eighteenth century, when his plays survived the most inadequate translations or free adaptations in highly successful performances, as was, for example, the case with Tsarina Catherine's the Great disarmingly self-confessed "free but weak translation" of *The Merry Wives of Windsor* (1786) (Stříbrný 2000, 29), or, again, in the nineteenth century, when the libretti and the music of Rossini's, Nicolai's, Berlioz's, and especially Verdi's operas dissolved or drowned Shakespeare's words and yet charged the situations, gestures, spaces, and images of his plays with new and fascinating energies.

Due to the theatrical medium for which it was written, Shakespearean drama is more open to new readings than epic poetry or novels are. In dramatic texts there is no narrator that would control the reader's access and guide his or her approaches and responses. This is particularly true of Shakespeare's plays: even the stage directions, which in other historical forms of drama fix what is to be seen on stage, are minimal and, what is more important, here the characters seem to speak entirely from their own position and do not lend themselves to serve as mere mouthpieces to the author's intentions. This turns Shakespeare's dramas into open texts, which present a spectrum of perspectives crisscrossing and qualifying each other rather than project one single, overarching point of view. Instead of an overall normative construction of meaning, "all that is conveyed to the receiver is the perspectival relativity of all value norms" (Pfister 1988, 68). This again opens up Shakespeare's plays to a wide range of possible stagings, interpretations, and appropriations and makes for canonical longevity. It is this openness that draws us again and again into the complex mirror hall of ambiguities, ironies, and contradictions, as the New Critics described Shakespeare's dramatic poems, or into the labyrinth of an interminable semiosis, as the more recent jargon of poststructuralism and deconstructionism has it. "Shakespeare und kein Ende": this is how Goethe put it in 1815, he, too, locating Shakespeare's canonical status in the continuing power of his plays to provoke new and subvert canonical readings (Goethe 1963, 287).

I am not arguing for an "anything goes" in Shakespearean performance and interpretation here; my point is, rather, that the structural openness and indeterminacies of Shakespeare's texts and their self-deconstructive potential (Lubrich 2001) have been a crucial prerequisite for their transcultural and European canonization. Because *Henry V* could be read both as a celebration and a deconstruction of national greatness and ideal kingship; because Coriolanus could be staged both as the quintessence of male strength of character and as a pathologically disturbed protofascist; because *The Tempest* could be understood both as a colonial dream and its nightmare shadow; because Shylock could appear as both an anti-Semitic fantasy and deeply human; because Shakespeare's plays could be both rejected as the work of a "patriarchal bard" complicit with the misogynous gender division of his time and endorsed as critical experiments with new gender roles: because his art could be celebrated both as an expression of pure nature and natural genius and the supreme achievement of self-reflecting sophistication . . . because, to sum up, the most diverse, even mutually contradictory positions left, right, and center could find confirmation in Shakespeare and his works could "paradoxically serve both sides in their respective efforts to draw ideological lines and define national identities" (Schabert 2000, 610; my translation) has Shakespeare remained not only a part, but at the very core of the European canon.

Beyond that, there are limits that we are more painfully aware of these days than in the recent past of multicultural euphoria. The collapsing twin towers of the World Trade Center mark the limits not only of a global economy but also of a global cultural canon.

Notes

1. Cf. the various publications of Jan and Aleida Assmann, in particular Assmann and Hölscher (1988), Assmann and Harth (1991a and 1991b).
2. This, as all Shakespearean quotations here, is taken from *Shakespeare* (1997).
3. For the particular use of "performance" and "performativity" here, see Pfister (2001) as well as Fischer-Lichte and Wulf (2001).
4. Cf. the comparative approaches in Bauer (1988) and Larson (1989).

For the present situation cf. Hattaway, Sokolova and Roper (1994) and Joughin (1997a). For a comparative study of Shakespeare's impact upon East European cultures cf. Stříbrný (2000).

5. Thanks to Markus Marti for having drawn my attention to their presence in the play.

6. Gadamer (1975, 269–75). Cf. also Küpper (1997, 58).

7. "The English language is to-day a most copious, most flourishing, most pregnant Tongue, and worthy that a Foreigner should apply himself to learn it, if not sufficiently to speak it, at least enough to understand their stupendous Comedies and Tragedies"—quoted from Yates (1934, 324).

II
Applying

The Translator's Visibility: The Debate over a "Royal Translation" of *Hamlet*

Helena Agarez Medeiros

UNTIL THE LAST QUARTER OF THE NINETEENTH CENTURY, SHAKEspeare's texts were virtually unknown among Portuguese readers, with the exception of an intellectual elite who could read his plays in French translation. In fact, only in 1877 was a play by Shakespeare translated directly from the English text, thus breaking the overall pattern of this playwright's reception in Portugal. To this date, only two of his dramas had appeared in translations,[1] most of them based on the French versions by Ducis.[2] However, even if they were not familiar with the texts themselves, Portuguese audiences were widely acquainted with the characters of Shakespeare's main tragedies. Operatic adaptations of Shakespeare's works were often brought to the Portuguese stages by foreign companies and the translations of the corresponding libretti were given wide circulation among the bourgeoisie and the upper classes. In addition, itinerant theatre companies visited Portugal frequently and played Shakespeare in French and Italian. (The performances of Rossi and Salvini were particularly appreciated and widely commented on; indeed, they would become the yardstick against which future Portuguese performances would be assessed).

In September 1877, Luís I, who had been king of Portugal for sixteen years, published a Portuguese version of *Hamlet*, the first of what was to become a series of his full text and direct translations of Shakespeare's dramas.[3] This date is now commonly accepted as the turning point in the reception of Shakespeare in Portugal. The cover of this "Portuguese translation" of *Hamlet* did not include any reference to the translator. The translation was published in a luxury edition of very small circulation—the copies were meant as personal gifts from the king to people of his choice. The identity of the translator was kept secret, but each copy was signed by the king.

On 11 September 1877, two Portuguese daily newspapers (*Diário da Manhã* and *Jornal da Noite*) published different excerpts from the king's text on the front page. Only the latter referred to "His Majesty King D. Luís" as the author of the translation, whereas *Diário da Manhã* decided not to betray what was supposedly the king's desire for anonymity. However, the secret had long been lifted since, in December 1876, Portuguese newspapers printed translations of articles that had appeared a few days before in two English papers. *The Times* and *The Athenaeum* had publicized the forthcoming Portuguese version of *Hamlet* and disclosed the identity of the translator. Nine months after the information that, curiously enough, came to Portugal from England,[4] the "royal translation," as it became immediately known, was given wide coverage in the Portuguese press. Almost every national newspaper and journal and much of the local press published articles in praise of the translation, either written by Portuguese journalists and intellectuals or translated from foreign newspapers (the English *Times* and *The Athenaeum*, the French newspapers *Le Gaulois*, *Le Figaro*, and *Journal des débats* and the Spanish *Solféo*). Even if the general tone of the majority of these reviews was highly laudatory, a few voices of dissent cried out against the translation and strongly criticized what they perceived as ignominious demonstrations of courtly flattery on the part of the authors of the favorable reviews. In turn, those who praised the king regretted the fact that "the Republicans" had decided to attack him "in the neutral field of literary discourse."[5] The debate raged between September 1877 and July 1878 at least,[6] and reached its peak in January 1878, with the publication of Alfredo Ansúr's virulent manifesto *Le roi traducteur ou Vive la république*.

This paper seeks to draw the contours of what turned out to be a debate between monarchists and republicans on the occasion of the "royal translation" of *Hamlet*. An analysis of the texts published in the Portuguese press during the above-mentioned time span allows for the hypothesis that the debate served strongly marked political purposes at a time when the Portuguese political regime suffered increasingly frequent bouts of criticism.[7] Given these circumstances, a brief overview of the political situation at the time of the publication of this translation of *Hamlet* is in order.

King Luís was Portugal's fifth constitutional monarch and reigned between 1861 and 1889. His was a period marked, on the economic level, by a liberal project designed to foster Portugal's industrial development and improve its road and railway systems through extensive loans of foreign capital and heavy taxes. The Party of Regeneration was the political instrument of this wave of modernization that had begun sweeping the country in the mid-1850s. In political terms, although very few major disruptions affected Portugal, this reign was characterized by a marked instability with frequent changes of government—in 1870, for instance, five different cabinets ruled the nation—and parties violently attacking each other in their struggle for power. In 1876, the country's two major parties—the Party of Regeneration and the Progressive Party—began alternating in power, with the king playing the umpire.

The Party of Regeneration ruled between 1871 and 1877, giving Portugal its longest period of political stability in the nineteenth century. The 1870s were also the decade in which the Republican party laid its foundations. In 1873, the "Federal Republican Center of Lisbon" was founded; three years later, on 2 April 1877, the Republicans (until then divided into different factions) perfected their union through the foundation of the "Republican Democratic Center," and in January 1878 the first Republican deputy was elected as a member of Parliament. Republican centers, clubs, associations, and periodicals were the means whereby the struggle for a radical constitutional change was set in motion in the 1870s.[8]

On 5 March 1877, this long period of stability came to an abrupt end when Fontes Pereira de Melo, head of the Regeneration government, withdrew from office on (allegedly) personal grounds, causing the cabinet to resign and the king to form a new government. Strongly partial to the Party of Regeneration, the king considered this removal from power to be temporary and appointed the Duke of Ávila, a man with undefined political allegiance, to form a government. This contrasted with the system the king had implemented the previous year, whereby the resigning cabinet should be replaced by the country's second major party.

Until the end of the Ávila government (January 1878),

strong attacks on the king were published almost daily in Portuguese newspapers—he was accused of disobeying the Constitutional Charter by deciding to rule instead of merely reigning. The charge was that the king was trying to "while away" the time during which his favorite party would be absent from power by appointing a politically harmless minister in total disregard of the nation's wishes, thus abusing his powers. In doing so, he had brought upon himself full responsibility for the turn of events, a responsibility that, according to article seventy-two of the charter, he should be deprived of as a mere reigning figure,[9] "the nation's supreme head of State" (article seventy-one). Periodicals of the opposition and those published by the Republican Party emphasized the king's alleged complicity with the Regenerators' corrupt government, his disregard for the nation's will, his disrespect for the Constitutional Charter, his susceptibility to flattery and, above all, his show of "personal power" (the phrase became commonplace in the contemporary press).

When, in August 1877, the party of Regeneration proclaimed itself "the king's party," diatribes against the king flooded the press: the monarch was accused of stepping down from his high office as the nation's foremost magistrate to become the head of a political party—another proof of "personal power" that evidently could not be conceived of in a constitutional monarchy.

The Republicans saw in this event another proof of the monarchy's "rottenness" (this term's equivalent in Portuguese, "podridão," had, for a few years, been frequently applied to characterize the state of internal politics, namely in periodicals) and, consequently, the urgent need for a change in the political setup.[10] In January 1878, the "King's Party," as it came to be known, was in power again and violent attacks on the king were once again given wide coverage in Portuguese newspapers. The slanderous allegations against Don Luís and the "rotten" state of Portugal went on undisturbed until the fall of the Regeneration government in May 1879.

This, in very broad strokes, was the political context in which the "royal translation" of *Hamlet* saw the light of day. On 16 September 1877, a literary journal (*Revista Literária do Porto*) that would soon publish a strongly hostile review of the king's translation asked: "Has any particular idea motivated this translation or was the king merely trying to convey his commitment to fine literature? It is only natural that, while writing Shakespeare's magnificent scenes, his majesty should be thinking of our politicians."[11] A few months later, in his manifesto *Le roi traducteur ou Vive la république*, the Republican Alfredo Ansúr claimed that the king's choice had been "tactless" since the play he had translated depicted his own situation as a monarch.

According to the authors of these remarks, the translation of *Hamlet* could have served the purpose of unveiling, through a process of analogy, Portugal's political environment at the time. However, apart from the aforementioned comments, the published reviews of the "royal translation" failed to look into this translator's ideological motivations, and merely brought out examples of translation errors or "infidelities" taken from the published excerpts.

The favorable reviews that appeared in the press almost invariably began by stressing the invaluable service the king had done to Portuguese literature: this translation of a Shakespeare play was seen as the means to fill in a gap Portugal should be ashamed of, being the only country in Europe still deprived of translations of the "great Bard." King Luís was considered to have paid deserved homage to another king—the majesty of birth bowing before the majesty of genius—and thus performing a highly patriotic duty. The claim was that the "throne" occupied by Shakespeare in international literature turned the effort put into this translation into an event worthy of praise, regardless of the quality of its outcome.

In fact, King Luís's task was considered all the more commendable when seen in the light of late-nineteenth-century Portuguese theory of translation, still dominated by the postulate of impossibility.[12] The motto "traduttore, traditore" (common in translation prefaces and reviews) was considered axiomatic, insofar as any translation that failed to give both the words and the sense of the original was inevitably "unfaithful" and thus seriously flawed. Moreover, Shakespeare was considered the most difficult author, and *Hamlet* his most untranslatable text. The extreme, insurmountable difficulty of translating Shakespeare, and this tragedy in particular, is discussed in at least ten of the thirty-six texts analyzed. It is allegedly due to this author's "bold images," "refined irony," use of obsolete words, intricate sentences, and the abundance of idiomatic expressions. Having stated this much, those who praised the king were unanimous in regarding this translation as "unimpeachable,"[13] "perfect,"[14] "excellent,"[15] so "faithful"[16] that it was even approved of by English critics.

The king's detractors—invariably Republicans—also underlined Shakespeare's greatness but strongly opposed any claims of fidelity on the part of those who applauded the translator's work. Instead, the king was accused (namely by Alfredo Ansúr) of "disrespecting," even "murdering" Shakespeare. In fact, he had uprooted *Hamlet* from its origins as a text *ad usum populi* and turned it into a text *ad usum Delphini*; he had cured Hamlet of his madness, cleaned him up and made him eligible for tea in the house of prudish families.[17] This civilized, courtly *Hamlet* was seen as a "pseudo-literary transfiguration of one of the most sublime creations of the English poet,"[18] an utter "disrespect" for Shakespeare.[19] To this Valentina de Lucena replied, on 21 October 1877, that the king was entitled to the "whim" of rewriting Shakespeare, of protesting against the "barbarisms" and "oddities" of this "great savage," thus giving of him an image he believed best suited contemporary society.[20]

As far as this translator's attitude to the original text was concerned, the two poles of dissent had been established: on one side stood those who believed the king had done what was expected of him (rendering faithful homage to Shakespeare), on the other stood those who claimed he had disrespected the "great bard" by adapting him to a "civilized" society. With the exception of Valentina de Lucena's remarks, this debate brought to the fore the importance of a "faithful" translation of Shakespeare, at a time when Portuguese theater companies lived almost exclusively on adaptations or imitations of foreign drama. These practices were not only widely accepted by audiences, but also fiercely defended by dramatists and translators in theoretical terms. In fact, an adaptation or an imitation were, theoretically as well as legally, considered equivalents of an original text, whereas a literal ("faithful") rendering of a dramatic work was regarded as a second-rate activity, and paid accordingly. Because complete faithfulness in translation was considered impossible, a literal rendering of a text could not become an equivalent of the original work, but a mere shadow of it. Adaptations and imitations, on the other hand, could offer evidence of real literary talent.

Just as he should limit himself to reigning instead of wanting to rule, King Luís should limit himself to translating instead of taking the liberty of adapting. Fidelity both to the Charter and to Shakespeare's text was expected of him. Both in political and literary matters, the king was supposed to assume a position of submission, avoiding the imposition of his own reading of *Hamlet* as he should avoid the imposition of his own political preferences. During the aforementioned political crises, the king was repeatedly accused of displays of "personal power." Similarly, this translation was referred to as an act of "personal power": the king had stepped down from his throne to enter a realm to which he did not belong, since he had never given proof of his literary skills by publishing an original work.[21]

Anonymity was another feature of the translation that gave rise to many comments: Monarchist critics attributed the omission of the king's identity to "excessive modesty," whereas Republicans saw nothing but a display of cowardice, a subterfuge designed to avoid harsh criticism on the part of those who were inevitably prone to it (themselves, mostly) and to attract the flattery of those who depended on the monarch's favors (and who were offered signed copies of the text). King Luís was accused of trying to escape responsibility for his actions by obtaining as a translator the immunity he was granted as monarch. In short, he seemed to think the constitutional prerogative of article seventy-two of the Charter should lose none of its validity when applied to the literary field.

Even though the analysis of the reviews this translation received could take us much further, I will, for the moment, limit myself to a few final remarks on a recurring issue in these texts: the contradictory evaluation of the king's linguistic and exegetic skills. In laudatory reviews, strong emphasis was laid on the king's flawless mastery of both the English and Portuguese languages as well as on such a perfect understanding of "the author's thoughts" that Shakespeare's "hidden beauties" were actually "enhanced."[22] According to these critics, the king gave ample evidence of outstanding intellectual abilities, thus adorning his dynasty with "new laurels" of a spiritual nature.[23] In the other camp, both Silva Pinto (in his review published by the *Revista Literária do Porto*) and Alfredo Ansúr, in his long abuse against King Luís, accused him of ignorance of the English and Portuguese languages and of serious misinterpretations of Shakespeare's words. The translator's style is deemed "awkward," "appalling," with frequent (and violent) attacks on the syntax.

Deprived of his powers as political ruler and military leader, the constitutional monarch's dignity ultimately rests in the superiority of his education and social skills, which alone should set the highest standards of his country's civilization. To deny the king acknowledgment of these faculties amounts to undermining his position as the nation's foremost representative, thereby denigrating monarchy itself.[24]

In a historical juncture of severe antiestablishment activity, King Luís's translation of *Hamlet* was used as a weapon in the Republican challenge to the legitimacy of monarchic rule. In the realm of politics, the king was chastised for ruling instead of complying with his institutional role of arbitrator, deprived of real power of intervention, but also of real responsibility. This call for submission on his part (to the Charter, to the nation, to the ruling government) was echoed by a call of a different nature—the king was expected to surrender to Shakespeare's genius by translating his dramas "faithfully." This was one of the first moments in the history of Shakespeare's reception in Portugal in which his works were accepted almost unanimously without reservations, without denigrating references to his barbarism or rudeness. Shakespeare was the exception to the rule whereby dramatic works ought to be adapted to the taste of Portuguese audiences—the words of this great genius could neither be adapted nor imitated. Their superiority deserved the respect granted to the words of the Gospel, even if the ultimate aim of the translation—complete faithfulness—was deemed unattainable. This translation of *Hamlet* was indeed the first of a series of Portuguese renderings of Shakespeare's dramatic works based directly on the original text, even though its influence on the prevalent theories of translation concerning dramatic works was scarce.

Trying to govern, King Luís was brought to Republican trial, just as trying to become an author at the expense of Shakespeare earned him severe criticism. Whether in politics or in literature, the Republican message was that this king's tendency to abuse power, to set forth his own set of values and to avoid responsibilities was a sign of the "rotten" state of Portuguese monarchy.[25]

NOTES

1. Different versions of *Othello* appeared in the 1770s (unspecified date), in 1834, in the 1850s (again, the date is unknown), and in 1856. In 1874, the leading Romantic poet António Feliciano de Castilho published his indirect translation of *A Midsummer Night's Dream*.
2. Ducis produced the following Shakespearean adaptations for the French stage: *Hamlet* (1769), *Roméo et Juliette* (1772), *Le Roi Lear* (1783), *Macbeth* (1784), and *Othello* (1792). His version of *Hamlet* was particularly successful—the Comédie Française repeatedly brought it to the stage until 1851.
3. Only six of the king's translations were published: *Hamlet* (Lisbon: Imprensa Nacional, 1877), *O Mercador de Veneza* (Lisbon: Imprensa Nacional, 1879), *Ricardo III* (Lisbon: Imprensa Nacional, 1880) and *Othello* (Porto: Imprensa Portuguesa, 1885). However, he also translated *Romeo and Juliet* (*Romeu e Julieta*), *The Taming of the Shrew* (*A Esquiva Domada*), *The Rape of Lucrece* (*O Estupro de* Lucrécia), and *Venus and Adonis* (*Vénus e Adónis*).
4. This would undoubtedly deserve specific investigation, but it is beyond the scope of the present paper.
5. Pinheiro Chagas in *Diário da Manhã*, 27 December 1877.
6. References to the "Royal translation" followed the publication of another translation of *Hamlet* by poet laureate Bulhão Pato in 1879. The two texts were then widely compared.
7. I have analyzed thirty-six articles and reviews published between 11 September 1877 and 10 July 1878 in periodicals belonging to different political factions (Partido Regenerador, Progressista, Republicano). The corpus used for this paper also includes Alfredo Ansúr's *Manifesto*, published in Lisbon in January 1878.
8. Two influential newspapers of wide circulation in Lisbon were founded : *O Rebate* (1873) and *Democracia* (1874).
9. Article seventy-two reads: "The person of the king is immune and sacred. He is not liable to any sort of responsibility" (my translation).
10. It is, therefore, significant that the king should have avoided this term in his translation. In fact, the Portuguese rendering of "Something is rotten in the state of Denmark" (1.4.90) reads: "Algum vício há na constituição da Dinamarca" (literally: "There must be some vice in the constitution of Denmark").
11. *Revista Literária do Porto*, 16 September 1877, p. 71, anonymous remarks (my translation).
12. In Portugal, nineteenth-century authors did not produce a corpus of texts dealing with general aspects of translation, or developing particular theoretical approaches. All that can be said about Portuguese theory of translation derives from the analysis of prefaces, notes, and reviews of translated texts.
13. *Comércio do Porto*, 11 September 1877; *Revista Literária do Porto*, 16 September 1877. None of these reviews were signed.
14. Charles Sellers in a review first published in *The Times* (27 November 1877) and then translated into Portuguese and published in *Comércio do Porto* and *Diário Popular* (17 December 1877).
15. *Journal des débats* (article quoted in *Diário do Comércio* on 19 October

1877) and *Diário da Manhã* (27 December 1877, review signed by Pinheiro Chagas).

16. William Allen in *The Financial and Mercantile Gazette* (1 October 1877) and Pinheiro Chagas in *Diário da Manhã* (29 December 1877).
17. Ramalho Ortigão in *As Farpas*, 1881.
18. Augusto Soromenho writing under the alias of Abdallah in *Jornal do Comércio*, 20 January 1878.
19. Silva Pinto in *Combates e Críticas* (1882), a volume in which he reprinted and further commented on his attacks on the translation and the reactions they got from several of the king's "flatterers."
20. Alias used by Maria Amália Vaz de Carvalho (distinguished writer and literary critic) when writing for *Diário Popular*.
21. Ramalho Ortigão in *O Ocidente*, 15 January 1878.
22. *Comércio do Porto*, 11 September 1877 (the review was not signed).
23. Charles Sellers in *Diário Popular*, 17 December 1877.
24. "Le manque de talent est défaut principal / De cette dynastie, en siège au Portugal" (Ansúr, p. 29).
25. The "royal translations" of Shakespeare's dramatic works are the subject of two previous papers the reading of which is highly recommended: Homem (2001) and Mesquita (2003).

Bibliography

References to Reviews of the Translation

O Círculo n° 73, 23 December 1877.

Comércio do Porto, 11 September 1877.

Correspondência de Portugal, 14 September 1877.

O Cri-Cri, 17 June 1877; 2 September 1877; 16 September 1877; 27 January 1877.

Democracia, 20 October 1877.

Diário da Manhã, 16 December 1876; 4 January 1877; 11 September 1877; 27 December 1877; 29 December 1877; 9 November 1877; 10 July 1878.

Diário do Comércio, 29 September 1877; 17 October 1877; 19 October 1877.

Diário Popular, 29 September 1877; 1 October 1877; 21 October 1877; 17 December 1877.

The Financial and Mercantile Gazette, 1 October 1877; 1 January 1877.

O Imparcial, 18 September 1877.

Jornal da Noite, 11–12 September 1877.

Jornal do Comércio, 20 Jan 1878.

Journal des Débats, 17(?) October 1877.

Le Figaro, 20 September 1877.

Le Gaulois, 12 October 1877.

O Ocidente, 15 January 1878.

O Pai Paulino, 17 September 1877.

O Primeiro de Janeiro, 14 September 1877.

Revista de Leiria, 16 September 1877.

Revista Literária do Porto, 16 September 1877; 7 October 1877; 14 October 1877.

The Atheneaum, 1 December 1876; January 1878.

The Times, 27 November 1877.

Periodicals on the Political Situation

Comércio do Porto, 4 September 1877; 2, 9, 16, 23, 30 October 1877; 6, 13 November 1877.

O Conimbricense, 17, 28 April 1877; 23 June 1877; 14 August 1877; 1, 5 February 1878.

Correio da Tarde, 8 March 1877; 2 November 1877.

Correspondência de Portugal, 15 March 1877.

Democracia, 7–11, 23 March 1877; 7, 19 June 1877; 28 August 1877; 4, 11–13, 21–29 September 1877; 4, 13 1877.

Diário Popular, 30, 31 January 1878; 1, 2, 4, 8, 9, 11, 18 February 1878.

Diário de Portugal, 30 January 1878.

O Progresso, 7 September 1877; 27, 29 January 1878; 6, 12, 13, 15 February 1878; 3, 4, 5, 13 March 1877; 7 April 1877; 17 June 1877; 1, 8, 18 27 July 1877; 2, 3, 7, 10, 14, 24, 31 August 1877; 1, 4, 7, 8, 9, 11, 12, 14, 15, 20, 21–29 September 1877; 13, 25 December 1877.

Shakespeare and Cervantes in 1916: The Politics of Language

Clara Calvo

THE TERCENTENARY CELEBRATIONS OF THE DEATHS OF SHAKEspeare and Cervantes in 1916 in England and Spain were immersed in discourses of nationalism and colonialism. Not surprisingly, the respective national languages of these two countries were frequently appropriated by patriotic and imperialistic constructions of national identity and both Shakespeare and Cervantes played a part in them, even if they did so rather as national heroes than as literary artists.[1]

During the celebrations, both in England and Spain, love for one's language was often equated with love for one's country. By 1916, both Shakespeare and Cervantes already enjoyed the status of national poets but around this time they were also increasingly regarded as national heroes. In the discourses that emerge from texts produced around the time of the 1916 Tercentenary, Shakespeare and Cervantes are not primarily, or at least not only, remembered for their literary creations. They are often, in fact, celebrated for having brought their national language to such a degree of perfection that they deserve the honors of true patriots and thus become national icons. The discourses of linguistic nationalism extant around 1916 in England and Spain follow, interestingly, very similar patterns and it is these patterns, and the role played by Cervantes and Shakespeare in them, that I will aim to clarify.

Shakespeare and Cervantes, as is well known, died on the same date, but they did not die on the same day, due to the eleven days' difference between the Julian and the Gregorian calendars.[2] Three hundred years later, both England and Spain felt the need to pay homage to the foreign, as well as the national bard. In Spain, Shakespeare was remembered in the *Real Decreto*, or royal decree, which in 1914, that is, two years in advance, gave directions for the tercentenary celebrations.[3] The Spanish Royal Academy also celebrated Shakespeare by setting up a prize for the best study in Spanish of critical literature on Shakespeare.[4] In England, Cervantes was not forgotten either. Professor Israel Gollancz, president of the Shakespeare Association in 1916 and honorary secretary of the committee for the Shakespeare Tercentenary, was also honorary secretary of a committee in charge of raising funds to endow a chair of Spanish, which would bear the name, the Cervantes Chair, at King's College London. The Duke of Alba, representing the Spanish Royal Academy (*BRAE* 1916, 245) and the Committee for the Cervantes Tercentenary, was invited to address the audience attending the Shakespeare Tercentenary meeting held at Mansion House on May Day 1916, presided over by the king and queen.[5] The British Academy celebrated the Cervantes Tercentenary with the first annual "Master-Mind Lecture" delivered by Professor Fitzmaurice-Kelly on "Cervantes and Shakespeare" (Fitzmaurice-Kelly 1916).

Despite being the tercentenaries of two national poets who respectively were seen to represent "Englishness" and the "spirit of the Spanish race," celebrations crossed their national borders and spread throughout the Western world: France, Germany, Italy, and many American countries also joined in. There were celebrations for Shakespeare in New York, San Francisco, Chicago; for Cervantes in Buenos Aires and Mexico; and for both Shakespeare and Cervantes in France and Germany. Yet what might have been just a cultural festival grew into a highly political affair, partly due to the First World War, which had Englishmen and Germans fighting each other in the trenches and Spain remaining staunchly neutral, and partly due to the institutional appropriation of both Cervantes and Shakespeare as patriots and national heroes. As a result, the celebrations of the double tercentenary in England and Spain were very different in intensity but were both deeply steeped in discourses of nationalism, colonialism, and race, having in the end little to do with literature.[6]

Following Michel Pêcheux, discourses are understood here as groups of utterances or texts that have a similar effect and do not exist in isolation but in dialogue with other discourses (Pêcheux 1982). Since a discourse is not, as Sara Mills states, "a disembodied collection of statements, but groupings of utterances or sentences, statements which are enacted within a social context, which are determined by that social context and which contribute to the way that social context continues its existence" (Mills 1997, 11), it is possible to show how the discourses of nationalism, colonialism, and race present in the celebrations of the double tercentenary are determined by their sociohistorical context and how in turn they contribute to the reassertion of notions of cultural identity and supremacy. The presence of similar discourses in the celebrations of the tercentenaries of two different writers in two distinct countries shows how institutions from two different cultures contribute in similar ways to the emergence, reproduction, and circulation of discourses.

This is the case even though the deaths of Cervantes and Shakespeare were, in the end, very differently commemorated in Spain and England. Initially, both countries made preparations for grand-scale celebrations. Homages, exhibitions, lectures, sermons, and school festivals dedicated to Shakespeare and Cervantes were going to take place in Spain and England in April 1916. Yet, four months before the festivities were due, in January 1916, Spain canceled all the official celebrations due to the Great War, despite being a neutral nation, whereas Britain, deeply involved in the conflict, went ahead and celebrated its bard throughout the country. Reasons dictating this difference in behavior were clearly political. The Spanish government officially called the festivities off with a second royal decree, giving among its reasons that foreign guests would not turn up due to the war, turning the celebrations into a local rather than an international affair, and the tercentenary commemorations would not be up to what Cervantes deserved (*Real Decreto* 30 January 1916, 234). In a sense, then, cancellation was called for by the official policy of noninvolvement. Britain, instead, was keen to claim Shakespeare back from the Germans, who had appropriated the English playwright as their own "national bard" in the nineteenth century (Bate 1997, 184). The German romantics—Goethe, the Schlegel brothers, Schiller—had elevated Shakespeare to the podium of greatest writer and German scholarship was at the turn of the twentieth century leading the field of Shakespeare studies. Also, around this time, there were more Shakespeare performances by professional companies in Germany than in Britain and the 350th anniversary of Shakespeare's birth had been lavishly commemorated at Weimar (Engler 1991, 107–8). Although before July 1914 German professors had been invited to take part in preparations for the celebrations to be held in London, in April 1916 Germany and Britain had to conduct separate homages for a bard both nations claimed as their own (Habicht 2001, 449–54). In Britain, celebrating Shakespeare was a form of drawing the line and defending the spiritual property of a nation that lived at the time under permanent fear of a German invasion. Henry Arthur Jones voiced this fear in *Shakespeare and Germany (Written during the Battle of Verdun)*:

> With this constant evidence before us of German temper and methods, it will be well for England to be prepared for the characteristic official announcement which will doubtless be made in Berlin on 23rd April of the final and complete annexation by Germany of William Shakespeare, with all his literary, poetical philosophical and stage appurtenances, effects, traditions, and association and all the demesnes that there adjacent lie. Meantime we may ask by what insolence of egotism, what lust of plunder, or what madness of pride Germany dares add to the hideous roll of her thieveries and rapes this topping impudence and crime of vaunting to herself the allegiance of Shakespeare? (Jones 1916, 3–4)

Feelings such as these explain why in 1916 Shakespeare and Cervantes were celebrated more as cultural capital with symbolic power than as playwright and novelist. Some of those writing at the time of the tercentenary were aware of this. In the 1916 Annual Shakespeare Lecture for the British Academy, entitled *Shakespeare after Three Hundred Years*, J. W. Mackail saw that literature was not what the celebrations were about:

> This is the tercentenary, not of any work or word of Shakespeare's but of his death. I come (it might almost be said) to bury Shakespeare, not to praise him. It would be using the occasion amiss to make it one of mere customary and recapitulated eulogy. For the time is one which calls on us to revise all our values. (Mackail 1916, 3–4)

Both Shakespeare and Cervantes wrote in a language that was not the only language spoken in their respective countries, yet in both cases the language they wrote in has become symbolic capital providing the illusion of a homogeneous cultural identity in two states, each of which came into existence out of more than one "nation." To this, the imperial past of both England and Spain adds a complicating dimension. Shakespeare's English is the language of Britain and its Empire; Cervantes's Spanish is the language of Spain and its South American ex-colonies. In the tercentenary celebrations for Shakespeare and Cervantes, English and Spanish often appear as symbols of national identity. To love one's language implies loving one's nation; being proud of the supremacy of one's language in other parts of the world is a recurrent element in the discourse of patriotic feeling.

This symbolic power of English and Spanish as cultural capital erasing difference and bringing different peoples under the banner of a shared cultural identity is present in many texts produced by the double tercentenary. In the *Real Decreto* of 22 April 1914, Cervantes is presented as the reason why "Spain is and will always be famous in the world" (175)[7] and celebrations of the tercentenary of his death are not conceived as a literary feast but rather as "a feast for humankind, a glorious banquet of the soul which learned men of all nations ought to attend, and particularly those of the great Hispanic family, who are linked by their thinking and their feeling for the rich and beautiful language of the author of *El Quijote*" (175).[8] It is the language of Cervantes, with its unifying power, its capacity to obliterate differences between colonized and colonizer, fusing both in "la gran familia hispana," that is being celebrated in the nationalistic discourse of this royal decree. Cervantes and his work have become an icon of national identity and the language he wrote in is the symbol of a homogenized cultural identity, the Hispanic race.

In Britain, language also plays a role in the nationalistic discourse contained in celebratory publications triggered by the tercentenary. Shakespeare's England and Shakespeare's language are used in *A Book of Homage to Shakespeare*, a volume edited by Sir Israel Gollancz in 1916, "to assert the continuity of a single national identity" (Kahn 2001, 458). Language and national identity are also granted a prominent role in the opening paragraph of "Notes on Shakespeare the Patriot," a brief lecture written by Gollancz and published in the *Shakespeare Tercentenary Observance*, a booklet that was to be read in schools throughout the country on Shakespeare Day (3 May 1916). Gollancz begins stating that

> It were well if every year a Shakespeare Day were observed, when those who speak the speech of Shakespeare might reverently pay homage to his memory, and be reminded of all that he stands for on the roll of British fame and of the universal recognition of his exalted genius. (Gollancz 1916, 11)

This leaves no doubt about the obligation for all those who speak English to admire the "roll of British fame," suppressing, or ignoring, the national identity of other non-British English-speaking nations who may not feel for famous Britons the regard Gollancz expects them to feel. After exposing schoolchildren to what he considers Shakespeare's patriotic speeches in *Richard II, Henry V*, and *The Winter's Tale*, Gollancz sees in Shakespeare's "love" for his native language an act of patriotism: "As a patriot Shakespeare cared no less for the speech of his native land than for its cherished history and its very soil" (Gollancz 1916, 18). Language and nation were for Shakespeare, according to Gollancz, one and the same thing and he gives as evidence the speech of Thomas Mowbray, Duke of York, in *Richard II*. Mowbray, when he is banished from his native soil, regrets most of all being banished from speaking and listening to his native English (Gollancz 1916, 19). This love of his native country and speech is, Gollancz continues, no mere poetic fervor since "it is solidly based upon his belief that English ideals make for righteousness, for freedom, for the recognition of human rights and liberties" (Gollancz 1916, 21). These words were meant to be read in English schools at a time when the proclamation of the Irish Republic had led to the execution of several Irish nationalist leaders, events that would inspire W. B. Yeats to write his poem "Easter 1916."[9] Yet, in a year that would later be labeled "The Year of Battles" because it saw the battles of Verdun, Jutland, and the Somme (Keegan 1998, 277), Gollancz's view of national identity is perhaps, in spite of the Easter Rising and strained Anglo-Irish relations, not altogether startling.[10] It is less easy, though, to explain how "Shakespeare's language" was seen as a constitutive element of national identity.[11]

The contradiction lying behind the equating of Shakespeare's language with British cultural identity has been exposed by Holderness and Murphy (1997). Early Modern English, they argue, is so different from current British English that we can say that most people nowadays read Shakespeare in modern "translation," that is, once typographical, orthographical, and even semantic differences have been smoothed out by editors (Holderness and Murphy 1997, 25). Appropriating Shakespeare's language as icon of national identity is also paradoxical because his dramatic works often play out linguistic diversity. *Henry V* contains a well-known example when, in 3.2, the Welsh, Irish, and Scottish captains—Fluellen, Jamy, and Macmorris—fight for the same king while retaining linguistic features from their own nonstandard language. They remind us that the wish to see "Shakespeare's English" as a binding, unifying force in British national identity is simply a myth. Shakespeare's plays also enact a different kind of linguistic difference. The swift changes from verse to prose or vice-versa sometimes signal to us that social inequality exists and that princes do not usually speak the same language as beggars. Projecting the cultural and national identity of "standard English" as the language of Britain was nevertheless an integral part of the celebrations of the 1916 Shakespeare tercentenary. Perhaps, in the same way that Shakespeare had to be retrieved from the Germans, English had to be brought back from the colonies.

In Spain, the discourse linking language and national identity was taken even further, jumping from the two-dimensionality of the printed page to the three-dimensionality of architecture and sculpture. In 1915, as part of the projected tercentenary celebrations, a contest took place to assign the building of a monument to Cervantes to an architect and sculptor. There was already a statue of Cervantes in Madrid, opposite the Palacio de las Cortes (see illustration, p. 85), but this was felt not to be enough. The new monument had to be, according to the *Real Decreto*, 29 March 1915, which gave regulations for the contest, a symbol of the Spanish nation, the Spanish race, the Spanish language.[12] It had to be a monument not to Cervantes the man or the writer but rather to "the greatest nobility of the Spanish wit and the highest degree of beauty reached by the Castilian language" (*Real Decreto*, 29 March 1915).[13] In the *Monumento a Cervantes* by sculptor Collaut Valera and architect Martínez Zapatero,

Statue of Cervantes in Madrid, opposite the Palacio de las Cortes.

which won the contest and still stands today in the Plaza de España in Madrid, there is a *fuente del idioma castellano* (a fountain of the Spanish language) whose upper level is adorned with the crests of all the South American countries (see illustration, p. 87). This fountain was consciously designed to stand as a symbol of the linguistic brotherhood existing between Spain and its former colonies. Running from the upper to the lower level, the water (which represents the Spanish language) covers completely the crests with a uniform watery curtain creating for us today an obvious allegorical message. The linguistic diversity of native American civilizations is suppressed. At a time when Catalan nationalism was once more coming to the surface, the language of Cervantes was called upon to serve as icon of a national and colonial identity, of a cultural "sameness," that was not quite true to life. Ironically, in *El Quijote*, Cervantes reminds his readers of the multilingual nature of his country since one of the first adventures of Alonso Quijano involves fighting with *el Vizcaíno*, a Basque whose mother tongue is probably not Castilian and who speaks the language of Cervantes with very odd syntactical choices. In the second part, Don Quijote is stopped on his way to Barcelona by the fellows of the famous highwayman Roque Guinart who address him in Catalan. *El Quijote* itself, as Cervantes humorously says, had its origin in some papers written in an Arabic language by Cide Hamete Benengeli, which he stumbled across while taking a stroll.

In England, the tercentenary celebrations also brought back the desire of building a Shakespeare memorial in London. In 1904, a wealthy Stratford brewer, Richard Badger, had offered the London County Council the sum of £2,500 to raise a memorial to Shakespeare. A Memorial Committee was formed that included bishops, judges, ambassadors, and Professor Israel Gollancz. In 1905 the committee considered honoring Shakespeare first with a statue, then with a museum that would be a "temple" for the national bard. In the same year, a letter of protest against this scheme was sent to *The Times*, signed, among others by J. M. Barrie, A. C. Bradley, and A. W. Pinero. The scheme was then abandoned but in March 1916, no doubt spurred by the spirit of tercentenary celebrations, the Memorial Committee settled on a statue of Shakespeare to be raised in Portland Place at a cost of £100,000. By then, Richard Badger, who had died, had increased his legacy to the sum of £3,500. The municipality of

Monumento a Cervantes **by sculptor Collaut Valera and architect Martínez Zapatero.**

Venice also offered to contribute with 1,000 Italian lire. Yet, the longing for a Shakespeare statue was not shared by everybody, at least in London, and in May 1916 a demonstration was organized against the statue and in demand of a National Theatre as the only fitting memorial to Shakespeare. Speeches were given, among others, by A. W. Pinero and Bernard Shaw. The opposition to the statue and the plea for a National Theatre indicate that at least some were aware of the fact that what the official Shakespeare committees were celebrating was a national hero, not a playwright.[14] This perhaps influenced J. M. Barrie's choice of topic for a one act farcical play, *Shakespeare's Legacy*, first performed at Drury Lane Theatre on 14 April 1916, at a matinée for the benefit of the YWCA (Young Women's Christian Association), whose working conditions as ammunition workers were in need of improvement. Barrie imagines a recently married Scottish woman, Mrs. Bantry, playing with Shakespeare's manuscripts as a child, because contrary to what is generally believed, Shakespeare was not born in Stratford but in Glen Drumly, and he is therefore not English but Scottish. To this, Mr. Bantry, the husband, who is English and will soon go back to the trenches, objects strongly:

> *Husband* (firmly): Pardon me, dear. Shakespeare wasn't Scotch. Everything else we give you, but—dash it all! (Barrie 1916, 14).

In Spain, around the same time, in May 1916, the weekly *España* paid homage to Cervantes and Shakespeare with two articles by the Spanish philosopher Ortega y Gasset and by Federico de Onís on Cervantes and one article on Shakespeare by José de Armas y Cárdenas. This article does not deal with Shakespeare's work, his genius, his contribution to world literature or his knowledge of human passions; it is an article about England's national character and Shakespeare the man deserves a place in it as England's most illustrious son. Shakespeare, for the Cuban-born writer José de Armas, embodies England's national spirit: "In Shakespeare one finds England itself, with its flaws and its virtues ... To know England is to admire it and to admire it is to understand Shakespeare" (Armas 1916, 11).[15] José de Armas was also one of the four Spanish-speaking contributors to Israel Gollancz's *A Book of Homage to Shakespeare*, with a sonnet that follows the rhyme pattern of the Shakespearean rather than the Spanish sonnet with three quatrains and a final couplet instead of two quatrains and two tercets (Armas 1916, 434). In this sonnet, Shakespeare and Cervantes discuss not their respective literary achievements but the First World War.[16] Shakespeare compares England (*Albión* in the sonnet) to Don Quijote, from whom it has, like an errant knight, taken the sword to defend France from the evil Caliban:[17]

ESPAÑA

1916

REDACCION Y ADMINISTRACION, CALLE DEL PRADO, 11
APARTADO DE CORREOS NÚM. 139.—DIRECCION TELE-
GRAFICA, ESPAÑO.—TELEFONO 5.233.

PRECIOS DE SUSCRIPCION: MADRID Y PROVINCIAS,
UN SEMESTRE, 2,50 PESETAS.—UN AÑO, 5 PESETAS.
EXTRANJERO: UN AÑO, 12 PESETAS.

Núm. 10 Cts.   SEMANARIO DE LA VIDA NACIONAL   Núm. 10 Cts.

EL CENTENARIO DE CERVANTES Y DE SHAKESPEARE
—Don Quijote. Amigo Hamlet admírate y alegrate de las salvas que están haciendo en honor de nuestro Centenario

Cartoon showing Hamlet and Don Quijote in conversation (see note 16).

CONVERSACIÓN DE DOS ALMAS	TWO SOULS IN CONVERSATION
Shakespeare y Cervantes	Shakespeare and Cervantes
—Mira, hermano español, como en la guerra Se olvida el hombre de la edad dorada; Mares de sangre inundan a la tierra— ¿Quién piensa ya en Lepanto, ni en la Armada? ¡Triste verdad! De nuevo siente el mundo De cruel Attila el ominoso estrago; Muere infeliz Cordelia, triunfa Edmundo, Y su canto infernal entona Iago;	—Look, Spanish brother, how in war, Man tends to forget the Golden Age, Seas of blood are seen to flood the Earth— Who thinks now of Lepant or the Armada? —Sad truth, indeed! Once again the world feels Of cruel Attila the hideous havoc Innocent Cordelia dies, Edmund triumphs And Iago sings his hellish song.
En Flandes reina Calibán artero Y a Francia heroica hiere con su azote . . . —Pronto, hermano caerá; porque el acero Ha recogido Albión de Don Quijote; Vive en ella su espíritu gigante, Y vence ¡ al fin ! tu caballero andante.	In Flanders artful Caliban reigns And heroic France he lashes with his whip . . . —Soon, brother, it will fall, as the steel Albion has taken from Don Quixote; his gigantic spirit lives in her, and finally! your errant knight wins.

This sonnet illustrates how the tercentenary celebrations in honor of Shakespeare and Cervantes were not primarily concerned with their literary legacies but with the iconic projection of two writers into national heroes and emblematic embodiments of cultural identity. The identification of England with Don Quixote recalls Ferdinand Freiligrath's association of Germany with Hamlet and Salvador de Madariaga's reading of the Spanish government's neutrality policy in the Great War as a Hamletian postponement of action in "El monólogo de Hamlet," an article published in the weekly *España* (Madariaga 1916). In the texts written during the tercentenary celebrations, Germany is no longer Hamlet; it is instead equated with Caliban, Iago, Edmund, and even Macbeth (Jones 1916, 23).

Gollancz's *A Book of Homage to Shakespeare* was a multilingual, multicultural volume put together to celebrate the 1916 Tercentenary and designed, as the editor observes in the preface "to symbolise the intellectual fraternity of mankind in the universal homage accorded to the genius of the greatest Englishman" (Gollancz 1916, vii).[19] Shakespeare is a universal genius, but he is a product of England. Gollancz's discourse often reveals this tension between world fame and national glory. His preface ends with a promise "to devote the book's profits (i.e., the profits of a book intending to show how Shakespeare's legacy belongs to the entire world) to Shakespeare—and to Shakespeare's England" (Gollancz 1916, x). The tension between Shakespeare the national hero and Shakespeare the universal genius is also evident in Francis Colmer's *Shakespeare in Time of War*, another publication triggered by the 1916 Tercentenary and consisting in an anthology of passages from Shakespeare's plays arranged by topic:

> Milton and Tennyson are not national poets in the full sense of the word. There is only one poet who has identified himself deeply with the nationality of our race and who has made himself the mouthpiece to interpret it in every mood and aspiration, who is himself, indeed, the typical Englishman. Our one and only national poet is William Shakespeare—national, not merely in an insular, but, one might almost say, in an imperial sense. (Colmer 1916, xvii)

The same tension between universal genius and national hero can be found in Spain during the Tercentenary in relation to Cervantes. In a leader published by the weekly *España*, Luis Araquistain, future President of the Spanish Republic in its Mexican exile after the Spanish Civil War, argues that if Cervantes is a universal genius, he is also "that cardinal figure of the Spanish race" ([Araquistain] 1916, 13).[19]

It seems therefore the case that, in the context of the 1916 Tercentenary celebrations, both Shakespeare and Cervantes, and the languages they wrote in, became cultural capital that was symbolically appropriated and molded into icons of patriotic enthusiasm in their respective countries with the help of very similar discourses of nationalism, colonialism, and cultural supremacy. The role played by the politics of language in the tercentenary celebrations is, then, to render possible this apparent contradiction that makes of Shakespeare and Cervantes both universal geniuses and national poets.

Notes

This study is part of research project PB98-0398, financed by the Spanish Ministry of Education and Culture.

1. Two articles dealing with the 1916 Tercentenary of Shakespeare's death, Habicht (2001) and Kahn (2001), became available after this study had already been delivered as a paper at the conference "Shakespeare in European Culture" held at the University of Basel in November 2001. This paper continued my research on the 1916 celebrations, which started with "Shakespeare and Spain in 1916: Shakespearean Biography and Spanish Neutrality in the Great War," a paper presented at a seminar on Shakespearean biography at the ISA conference in Stratford in 2000. It has been reassuring to find that some of the material used and the conclusions reached by Habicht and Kahn coincide with my own. I have, however, extended the discussion, as my main aim here is a joint exploration of the tercentenary celebrations held for Shakespeare and Cervantes in England and Spain, foregrounding the role played by language in the construction of national and cultural identities and showing at the same time how, in two countries very differently involved in the Great War, "national languages" are appropriated in discourses of patriotism and colonialism, at the expense of linguistic diversity. Since I have had the chance to revise the text of this paper before publication when Habicht (2001) and Kahn (2001) were already in print, I have incorporated here references to their work to point out connections for the benefit of the reader.

2. In 1616, Spain was already using the Gregorian calendar, whereas England was still operating under the Julian calendar. The estimated difference between the two calendars at the time of the deaths of Shakespeare and Cervantes was between ten and eleven days. Shakespeare therefore died, approximately, eleven days after Cervantes. See Miranda y Marrón (1904, 15).

3. The royal decree giving directions for the celebrations also nominated the members of the honorary and executive committees (*Real Decreto*, 22 April 1914, 175–76). The members of the honorary committee were mostly members of the government and politicians.

4. In its ordinary session of 6 April 1916, the Royal Academy "passed a resolution to the effect that, in order to correspond in the best possible way to the interest in the glory of Cervantes shown by the British Academy and the Government of England, a literary contest would take place to commemorate the tercentenary of the death of the great English poet William Shakespeare" [acordó que, a fin de corresponder del mejor modo posible al interés que por la gloria de Cervantes han manifestado la Academia Británica y el Gobierno de Inglaterra, se publicase un Certamen literario con motivo de solemnizarse el tercer centenario de la muerte del gran poeta inglés Guillermo Shakespeare] (*BRAE* 1916, 245). This literary prize, advertised in the official Spanish newspaper *Gaceta de Madrid* on 23

April 1916, would be awarded to a study on "Shakespeare in Spain: Translations, Imitations and Influence of the Works of Shakespeare in Spanish Literature" [Shakespeare en España. Traducciones, imitaciones e influencia de las obras de Shakespeare en la literatura española] (see *BRAE* 1916, 247). The deadline for submission of manuscripts was 23 April 1917. A year later, the *Boletín de la Real Academia Española* (*BRAE* 1917, 261) recorded that only one study was submitted and in 1918 a book bearing as title *Shakespeare en España* was published (Juliá 1918). Another book bearing the same title appeared in 1920 (Ruppert y Ujaravi 1920).

5. The Duke of Alba was one of the only two representatives from a non-British ex-colony to address the Shakespeare Tercentenary Meeting at Mansion House, in the course of which the king and queen were presented with a copy of *A Homage to Shakespeare*, a costly book edited by Israel Gollancz. A beautifully decorated program in the style of William Morris's designs for the works of Shakespeare at the Kelmscott Press and entitled *Shakespeare May Day 1916* was printed for the occasion.

6. Kahn (2001) thoroughly shows how issues of colonialism, race and the British Empire are overwhelmingly present in Gollancz's contribution to the Shakespeare Tercentenary celebrations.

7. "por cuyo inmarcesible nombre es y será gloriosa España."

8. "una fiesta de la Humanidad, un grandioso banquete del espíritu al cual concurran los hombres cultos de todas las nacionalidades, y especialmente de la gran familia hispana, que tienen por vínculo de su pensar y de su sentir la rica y hermosa lengua del autor del Quijote."

9. The seven Irish nationalist leaders who signed the Proclamation on behalf of the Government of the Irish Republic read on Easter Monday on the steps of Dublin's General Post Office were sentenced to death. Three of them were executed precisely on Shakespeare Day (3 May): Thomas J. Clarke, Thomas McDonagh, and Patrick H. Pearse. They had surrendered on Sunday, 30 April, the day when sermons in honor of Shakespeare were read in Stratford, London, and other English towns.

10. Habicht (2001, 450–51) has shown how Gollancz edited, or rather censored, the English translation of Douglas Hyde's contribution to *A Book of Homage to Shakespeare* (Gollancz 1916). Hyde, who was leader of the Gaelic League, had submitted a poem in Gaelic that contained references to Irish hatred of England for its colonial and "deceitful" domination of Ireland. Gollancz toned them down or simply deleted them.

11. On the role played by Shakespeare in the construction of a unified national identity in Gollancz (1916), see Kahn 2001, 458–67.

12. The *Real Decreto*, 29 March 1915, insisted several times on the fact that what the monument to Cervantes was to commemorate was not "the genius of an artist" [el genio de un artista]: "Despite having been so extraordinary the figure in which the soldier at Lepant, the brave prisoner who conspired to take Argel and the novelist which put an end to romances are blended, it is greater than his personality the representation which centuries have awarded him; first, because his work shows the most noble side of the national spirit; second, because he raised the language to a such a high level of splendour that thanks to him Castilian is worldwide called the *language of Cervantes*" [Con haber sido tan extraordinaria aquella figura en quien se confunden el soldado de Lepanto, el cautivo valeroso que conspiró para conquistar Argel y el novelista que acabó con

los libros de Caballerías, aún es más excelsa que su misma personalidad la representación que los siglos le han reconocido; primero, porque su labor refleja lo más noble del esprítu nacional; segundo, porque llevó el idioma a tan alto grado de esplendor, que por él se llama en el mundo entero al castellano la lengua de Cervantes] (*Real Decreto*, 29 March 1915, 936).

13. "la mayor nobleza del ingenio español y el más alto grado de belleza á que llegó la lengua castellana" (*Real Decreto*, 29 March 1915, 936).

14. For the opposition to a new Shakespeare statue in London and the demand of a National Theatre see *Shakespeare Memorial: The Plea for a National Theatre* (London: Daily Chronicle, 1916).

15. "En Shakespeare está Inglaterra toda, con sus faltas y sus virtudes ... Conocer a Inglaterra es admirarla, y admirarla es comprender a Shakespeare."

16. The cover of the issue of the weekly *España* dedicated to the tercentenary bears a cartoon showing Hamlet and Don Quijote in conversation (see illustration, p. 89). In the caption, Don Quijote says to Hamlet: "Amigo Hamlet, admírate y alégrate de las salvas que están haciendo en honor de nuestro Centenario" (Friend Hamlet, admire and be glad of the cannonade being fired to honour our Centenary). This wry joke on the Great War shows how literary matters in 1916 remained on the back burner (*España* 2, no. 67: 1).

17. The English translation is mine and has no claim to be more than a literal rendering of the meaning of the Spanish original, for which purpose meter and rhyme have been sacrificed.

18. The other three Spanish contributors to Gollancz's book were Alfonso Merry del Val, Spanish ambassador in London; Antonio Maura, then president of the Royal Academy; and writer Armando Palacio Valdés. For a detailed analysis of Gollancz's *Homage* see Kahn 2001.

19. "esa figura cardinal de la raza española." The weekly *España* was an attempt to give a voice to what Ortega called "la España vital" [*vital* Spain], which was meant to oppose "la España oficial" [official Spain]. Ortega no doubt means *vital* to be understood in opposition to *official*, so "vital" should be taken in the sense of "energetic" and "alive," as opposed to official Spain which is "passive" and "dead." See Ortega 1961, 271–75.

Camel, Weasel, Whale: The Cloud-Scene in *Hamlet* as a Hungarian Parable

Péter Dávidházi

A FEW CASUAL WORDS UTTERED IN PASSING, THE CLOUD-SCENE OF *Hamlet* lasts hardly more than a minute. At first sight the brief encounter between Hamlet and Polonius may seem funny but insignificant in the ominous second scene of the third act. We have just seen the mouse-trap play within the play, after which the queen, deeply upset, sent Rosencrantz and Guildenstern to her son with the message that she would speak with him in her closet before he went to bed. Now Polonius enters with the same message but in a more urgent manner: she would have a word with Hamlet, "and presently." So the prince has to obey her wish, and there is not much time left for idle words, yet we see him looking up and pointing toward the sky with the unexpected and seemingly whimsical question: "Do you see yonder cloud that's almost in shape of a camel?" Polonius may be taken off guard by the swift and discontinuous change of the subject of their conversation from the Queen's request to the cloud's shape, but his prompt answer shows no surprise: "By th' mass, and 'tis like a camel indeed." But this agreement does not satisfy the prince for long: "Methinks it is like a weasel." Polonius is quick to find the ground for justifying the new simile: "It is backed like a weasel." Then comes the third and final challenge: "Or like a whale?" On the face of it, the old courtier could not agree more: "Very like a whale." At last Hamlet looks satisfied: "Then I will come to my mother by and by," he says, as if to indicate by the "then" that something necessary was finally accomplished, a prerequisite of his visit to the Queen, something meant (or feigned) to be both indispensable and logical, at least within the system of his pretended madness. The scene is practically over: Hamlet dismisses everybody and after strengthening his resolution to confine himself to verbal cruelty ("I will speak daggers to her but use none") he leaves the stage (3.2.338–60). Enter Claudius, Rosenkrantz, and Guildenstern. We are so much carried away by the fascinating plot, by the inexorable unfolding of tragic fate, that there is no time to ponder upon the probable significance, if any, of the cloud-scene, and as Polonius himself is killed not much later in the same act, we may tend to forget about the strange little interlude altogether.

As regards its overt dramatic function, the cloud-scene seems to be deceptively simple, suggesting a meaning neither unexpected nor terribly profound at first sight. If we analyze it in terms of dramatic propriety, looking at the immediate context and taking into account the purpose and character of the person who initiated the dialogue, then Hamlet is probably trying to make yet another hint at his own evasiveness, just as he did in the preceding little episode, when he repeatedly (also three times) asked Guildenstern in the presence of Rosencrantz to play on a recorder, and when Guildenstern finally was unable to do it, and admitted to lack the necessary skill, Hamlet retorted with spelling out the lesson for both of them: "'Sblood, do you think I am easier to be played on than a pipe? Call me what instrument you will, though you can fret me, you cannot play upon me" (3.2.334–36). Those two are still around him when he is teasing Polonius about the shape of the clouds, and although the lesson to be learned is summed up in an aside this time, it is nevertheless a similar conclusion concerning all the three of them: "They fool me to the top of my bent" (3.2.345–46). *My* bent, of course, because whatever they may think, *he* is the one who defines the limit. In this context Hamlet seems to have dreamt up the cloud-scene to make all his three observers realize that his whimsical, apparently insane intentions would be at least as difficult to fathom out or pin down as it is hopeless to identify the ever-changing shape of the clouds. With this purpose in mind, the sudden and unpredictable initiation of the subject or subsequently the sharp and startling shifts of opinion are meant to be feigned symptoms of sheer madness, calculated to convince Polonius, and by his inevitable report, Claudius, that the prince is utterly but harmlessly out of his mind, hence represents no real threat. If so, Polonius may have been taken in by the device, but it was not enough to deceive the more suspicious Claudius, who considers Hamlet something like a loose cannon, promptly commands Rosencrantz and Guildenstern to get rid of him, and the two villains leave before Polonius can have a chance to report anything.

This interpretation reduces the various possible meanings of the dialogue to one single element, the common denominator between the difficulties of playing the recorder and identifying the clouds, but what it highlights, the theme of unknowability, is one of the main problems of both Hamlet and Polonius not only this time but in practically all their encounters. Just as Hamlet seeks to evade identification by pretending madness, Polonius is playing roles or using mimicry; whatever they tell each other about anything is highly ambivalent, with no guarantee that it is meant seriously, and no indication of their real opinion. Hiding ulterior motives and tactical considerations, their utterances keep negotiating between purpose and possibility, so they are meant to be tentative, elusive, hypothetical. As Northrop Frye pointed out, scholars had often been prone to misread Polonius by accepting Hamlet's melancholic views on him as Shakespeare's (Frye 1986, 83), and one may add that they (we) have remained too close to Dr. Johnson's reading of Polonius's behavior as marked by *unintended* symptoms of senility, his inconsistent and pompous speech as "dotage encroaching upon wisdom," his lapses into confused verbosity as temporary losses of intellectual control: "the mind in its enfeebled state cannot be kept long busy and intent, the old man is subject to sudden dereliction of his faculties, he loses the order of his ideas, and entangles himself in his own thoughts" (Johnson 1986, 327). But it is more probable that he is *playing* the old fool in order to take his victim off guard, and to observe him all the more easily. After all he is an informant, and the safety of his own children is at stake. Had he been as genuinely senile as he may sound, he could not have taught Reynaldo (as if absentmindedly yet so efficiently) the subtle tricks of spying, like how to gain confidence by tentative and devious questioning, he could not have kept in mind his "drift" so firmly all through his digressions (2.1.39), and he could not have been so proudly aware of his pedagogical accomplishment at the end of the session. "See you now, / Your bait of falsehood takes this carp of truth, / And thus do we of wisdom and of reach, / With windlasses and with assays of bias, / By indirections find directions out. / So, by my former lecture and advice, / Shall you my son" (2.1.60–66). No, what he says about the clouds cannot be taken as his sincere opinion, just as Hamlet's similes are no indication of what he thinks about them.

Their respective role-playing makes their three successive agreements no indication, let alone proof, of what they see, and we as spectators cannot even be sure that there are any clouds above them whatsoever. At the end of the cloud-scene we are reminded that " 'Tis now the very witching time of night" (3.2.349), so it must be dark outside, and their little dialogue takes place in the palace where torches are the only source of light, so the shape of "yonder clouds," supposed to be seen by them through a window (in the late nineteenth century Edwin Booth as Hamlet made Polonius look out), is impossible for us to ascertain. From the point of view of the audience there is a great difference between the recorder-scene and the cloud-scene: we could actually see the recorder, to play on it would have required only some well-definable expertise from Guildenstern, and we could have heard and *judged* the quality of his performance; the shape of the clouds would be, even when visible, far too changeable to be identified without a greater degree of imaginative closure, and if we only hear about them from two notorious pretenders, we cannot have any reliable information to form a judgment. Taken as a parable of knowing, the cloud-scene would be deeply agnostic, but so far with nothing especially Hungarian or East-Central-European about it.

Yet however puzzling the ultimate indeterminacy of its meaning, the little dialogue recalls a situation familiar to us all and still far too general to be specifically East-Central-European: that of *interpretation*. Interpreting visual phenomena is of course not the same as interpreting written texts, nevertheless the scene may justly remind a literary critic of his or her own predicament. It is hardly surprising that János Arany (1817–1882), an inspired Hungarian translator of *Hamlet* (1867) and a major poet as well as an interesting protostructuralist literary critic of the mid-nineteenth century, spontaneously associated his difficulties in identifying the vaguely diffuse meaning of (second-rate) contemporary Hungarian poetry with the excruciating task Hamlet set to Polonius in the cloud-scene. "The reader of poems often feels himself in Polonius's situation," he complained in 1861, reviewing a volume of poems by one of the many poetasters,

> the author-Hamlet keeps showing him bits of clouds, and in response he is sympathetically rubbing his eyes and his spectacles to make his stubborn imagination recognize *that* which Hamlet happens to see, and when failing to do so, he just repeats Polonius-like: all right, let it be a whale, I don't mind, or, if less polite or compelled to sincerity by his job, he flatly denies the proposition, saying that it is no whale, no weasel, no camel, thank you, but sheer inflated vapour (Arany 1968, 290).

Arany's neoclassicist critical assumptions usually made the cloud-scene analogous with the impossible task of interpreting *bad* poetry, a poetry "trying to display ideas without body for our sensory perception" and "seeking to capture the clouds" (Arany 1968, 291), like an epic in which characters or events "are clouding in confused indeterminacy in front of the reader's eyes" (Arany 1962, 403–4). Yet Arany used critical norms implying the cloud-scene analogy too often to confine its relevance to bad poetry only, and probably he realized its emblematic validity for the interpretation of *any* work of art. His applied commentary to the scene indicates his awareness of its more general hermeneutic implications:

> When the good old Polonius, for the sake of the Danish prince, imagines a piece of cloud as a camel, a weasel, or a whale, what he is doing is not as wildly foolish as it may seem. Indeed, to something as empty, indefinite, diffuse, and blurred as a patch of cloud, who could render a definite, solid, and constant image, or who could be sure that what he sees as a pilgrim, is not imagined by another spectator as a palm, a cliff, or a fountain . . . ? Every single spectator has to add a piece of his own fantasy to the view, to fill the void, to round off the shape, and to capture the image for at least a moment before it returns to its original nothingness. (Arany 1968, 290)

This is not far from the act of interpretation as seen by much later theorists, like Roman Ingarden in 1931 and (though somewhat differently) by Wolfgang Iser in 1976, that the reader's task is to resolve the indeterminacies (*Unbestimmtheitsstellen*) in the literary work of art, that is, to complete its vacant places by spontaneous acts of the imagination, usually in a smooth and satisfactory manner, but occasionally disturbed by the phenomenon called "opalising" (*Opalisierung*), when the reader is compelled to oscillate between equally plausible ways of completion (Ingarden 1965, 261–70; Iser 1984, 267–80). Neither is it far from the central tenet of *Gestaltpsychologie* that our perception is an involuntary grouping of sensory data into units by closing any gaps that would disturb our sense of their wholeness. It is also remarkably near to Wittgenstein's notion, spelled out toward the end of *Philosophical Investigations* (between 1947 and 1949) partly in response to Wolfgang Köhler's *Gestaltpsychologie*, that to see something is always to see it *as* something by an act of interpretation implied in seeing and accomplished with the help of our imagination, by a process that is effortless and undisturbed as long as a change of aspect (*Aspektwechsel*) will not make the same image look like something else. Even nearer to the interpretive analogies of the cloud-scene, Wittgenstein emphasized the subtle difference between actually seeing (or hearing) an artistic phenomenon as something and merely *knowing* that one is expected to see or hear it like that. Nearest of all to Polonius's task are Wittgenstein's examples of the situation when somebody is trying to prescribe the implied interpretation for our sensory organs by referring to the intention of the artist: "in conversation on aesthetic matters we use the words: 'You have to see it like *this*, this is how it is meant'; . . . 'You have to hear this bar as an introduction'" (Wittgenstein 1997, 202e).

Yet however appositely Arany used the cloud-scene to illustrate some interpretative problems of poetry, the associative leap of his application makes one wonder what it was in this tiny episode that made it so memorable for a mid-nineteenth-century poet who lived in an East-Central-European country still shaken by the 1849 defeat of its fight for independence against the Habsburgs, still shocked by the final blow received from the tsarist troops as yet another historical lesson of what it means to be small on the map between antagonistic (or even *friendly*) superpowers. Arany had been nurtured by a literary tradition that often extolled *Hamlet* for aesthetic and patriotic reasons but so far never substantiated either its beauty or its political relevance by referring to this particular detail. True, for a poet the scene may have been distinguished, partly at least, by something historically and regionally as unspecified as the age-old cloud-motive itself, one of the renewed favorites of Romantic poetry in general, an endlessly variable theme that had never ceased to fascinate Arany's imagination. In his essays and letters he considered the very fascination with the changing clouds the hallmark of a genuine artistic sensibility, a disposition unmistakable even in social dropouts like the fool of the village in one of his poems, who watches the clouds nostalgically for hours, spellbound by their magic metamorphoses from a bull to a tower to a horseman to a big tree, and finally he sighs with a painful sense of bereavement at their ultimate dissolution. But most probably there was more than that in the little dialogue of Hamlet and Polonius for Arany to remember, and the key to this is a humble and innocent-looking little phrase in his comment on the scene: it is "for the sake of" the Danish prince that Polonius recognizes in the cloud first a camel, then a weasel, and finally a whale. At its place in the argument this phrase may do hardly more than state the obvious, yet it opens up an additional dimension, revealing a latent function of any act of interpretation, a hidden agenda Hamlet himself is deeply concerned with: the intricate negotiations about *power*.

Arany as an East-Central-European author in 1861, with all the painfully vivid experiences of a very oppressive postrevolutionary decade and all the crude and subtle forms of imperial retaliation, must have been especially sensitive to the cloud-scene in *Hamlet* because it offered one of the finest Shakespearean illustrations of the inescapable interplay between interpretation and power, where both are means and ends at the same time, interpretation being not only inseparable from the expectations of those in power but also a way of testing the limits of freedom. What the prince asks is spelling out his expectations in no uncertain terms. His question is not an uncommitted "Do you see yonder cloud and what do you think its shape is like?" but the tendentious "Do you see yonder cloud that's almost in shape of a camel?" an inquisition binding together the very act of *seeing* with the Wittgensteinian *seeing as* something, and prescribing the implied interpretation in a subtly dictatorial manner. The first question is crucial because its thinly veiled command is softened (as never again in the subsequent two questions) by the tentative "almost," a word indicating a gap in the supposed correspondence and thereby making the required first agreement look deceptively like the result of considerate judgments made by two independent minds. Moreover, the seemingly humble "almost" is a crucial part of the test: Hamlet makes his claim with a degree of acknowledged uncertainty that Polonius, should he think that he can afford to differ, could use to legitimate his dissent. But the old courtier knows immediately that it would be dangerous and foolish to contradict the prince, not only because (as Turgenev realized in 1860) for him as a courtier there was more at stake here than for a simple adult wisely accepting the mere whim of a sick and spoiled royal child (Turgenev 1963, 178), but because the odd question, so obviously irrelevant at its face value, is most probably a symbolic gesture to redefine the limits of their respective powers, at least on the surface. (Under the surface everything may remain unchanged, Polonius may keep spying on Hamlet for Claudius as before, and Hamlet can keep on feigning his madness for his hidden purpose.) Polonius recognizes that the three subsequent questions are meant to renegotiate the rules of their overt behavior, and he decides to reaffirm his own subordinate position. He has two children to protect, himself trying to survive in a formidable court where anything can happen. With no chance for real peace, you should at least try to prolong the truce, especially if you can do it simply by saying yes to a few harmless questions.

But are they harmless indeed, and is it really so easy and inconsequential to say yes? If we suppose that the little dialogue is a language game designed to discover and reaffirm the new distribution of power, then to accept (if only for tactical reasons) the terms of all the three questions is to give up the right to explicit defiance in such a docile and humiliating manner that after the lip service we cannot be the same as before. Arany must have known this psychological problem from personal experience, because he was subjected to similar questionings by the authorities after the defeat of the 1848 revolution, a fight for national independence he had been supporting not only as poet and editor, but also as a clerk in one of the revolutionary ministries. After the uprising was mercilessly crushed and his friend Sándor Petőfi killed on the battlefield, Arany was overwhelmed by bitterness, disillusionment, and a deep sense of shame and guilt for being a survivor. Employed as a professor in a country high school on the strength of his poetic fame and sheer intellectual excellence alone, having no university diploma whereby to secure his post, he could easily lose his job, the only source of income for his family. It was in this precarious and vulnerable position that he was commanded by the authorities to write a sincere account of his activities during the revolution and to verify his statement by submitting all the relevant documents for inspection. His apologetic confession is embarrassing to read even today, a century and a half later, and having learned many a new lesson about the infinite human capacity to enrich the arsenal of humiliation. The unusually complicated and often cumbersome syntax of his account indicates a painful awareness of the discrepancy between the condemnatory terminology with which everybody was expected to describe the revolution and his own cherished memories of a heroic, if ultimately hopeless, fight for independence.

> It was not at all for political reasons, but only because I could not get my salary for a year and a half, and consequently I was in great need, that I was compelled to accept, in order to provide for my family, a merely subordinate office from the revolutionary government. Thus it happened that I was employed as a mere clerk at the Ministry of Internal Affairs from 25 May to 30 June 1849, and temporarily I moved to Pest, but as soon as I realized what the state of affairs was like, I regretted my steps . . . (Arany 1966a, 103)

But in spite of all the minimizing formulae, despite the whole array of "mere," "merely," "only," "temporarily," "as soon as," and even "regretted," the authorities were not satisfied by his readiness to answer the first question and to answer it in the expected tone and terminology: they sent his confession back to him in 1853 with the second imperative to write a new and more exhaustive autobiography, to fill the lacunae of the first, and to give a detailed account of his literary activities during the revolution. The phrasing of the new admonition implied that a fully sincere confession may be rewarded by forgiving some minor offenses. Arany, anxious to protect his family, could hardly afford to ignore or resist the new command, and his second account was no less abounding in apologetic phrases than the first (Arany 1966b, 104–5). Although this second testimony complied with the required terms of renaming the past no less (and probably even more) resolutely than the first, it was by no means the last of his tribulations, and we can see from his letters that he was exposed to an equivalent of Polonius's third testing soon enough. "From time to time they tried to frighten me, tame me, train me, and intimidate me by diverse means, but I am still not docile enough for the yoke" (Arany 1982, 397). Thus he summed up his last few years for a friend in 1854, only a few years before the visit of Franz Joseph to Hungary, when he would be asked to write a celebratory poem for the emperor, a lucrative request he would turn down, and would compose a defiant ballad instead, *The Bards of Wales*, celebrating the poets who refused to adulate Edward I and were ready to die for their disobedience.

What Arany had to realize after the revolution was that the authorities wanted to tame him not only by making him confess and regret his involvement with the revolution but also by making him write about the revolution in the unambiguously condemnatory terms used and required by the authorities. To spell out his deeds to let the authorities know them was only part of the task, and bearing in mind the remarkable efficiency of imperial espionage, it was probably the less vital part. The ultimate purpose of the exercise was the very act of renaming, the symbolic acknowledgment of, and commitment to, an antirevolutionary language. In response to the oppressive demands of that postrevolutionary decade, and amid the vicissitudes of East-Central-European history ever since, the cloud-scene of *Hamlet* calls to mind something entirely different from the much-quoted parallel in *Antony and Cleopatra*. True, the similarities are striking in many ways: in the dialogue between Antony and Eros the clouds are also compared to animals by Antony ("Sometime we see a cloud that's dragonish, / A vapour sometime like a bear or lion, / . . . That which is now a horse, even with a thought / The rack dislimns and makes it indistinct / As water is in water"), and Eros does not try to contradict Antony's propositions any more than Polonius did, and even his "Ay, noble lord" or "Ay, my lord" or "It does, my lord" may be characterized by a similarly invariable readiness to agree. But the latent differences are obvious enough and go beyond the divergent meanings the two scenes attribute to the cloud metaphor, far beyond the subtle difference that for Antony "the evanescence of the cloud is used as an image of changes in one's identity, and the transience of things," whereas "underlying Hamlet's mockery is his sense not of transience but of indeterminacy" (Edwards 1989, 168). Unlike Polonius,

Eros for some time does not know what kind of language game they are playing; in spite of Antony's opening line about himself at the beginning of their dialogue ("Eros, thou yet behold'st me?") it is not until Antony's final explanation that Eros realizes that the parable is about his master's final inability to keep his identity. "My good knave Eros, now thy captain is / Even such a body. Here I am Antony, / Yet cannot hold this visible shape, my knave. . . . Nay, weep not, gentle Eros. There is left us / Ourselves to end ourselves" (4.14.1–22). More importantly, Eros is neither expected nor compelled to adjust his opinion to that of his master's; his agreements are not tactical and hide no ulterior purpose. Though he is a knave of Antony's, and their relation is no less hierarchical than that of Hamlet and Polonius, in their dialogue the dimension of power is irrelevant.

More similar to the cloud-scene in *Hamlet*, at least from this (East-Central-European) point of view are the forced acts of renaming Katherina is made to perform for Petruchio in *The Taming of the Shrew*. She is demanded to call the sun first the moon, then the sun, finally the moon again, and as long as she is reluctant to do so, Petruchio denies her request to take her back to her father's house, until in the end Katherina's defiance is (or pretends to be) broken. "Forward, I pray, . . . / And be it moon, or sun, or what you please. / And if you please to call it a rush-candle, / Henceforth I vow it shall be so for me." The ensuing dialogue resembles that of the cloud-scene in *Hamlet* precisely in its dimension of power.

> *Petruchio:* I say it is the moon.
> *Katherina:* I know it is the moon.
> *Petruchio:* Nay, then you lie. It is the blessed sun.
> *Katherina:* Then, God be blest, it is the blessed sun.
> But sun it is not, when you say it is not,
> And the moon changes even as your mind.
> What you will have it nam'd, even that it is,
> And so it shall be for Katherine.
>
> (4.5.1–22)

Petruchio is not yet satisfied, and makes Katherina greet an old man as if he were a budding maid, then apologize for her "mistaking eyes" (4.5.27–48). In all these lessons of the "taming school" Katherina is required to perform a mere speech act with or (as is usual in what we call soft dictatorships) without internal assent; she is not expected to believe that the sun is the moon or vice versa, only to pretend to be convinced by Petruchio. (As Hortensio urges her to obey: "Say as he says, or we shall never go.") Yet she realizes the far-reaching psychological consequences of the seemingly easy verbal exercise: as soon as she would say as he says, she would lose (give up) her formerly unconditional claim (and right) to an opinion of her own. The quick shift from the brutal methods (to deny her food, not to let her sleep, etc.) whereby Petruchio tried to break her will to the physically painless nature of such testing speech acts indicate that the dividing line East-Central-Europeans draw between hard and soft dictatorships is always relative, and the subtly intimidating methods of the latter rely on the traumatic memories of the former. After the defeat of the 1848–49 revolution many were executed or imprisoned, and Arany's task to write an appropriate verbal description of his behavior followed (and recalled) those executions and imprisonments the same way as Katherina's verbal task followed her physical ordeals and must have evoked their memory. When Arany wrote in 1861 that Polonius wanted to see the clouds as three subsequent animals *for the sake of* Hamlet, he knew the situation he was talking about.

The personal experiences of later Hungarian authors provided no less material dovetailing with the cloud-scene. To illustrate the grim historical associations lurking behind possible East-Central-European interpretations of the scene let it suffice to quote the distinguished literary historian, G. Béla Németh, who wrote a study, in the 1970s, on the post-1849 period of a Hungarian newspaper, and characterized its incorrigibly opportunist editor by saying that after the revolution "he could still easily see the cloud as a camel, whenever that was what the authorities wanted, but now the historical situation was such that he preferred to see it as just a cloud, hence the most characteristic feature of his paper was its divided loyalty" (Németh 1976, 442). Being able to mention *the* clouds without having to name the scene or even the play, the casual reference of the literary historian, significantly not a Shakespeare scholar himself, reveals that the cloud-scene became a well-known symbol for him and the readers he had in mind; the allusion also indicates that it was the power-relations of the scene that mattered for the members of this interpretive community, and *resistance* was their implied ideal of behavior for anybody in Polonius's situation. As Németh was the editor of Arany's collected studies and reviews, he knew very well Arany's complex interpretation of the scene, but most probably it was his own share of humiliating experiences that made him associate Polonius's responses simply with the dilemma of any individual vis-à-vis an oppressive regime. After having been expelled from Eötvös College in 1949, he had to accept a series of demeaning jobs during the hard dictatorship of the 1950s, and when he was allowed to teach in a high school in the early 1960s, he was soon commissioned with a series of philosophical seminars for his colleagues (the first test), as a result of which he was labeled a reactionary and was demanded to give (as the second test) a speech to celebrate April 4, the liberation from German occupation and the symbolic beginning of Soviet rule, and finally, as his speech was found lacking in enthusiasm for the new regime, he was warned that the only way to keep his job would be to apply voluntarily (as the third and most decisive test) for membership in the Communist Party. We may guess from the scholar's autobiographical essay how difficult it must have been to do so, but he finally complied, and although this enabled him to become a university professor with ample clandestine opportunities to incite and instigate his students to independent thinking, the haunting memory of his self-submission remained vivid enough to exclude any alternative interpretation of the cloud-scene, and make it a parable about power. His bitter parody of the party officials' reasoning may illustrate the situation in which this interpretation of Hamlet's questions and Polonius's answers seemed so inevitable: "Philosophy, literature, history? Come off it. The Party Center would decide, here and now, what you are supposed to say about somebody or something, and those who can repeat it with utmost precision will be rewarded" (Németh 1996, 15–16). From this point of view the epistemological evasiveness of the clouds, or of anything, is pathetically irrelevant.

Later generations, born after World War II, may have been far too young before 1956 to have intimidating memories of the Stalinist-style hard dictatorship. But growing up in the soft version of the 1960s and 1970s still felt like being compelled, if ever so subtly, to join a compulsory renaming exercise. In retrospect it seems that most of the ideological subjects a university undergraduate had to study were invented not so much for the usefulness, if any, of the information they had to offer, but for making sure that everybody accepted the evaluative terminology the Party sought to disseminate. Acceptance required no conviction: the key terms were to be kept intact, but the examiners cared less and less if the students really believed what they were talking about or merely recapitulated the lesson, say, in political economy, to get it over and done with. The deceptively smooth workings of the required terminology hinged on a master-term, the most guarded (because the most vulnerable) of them all, the label for 1956, "ellenforradalom," that is, "counterrevolution." After a painfully long reign of cautiously uncommitted terms like "tragic events" or "regrettable events," the subsequent renamings of 1956, from the first partisan (but semiofficial) attempt, in January 1989, to call it in a broadcast "an uprising of the people," to the post-1989 revival of the long-suppressed but privately cherished and ultimately ineradicable word "revolution," may epitomize the obvious connection between having the power to rule over the present and having the authority to rename the past. For the man of the street the official replacement of the term "counterrevolution" with "revolution" meant (and still means) much more than the change of the official name of the country itself from the Hungarian People's Republic, a typical coinage of the communist regime, back to the former name, the Hungarian Republic, that used to signify the promising but tragically short-lived form of state that had abolished the Hungarian Kingdom on 1 February 1946, and survived till 20 August 1949. In most cases, however, the renamings unearthed and retrieved former names that were nostalgically remembered by one section of the elder generations and resentfully by another, due to differences in upbringing, social position, ideological conviction, or sheer temperament. In the building of Eötvös Loránd University, my own alma mater in Budapest, there used to hang a carefully framed sign on the wall, with golden letters against a black background, indicating that you reached the Department of Dialectical and Historical Materialism, hence (so you were supposed to infer) anything idealistic, let alone metaphysical, would be deplored here as false, evil, obsolete, and reactionary. In 1989 the sign was promptly replaced by a new one of exactly the same size and colors, alerting you to the Department of Metaphysics, with the new implication that anything (Heaven forbid) materialist, whether dialectical or historical, would be duly branded here as vulgar, immoral, and totalitarian. The names of most streets, roads, squares, and many other topographical units that had been changed in the late 1940s and early 1950s to obliterate the traces of the previous regime, were quickly subjected to a new revision after 1989 either to reclaim their former names or to acquire brand new ones, with the tacit assumption that society at large would both accept the necessity and understand the rationale of all such changes. Yet that assumption was often unwarranted: the rechristening of "Liberation Square" as "the Square of the Franciscans" in Budapest was accompanied by a fierce debate whether what the Russians did in (and to) Hungary in 1945 could still be called liberation even if their troops, while truly liberating the country from German occupation, raped women, ransacked homes (with a curious predilection for collecting watches), and their invasion soon turned into a so-called "transitory stay," a euphemistic official term for something that lasted for four decades and was hardly less oppressive, especially in the 1950s, than any comparable sojourn of a superpower on Hungarian soil ever before. The landslide defeat of the first democratically elected government (1990–94) at the second election in 1994 could be explained in many ways, but as a student of Shakespeare I would suggest that it tried to rename too many clouds too suddenly not to elicit large-scale resistance.

All in all, the East-Central-European déja vu experience when watching the cloud-scene in *Hamlet* is overwhelming, and anybody old enough in the region to have witnessed at least one *translatio imperii* would not be surprised by the prince's first abrupt question, but would take it as the all too familiar opening gambit in the renaming game, and would expect, indeed could predict almost verbatim, all the rest. No wonder that in this region it is difficult to frown upon Polonius as nothing but a pathetic old fool, and not to recognize in his answers the epitome of all our humiliations. Characteristically not only of the Polish experience, the Polonius of Tadeusz Różewicz's poem "Conversation with the Prince" addresses Hamlet from the point of view of a powerless subject who cannot disobey ("I am deferential / you can impress / any mark upon me / you are the seal / I am the wax of the world"), and after revealing his identity behind Polonius's mask ("Prince / I am not a clerk / I am a contemporary / poet / the year is 1958") he can still reenact the cloud-scene almost verbatim ("You ask about the shape of yonder cloud / 'tis like a camel indeed / thou think'st it is like / a weasel / it is back'd like / a weasel / or like a whale? / very like a whale"), only to elicit derision from Hamlet, who will kill him anyway ("you laugh at me / good prince / you detect the windbag / behind the arras"), and the poem ends with a gruesome German line quoted from Gottfried Benn, "Das Hirn verwest so wie der Arsch," [the brain rots like the arse] (Różewicz 1982, 75). As the name itself refers to the country known as Polonia in Shakespeare's time, and clearly indicates somebody of Polish extraction, scholars have often wondered why Shakespeare would give such an unlikely name to a Danish courtier, so unlikely indeed that it was advisable at one point (as the bad Quarto shows) to change it to Corambis. One of the hypotheses is that he wanted to allude to one of his sources, *The Counsellor*, a recently (in 1598) published book on good government, translated from the Latin original of the Polish statesman Laurentius Goslicius. Well, plausible enough, but only because we have to preclude, alas, the alternative explanation that Shakespeare divined the vicissitudes of twentieth-century East-Central-European history, formed a character to match all the psychic requirements of survival, and after some hesitation found Polonius a better-sounding name than, say, Hungarus.

III
Staging

The British Personality of the Millennium: British Shakespeares, Amateur and Professional, in the New Century

Michael Dobson

THERE IS AN ODD SILENCE IN THE MIDDLE OF BRITISH CULTURE AT the moment, and one of its names is England. One of its others, I will be suggesting, may be Shakespeare. My illustration to these rather sweeping claims will be a description of some of the ways in which Shakespeare participated in British celebrations of the millennium. This may sound like a simple exercise in factual reportage, but in practice one of the only things that public events involving Shakespeare in Britain in the year 2000 made resoundingly clear was that in Shakespeare's own country—insofar as such a thing still exists, given all that has happened to redefine England and/or Wales and/or Scotland and/or Ireland and/or Britain since 1616—there is no longer anything approximating to consensus about either "Shakespeare" or "Britain" or "the millennium." The millennium was bound to be an ambiguous festival in a country that still has a state church but that has officially embraced multiculturalism, and it was inevitable that there would be some attempts to transfer attention from the celebration of the formerly national religion to the celebration of a supposedly still common national culture, represented by Shakespeare. But in practice both religion and culture took a backseat to politics, and in British public life, or perhaps "British" public life, the year 2000 was still heavily preoccupied with the implications of the year 1999. That much more momentous year saw the inauguration of separate parliaments for Wales, Scotland and Northern Ireland, and thus the reversal of a historical process, much-accelerated during Shakespeare's own lifetime and much-articulated in Shakespeare's own canon, by which England had long aspired to disappear as anything other than the normative core of a united Great Britain. In the year 2000, as far as the constitution was concerned, Scotland, Wales, and Ulster had now reappeared, but England had not, its voters represented only in the Westminster parliament of the former United Kingdom. The only English electorate that has achieved a comparable extra layer of representation, predictably enough, is the population of London, who have suddenly acquired a directly elected mayor: this discrepancy has still further increased the capital's sense of itself as an independent city-state with nothing to do with the rest of England whatsoever.

So with the national religion, the national culture and the national identity all in a thoroughly British muddle, millennial attempts to mark something definite and rich-with-shared-public-meaning by appeal to Shakespeare were always liable to achieve at most an inadvertent nostalgic pathos. It is of some interest that the title "Man of the Millennium" was conferred on Shakespeare by a poll of listeners to BBC Radio 4, the broadcasting channel formerly known as the Home Service: as its unchanged initials suggest, the BBC—the British Broadcasting Corporation—is one of the few national institutions so far unredefined by devolution, the national broadcasting service of a nation that does not quite exist any more. (One might contrast here the current fuss at the National Theatre in London, which is having to revise its charter in the wake of proposals made quite independently north of the border to establish a separate Scottish National Theatre.) There is some confusion, indeed, as to whether the voters in the BBC poll felt that they were conferring the title "Man of the Millennium" or "Briton of the Millennium" (the poll was in fact officially for "British Personality of the Millennium"). Some, doubtless, would have felt that the two were synonymous anyway, but the latter seems especially resonant: Shakespeare's strangely low profile in the British Isles at the moment may be directly related to the fact that he is indeed a definitive Briton, the national writer of history plays for a nation that is itself rapidly becoming history. I mean to complicate this familiar newspaper-editorial lament, however, by talking a little later about a much less visible and much more English Shakespeare, still deeply embedded in a distinctive if largely unacknowledged sphere of English public life. That is the Shakespeare of the amateur theater, an institution that also used Shakespeare to celebrate the millennium, but in ways much less widely reported in Britain and I suspect almost unknown in the rest of Europe.

More of that in due course: meanwhile, let us start from where we are, in the postmillennial hangover. At the time of writing, in the autumn of the year 2001, there is practically no Shakespeare being performed professionally in the capital whatsoever—less than I for one have ever known, and quite possibly less as a proportion of the available repertory than at any time since 1660. My own students, required this term to write about a live production of a Shakespearean tragedy or history, have been obliged to seek out a fringe production of *Othello* played in a basement near King's Cross Station by a cast of six, a cast that at some performances has outnumbered the audience. Other college groups have resorted to a revival of an adaptation called *The Yiddish Queen Lear*, reports of which are not favorable. Admittedly, as of a fortnight ago there is now a free-standing RSC *Merchant of Venice* running in the studio-sized Pit prior to a national tour of small venues, but otherwise—nothing. This lack of live Shakespeare can partly be explained by economic factors—lots of companies revived plays by the Man of the Millennium in 2000, and will not be able to repeat such large-cast extravagance for a while yet, and the American tourists who can normally be relied upon to subsidize Shakespeare in London are further discouraging such revivals by staying away in their droves in the aftermath of September 11. But it also has to be admitted, as the low attendances for the *Othello* suggest, that the interest in Shakespeare that briefly flared anew in Britain from the success of *Shakespeare in Love* in 1998–99 through the millennium has now quieted down to an almost deafening silence. The most striking symptom of this is perhaps the lack of media interest to date in what is currently happening to the nation's most conspicuous designated Shakespearean institution, the Royal Shakespeare Company. The RSC marked the year 2000 by performing a magnificent feat that it had not attempted since the Shakespeare tercentenary of 1964: under the heading of "This England," using four directors and three Stratford venues (and another three in London when it transferred), they revived both tetralogies of history plays from *Richard II* through to *Richard III*, briefly enabling theatergoers at one climactic point in the repertory to see all eight plays in sequence over three days. By contrast the RSC has marked the year 2001, its own fortieth birthday, by announcing, in May, the abolition of the repertory system on which its identity as a company has always been based, thereby guaranteeing that no such large-scale company project as "This England" will ever be possible again. The RSC management has just capped this, in October 2001, by revealing plans to demolish its headquarters, the Royal Shakespeare Theatre: they have apparently recognized at long last that the venue that saw Komisarjevsky's *Comedy of Errors* and Olivier's Coriolanus and Brook's *Dream* and Nunn's *All's Well* and Sher's Richard III cannot possibly be suitable for the high-quality production of Shakespeare. So far these developments have attracted surprisingly little attention outside the ranks of the stagehands and support staff who have been fired in their droves in Stratford and at the Barbican, or beyond the baffled membership of the RSC's mailing list. (There is a sufficient air of incipient mutiny among the actors, though, for there to be serious talk of secession, and we may yet see the company fragment into the Official RSC, the Provisional RSC, the Real RSC, the Continuity RSC, etc.) Such journalists as have bothered with the latest announcement, for example, have characteristically been much less interested in the status and nature of live Shakespeare than they have been in real estate, lamenting the proposed destruction of the theater only as a dangerous possible precedent for the demolition of other 1930s listed buildings. As with so much else in present-day Britain, the Shakespearean theater is news only in so far as it might affect property prices.

The Professional Millennium

In truth there was already something hollow or at very least conflicted about the public, professional Shakespeare celebrations of the preceding year which made this current postmillennial apathy almost predictable. The focus for the country's millennial celebrations was itself a notoriously hollow structure, the Millennium Dome, whose contents—kept secret until the building actually opened—were in marked contrast to the exhibitions held fifty years earlier for the millennium's chief precedent as a public event, the 1951 Festival of Britain. Shakespeare did get mentioned in the souvenir book, the modestly titled *Official Commemorative Album for the Millennium*, but when the Dome itself was royally and officially inaugurated, at a grand VIP gala party late on 31 December 1999, the building's content (or the lack of it) occasioned considerable surprise.[1] I have to confess that I was not myself on the guest list for that opening party (despite having written the bit about Shakespeare for the tacky souvenir book), but was instead at an alternative gathering on the other side of the river, directly opposite on Thomas Nashe's beloved Isle of Dogs. Here we millennial revelers had to content ourselves with a) watching a Pink Floyd–like light show playing on the Dome's jellyfishlike roof as the royal procession motored past downriver toward the festivities, b) indulging that brief, now-forgotten utopian hope that the entire Internet would crash at midnight, and c) speculating as to what exactly Her Majesty would have to be polite about when she got inside the Dome and looked around. Everyone at the party I was at assumed that there would be something by way of a Shakespeare section, which just shows what sort of class-fragment of throwbacks I associate with:[2] but in the event the Dome was so deliberately light on anything that could possibly connote old-style Britishness, so fearful of patriotic nostalgia, that there was no trace of the Man of the Millennium to be seen in any of the themed "zones" into which its cavernous interior was divided. The last thousand years seemed in practice to have dwindled to the last decade: there were no History or Culture Zones at all, just a nightmare perpetual 1990s present of the Money Zone (sponsored by the City of London), the Work Zone (sponsored by Manpower), the Body Zone (sponsored by Boots, L'Oreal, and Roche), the Talk Zone (sponsored by British Telecom), the Journey Zone (sponsored by Ford), and so on. It is easy to imagine how Shakespeare might have been included in any or all of these Zones, but the fact remains that he was not. He appeared fleetingly on video, but only to be ritually disavowed: in the specially commissioned episode of *Blackadder* projected at intervals on a giant screen, a present-day Blackadder time-traveled back to Elizabethan London and, meeting Shakespeare, kicked him painfully in the shins in the name of all the schoolchildren obliged to suffer in his name since his death.

Despite this, School Shakespeare did get into the Dome later, when large numbers of primary schoolchildren filed into the building to perform activities prescribed by the Shakespeare component of the National Curriculum on something called the Our Town Stage. If that sounds like a more suitable venue for Thornton Wilder than for William Shakespeare, it is hardly surprising, since this part of the Dome, the one bit specifically oriented toward the great native tradition of live drama, was sponsored by McDonald's. The activities performed in the name of Shakespeare on the Our Town Stage, though, did not exactly extend to performing Shakespeare, or at least not as we know it: although a press release boasted that every single one of Shakespeare's plays had been seen on the Our Town Stage over three days, this was no full-text twenty-four-hour marathon but a medley of the shortened single scenes and half-dramatized plot summaries that the National Curriculum regards as more than enough of Shakespeare for ten-year-olds to be going on with. It is worth mentioning here that Shakespeare's compulsory presence on the state school curriculum throughout Britain remains both controversial and contradictory: controversial in that many schoolteachers resent having particular approaches to the teaching of Shakespeare forced upon them, and contradictory in terms of what schools are actually required to do with, or vaguely near, the plays. Up to the age of eleven, students are required to do Tudor England, and do it often—apart from the odd Viking, everything between the Romans and Henry VII has vanished entirely from state school history, so that the subject-matter of all Shakespeare's history plays except the least-revived, *All Is True*, is rapidly vanishing forever from popular memory. Henry VIII's six wives and Elizabeth I's big dresses, though, come around again and again, with Shakespeare's life and times included as one mandatory element of the standard olde Ladybird account of Merry England. It is only at fourteen and sixteen that students actually have to write about prescribed single plays, and it is only then that they are told that sixteenth-century England was not merry at all but was in fact rife, as can be seen from Shakespeare's plays, with social inequality, sexism, racism, and so on. I am not necessarily suggesting that this was not the case, but it does seem to be true that the lasting impression given to British students by this two-phased introduction to the career of their national poet is that Shakespeare is, first, twee, and, second, objectionable.

Given the vacuousness of the Dome and the potential ineptitude of the National Curriculum, it is just as well that in the far off golden days of the year 2000 there was still a Royal Shakespeare Company, an organization that has intermittently been much more successful at relating Shakespeare's plays to contemporary British life and even at making them seem really exciting. The "This England" project, the RSC's own millennial event, now seems in retrospect to have been a perfect culminating specimen of the company's work—intermittently, it was indeed wonderfully successful at relating Shakespeare's plays to contemporary British life and at making them seem really exciting in the process. I am not about to describe the entire eight-play cycle in detail here—if you want that sort of thing, you can look it up in the *Shakespeare Survey*—but I do want to comment on one particularly interesting and much-discussed feature of the whole project. That is its refusal, unlike the Peter Hall–John Barton *Wars of the Roses* of 1964 or the Bogdanov-Pennington *Wars of the Roses* of the late 1980s, to adopt a single style or mode across the complete sequence of plays. Stephen Pimlott started the cycle with a modern-dress, white-box *Richard II* in the tiny Other Place; Michael Attenborough continued with a medieval-dress, sumptuously-lit *Henry IV Parts 1 and 2* in the 400-seat Swan; then Edward Hall put that play's survivors back into modern dress for a big-scale World War II–like *Henry V*, quite possibly the last Henry V that will ever be seen in the Royal Shakespeare Theatre. Michael Boyd then directed a whole different set of actors for the whole of the first tetralogy back in the Swan, all of it staged, again, in a stylized late-medieval look. To some extent, this eclecticism was purely pragmatic—RSC directors have not agreed about anything very much over the last few seasons, especially casting for a whole repertory season, and that is one important reason why the company's Artistic Director Adrian Noble has been able to sell them the idea of splitting up the RSC into a whole series of one-off subcompanies of no fixed abode, turning Noble into a West End impresario in the process. The chances of Pimlott, Attenborough and Co. teaming up to make shared decisions about the whole of "This England" as a sort of collective directorial cabinet were always pretty remote, even if that had seemed desirable. What is interesting, I think, is that it did not: the RSC did not want to commit itself either to a shared identity or style as a company, or to a shared view of which England "This England" sought either to represent or to play to. It was a deliberately inconsistent theatrical event both about and for a willfully inconsistent country: neither the lonely Blairite achievements of Prince Hal across the first tetralogy nor the ultimate defeat of the comparably single-minded PR-specialist Richard III at the close of the second were offered as parts of some larger overall statement or perspective about the making of the proto-British Tudor state that both might have served. Like postdevolution Britain itself, or the multiply zoned Dome in its capital, "This England" managed in the end to add up to rather less than the sum of its parts.

The Amateur Millennium

Elsewhere in 2000, though, Shakespeare was invoked in the service of a much more single-minded view of "This England," and one that seems likely to survive the break-up of Britain, which is so puzzling other areas of national discourse. It is an interesting exercise, I think, to subtract all those features of English popular national mythology and popular culture that are associated with the "British project" and see what England has left. Take away "Rule Britannia" and the last night of the Proms; take away John Bull; take away the imperial and postcolonial capital London; take away the Scottish and Dutch and German and in any case British or would-be British monarchy from James I onward; take away King Arthur; take away roast beef (if BSE and foot and mouth have not done that already); and what is there? There is a white flag bearing a red cross, occasionally worn by football hooligans; there is the Church of England; there is cricket; there is gardening; there is morris-dancing; and there is amateur theater. In short, there is what has been demonized over the last decade or so (by a national press terrified at the prospect of its nation dwindling to a province) as Middle England, a mysterious realm so unfashionable that its only current voices in national public discourse are provided by a few remnants of the Conservative Party, and certain residual provincial corners of the BBC Home Service—most obviously *Gardeners' Question Time* and *The*

Archers. Middle England is perhaps the last refuge of a vigorous, vernacular Shakespeare whose works are still felt to be at the center of an English national, or at least civic, culture. And so it was that amateur dramatic societies in market towns and suburbs the length and breadth of England, determined to marshal all their material, spiritual, and human resources in honor of Millennium Year, felt called upon to revive one Shakespeare play or another in the year 2000.

I am going to cite only one such revival as an example, the production of *The Winter's Tale* staged by the Lymington Players in southwest Hampshire. (Lymington, by the way, is a Georgian market town on a small estuary on the south coast: like many other English towns it used to have a professional theater, but in Lymington's case it had already lost it well before the coming of the cinema, lapsing into stagelessness soon after the harbor silted up in the early nineteenth century, ending the town's career as a naval base.) I should probably preface this account, though, with some general remarks about English am dram, since it has hitherto attracted little if any attention among professional Shakespearean academics in Britain, and is, I imagine, even less well-known among their colleagues on the European mainland. (I suspect, for example, that the British Council keep pretty quiet about the amateur theater.) Amateur dramatic societies supply a popular setting for murder mysteries (and reciprocate by providing the only contemporary home for any of Agatha Christie's dramatic works except *The Mousetrap*), but they are otherwise largely ignored in modern print culture: they are comprehensively shunned by scholars of contemporary Shakespeare, who are heavily biased in favor of the metropolitan (especially the work of big-name directors in subsidized companies) and, less prominently, the avant-garde. Theater professionals, meanwhile, are inclined to blench, cross themselves, and change the subject if am dram is even mentioned in their hearing. Amateur dramatic societies are equally avoided by professors of contemporary cultural studies, who have largely confined their attentions to the intellectual landscapes either of the élite or of the oppressed. Consequently, practically nothing you could call analytical has ever been written about am dram at all. It has inspired a great many how-to books, and a single classic satire, Michael Green's *The Art of Coarse Acting* (1964), but no great works of criticism or sociology or cultural history.[3] Despite the supposed intellectual fearlessness and freedom from snobbery of the postwar academy, some things, it seems, are still considered either beneath notice or completely taboo. And one of them—possibly the defining social blind-spot of professional academia, a profession in perhaps necessary denial about its own social status, perpetually afraid of tarnishing its cultural capital by association with mere schoolteachers—is amateur Shakespeare: public performances carried out, often by middle-aged white English people, dressed up, who do not even have the excuse of professional ambition or financial gain to mask their shameless, transgressive, and appallingly respectable pleasure in the works of their national poet. If I achieve nothing else in this essay, let me at least outrage the taboo against admitting that this kind of thing goes on once and for all. Yes, any readers who saw the *BBC South Today* feature on the Brownsea Island Open-Air Theatre production of *As You Like It* in 1981, that *was* me doubling Amiens, First Lord, and Jaques de Boys. Yes, my parents *did* meet as fellow members of the Stokesley Amateur Dramatic Society in the North Riding of Yorkshire. Yes, I *will* visit the primal amateur scene, however embarrassing for all concerned. If we are to avoid embarrassment, after all, we may as well give up the study of English culture altogether.

Invisible because unspeakably middlebrow it may be, but in the twenty-first century the amateur theater is still huge; far bigger than the professional theater. Admittedly, the number of societies has fallen since the glory days between the wars, but the last census conducted by the Central Council for Amateur Theatre, in 1989, estimated that Britain overall boasted 6,500 societies with 700,000 members and an annual audience of sixteen million—and these figures exclude school and university drama altogether. Despite the demographic problems involved in doing Shakespeare—a playwright who habitually wrote lots of roles for young men, who are in proverbially short supply in am dram—Shakespeare constitutes a significant proportion of this activity. (The Lymington Players, typically, perform three shows a year, one of which is always a Shakespeare.) If nothing else, the sheer scale of this phenomenon makes the occasional shrill claim that if the theory-crazed freaks in the universities do not all embrace humanism forthwith then

Shakespeare will be forgotten look pretty strange—Shakespeare is in fact an intensely popular writer, but a lot of his popularity is among people who apparently do not count as the populace. This massive survival of nonprofessional performance also greatly complicates, I think, what has become one of our dominant paradigms for thinking about the economics of Shakespearean drama right back to Shakespeare's own time, the notion of the commodification of culture. Despite Thatcherism, most human activity—especially around the arts—simply cannot be sustained on a "purely" economic basis: if everyone only acted rationally for financial gain, there would be no university academics, for a start, and no students for them to teach anyway, since child rearing would have vanished from the face of the earth. The early modern theater, though since the 1980s we have stressed its increasing professionalism and involvement in the rise of capitalism, belonged to a gift economy, and usually operated under the auspices of the civic. It turns out, looking at am dram, that there is still such a thing as society, and there is still theater that takes place in the space of the civic rather than on a purely commercial basis—if indeed there can be a "purely" commercial basis for an art form that, if you factor in the length of the apprenticeship and the structural periods of unemployment in calculating hourly rates, does not pay even many of its most successful professionals a living wage. It is quite ironic in this connection that during the rehearsal period of their millennial *Winter's Tale*, the Lymington Players invited a notable local Shakespeare specialist (based in nearby Southampton) to address the society about the play, none other than that expert on the commodification of early modern drama, Kathleen McLuskie, who regards talking to local amateur theater groups as a sort of obligatory community service. It might even be possible to cite McLuskie's career-long insistence on the defining commercial dimension of early modern theater as itself a feat of denial, since she is herself a notable ex-student actress, whose Doll Common in *The Alchemist*, for example, is still spoken of with awe and reverence among those who saw it. (Its director, incidentally, was another semilegendary academic figure, Mick Hattaway.) I probably do not need to add that the Lymington Players listened to her with exquisite politeness, and ignored everything she had to say about the play.

If Shakespeare's own activities were framed, at very least, by nonprofessional forms and arenas of performance—as his at once passionately supportive and utterly damning portrait of the rude mechanicals in A *Midsummer Night's Dream* suggests—then amateur drama in its modern form has been no less framed by Shakespeare, and the resort to Shakespeare to mark the millennium was inevitable. Whatever the commercial roles he may have served as a legitimating icon, Shakespeare has been and remains one of the signs of middle-English public culture, marking a legitimate space especially for that class that craves legitimate intellectual property above all else, and is prepared even to wear makeup in the village hall in order to make its claims to the national poet. The first modern am dram group in Britain, the Manchester Athenaeum Dramatic Society, 1847, performed more Shakespeare than anything else in pursuit of its stated aspirational aims, which were "to cultivate a taste for standard dramatic literature and poetry and to be a source of mutual improvement to its members." Perhaps its most important successor in founding the amateur theater movement of the next century characteristically entered the secular public realm via Shakespeare. In 1901 the Stockport Unitarian Sunday School Dramatic Society were denied the use of the Unitarian Hall after the church elders objected to their construction of a tunnel between the stage-right and stage-left wings, and instead broke away to produce their initial production, of *The Merchant of Venice*, as the Stockport Garrick Society (Taylor 1976, 38). The entire little theater movement, in which visionaries such as Barry Jackson (and less prominently my own grandfather, a Shavian Methodist called John Berriman) were so caught up during the 1920s and '30s, descended from this crucial move.

It is fitting, then, that the Lymington Players' millennial production of *The Winter's Tale* found itself in some rivalry for personnel with the local church's homemade millennial pageant-play about the history of the parish: religion and the stage have not been natural allies for a long time, and celebrating the man from Stratford as Man of the Millennium in any context was always liable to look disrespectful toward the man from Nazareth whose birthday party this year was supposed to be. Fortunately, though, there was no competition for venues or dates: the pageant took place in St. Thomas's church itself in the autumn of 2000, while *The Winter's*

Tale played for a week in the early summer in the Players' home venue, the Malt Hall at the Lymington Community Centre. The Lymington Players have the same sort of relationship to the Malt Hall that the RSC does to the Royal Shakespeare Theatre, complaining endlessly about its cramped backstage area and its acoustics, but unlike the RSC they will never get National Lottery money to bulldoze it. Their home performance space, considerably smaller even than the Other Place in Stratford, doubles as Lymington's only cinema: it boasts about fifteen rows of fold-down red plush seats, and a lethally shallow proscenium-arch stage, slightly bigger than the average mantelpiece, but not by very much. It can accommodate a small cinema screen quite comfortably, but actors pretty much have to face the audience continuously, and keep moments when they pass one another to an absolute minimum, or they are liable to fall off.

This is entirely typical for an amateur theater group, and since it makes the sort of in-depth, visually oriented designer Shakespeare currently favored by professionals impossible anyway, it helped to underline the profound aesthetic differences between this *Winter's Tale* and any I have ever seen staged in the commercial or subsidized theater. The costumes, for example, scrupulously eschewed any resemblance to real clothes, confining themselves to general low-budget gestures toward the Renaissance. Am dram generally takes a fairly dim view of modern-dress Shakespeare, and here everyone was in tights and robes, which more or less matched the pennants that, apart from a small throne, constituted the entire set for acts 1, 2, 3 and 5. (Think Donald Wolfit on a shoestring, in a shoe box.) What am dram likes about Shakespeare is everything method-trained professionals are embarrassed by—his perceived disdain for realism, his large gestures, his interest in fairy tale, and indeed his kinship with the genre closest to am dram's heart, pantomime. In fact most participants in amateur drama do not go to the professional theater much anyway, except to see *Dick Whittington* or *Mother Goose* at Christmas.

In pursuit of what its proponents continue defiantly to regard as an utterly mainstream style of performance, amateur Shakespeare may well produce effects that look completely avant-garde, and this particular *Winter's Tale* effortlessly achieved levels of alienation of which Brecht could only dream. For one thing, like any other amateur show, it included a much wider range of body types than are seen in the commercial theater, their unfamiliarity thrown into sharp relief by one another and by the tiny scale of the stage. Whereas the professional stage pretty much only uses actors who have standardized generic healthy well-proportioned bodies that could work in lingerie adverts if their agents could not come up with anything else, that is pretty much the one type of physique that the amateur stage never sees, offering a quite different sense of the human species as a result. This Leontes, for example, though not the greatest I have ever seen, was easily the tallest—in fact the director of the Lymington production, Liz Watson, was pretty dismissive of Sir Antony Sher's performance of the role in Stratford the previous year, on the grounds that he was obviously too short to be adequately kingly. Time, too, offered physical characteristics rarely seen on the professional stage. *The Winter's Tale* had been carefully chosen to mark the millennium, partly on the grounds that it dramatized a coming-to-terms with the past and a movement forward into a new generation, and partly because it offered scope for the full demographic spread of the Society's members, from the middle-aged schoolteachers in Leontes' court to the Bohemian shepherdesses recruited from their classrooms, right through to Time—who could aptly be personified here by the Society's longest-serving member, and hence the figure best-known to its core audience, a local woman of ninety-six called Helen Tew. She was even supplied with a topical elaboration of part of her speech, toward its close, twinklingly delivered as a sort of local gossip:

> ... You yesterday
> Who saw a full Millennium pass away
> May grant me sixteen years! Of this allow,
> If ever you have spent Time worse ere now ...

And so on. As these examples may suggest, the relations between actor and role are profoundly different in amateur Shakespeare, as they are in am dram in any case, as respectable people deliberately play villains at arm's length, or as recognized local villains are seen to be playing roles far nicer than themselves; with an audience that largely consists of the cast's friends, neighbors, and families, the theatrical contract is wholly rewritten. (Everyone in the hall knew, for example, that the performers playing Leontes and Hermione are married, and it did make a difference.) It can be hard work, but it pays off: in amateur theater, the suspension of disbelief becomes an act of massive communal achievement. I was lucky enough to see two really exceptional Paulinas during 2000 and 2001: one was Deborah Findlay's high-maintenance lady-in-waiting-who-lunches in Nicholas Hytner's big-scale, high-gloss production on the National's immense Olivier stage in the summer of 2001, but the other was the supremely unaffected widow called Hazel Gibbs who played the role within about two square feet of badly lit boards in the Malt Hall in Lymington the year before. There are worse ways of celebrating a millennium—we should bear it in mind for the next one.

The Winter's Tale sold out for all six of its performances, there was a small notice in the *Lymington Times*, and then it was heard no more: "This England" transferred to Plymouth and Newcastle and then London and then it closed, and the RSC practically abolished itself behind it; and the Millennium Dome stands empty and disgraced and unwanted beside the Thames. Where does that leave Shakespeare in Britain in the early twenty-first century? Alive in the English provinces but dying in the ex-British metropolis? Condemned to an exclusively middlebrow afterlife, keeping the aspirations and fantasies of the lower middle classes alive in church halls? Let me close by inviting some comparative investigation as to whether these phenomena have any counterparts in the rest of Europe. If Shakespeare is "popular" in continental Europe, with whom is he popular? What social formations do his plays seem to ratify? Does Europe too boast Shakespeares every bit as localized as the Shakespeare of Hollywood purports to be globalized? I look forward to being able to report the answers to these questions back in London, back in England—or even, if it is not stretching a point nowadays, in Britain.

Notes

1. On the Dome, the celebrations on Millennium Eve, and Shakespeare, see also Höfele (2001).
2. This party was hosted by Charity Charity, global creative director of

J. Walter Thompson Advertising and advertising correspondent for *The Oxford Companion to Shakespeare,* to whom many thanks. The guests included, surreally enough, the ex-RSC actor Stephen Moore, perhaps best remembered as Parolles in Trevor Nunn's *All's Well* or as Marvin the paranoid android in *The Hitch-Hiker's Guide to the Galaxy.*

3. The most important histories to date are Taylor (1976) and Rendle (1968). On the ideals and practices of the "Little Theatre" movement during its inter-war heyday, see especially Downs (1934).

4. *Amateur Theatre in Great Britain* (1989).

Accommodating Shakespeare to Ballet: John Cranko's *Romeo and Juliet* (Venice, 1958)

Nancy Isenberg

JOHN CRANKO'S CHOREOGRAPHY OF *ROMEO AND JULIET* IS ONE OF the most popular among ballet companies throughout Europe and beyond. But not everyone knows that it was originally created for the summer festival of the Teatro Fenice in Venice in 1958 and performed by the ballet corps of Milan's La Scala. A twenty-one-year-old graduate of the Scala ballet school was beginning her career as prima ballerina, dancing the part of Juliet; the music was Prokofiev's, and the choreographer was a young South African making his living in Europe.[1] The ballet was an immediate success and would enter into the repertoires of many ballet companies. The dancer in the role of Juliet—Carla Fracci—would go on to become Italy's ballet icon and perform the role of Juliet for forty years to come. John Cranko would take up residence in Germany, where as artistic director he would turn the Stuttgart Ballet into a world-class company.

This paper explores the success of that choreography by Cranko as a felicitous coming together of cultural circumstance, ballet convention, and narrative source. It follows a trajectory that begins with the Soviet version to which Cranko's work reacted and yet to which it is inseverably bound through the music score and libretto. My study then moves on to its transfer from the Soviet to the Italian context of the late 1950s. Underlying the very idea of a *Romeo and Juliet* ballet of course are the tools of the composer, librettists, and choreographers, used to accommodate Shakespeare's drama to this other genre. As I proceed to explore the elements of ballet convention at work here, what emerges is a much closer connection between *Romeo and Juliet* as ballet and its

Elizabethan source than would first appear evident. With all this, however, I do not overlook the way in which, as ballet, *Romeo and Juliet* offers its own interpretative perspective on Shakespeare's narrative.

Cranko was the first of a long series of choreographers outside the Soviet Union to tackle the Russian music score and libretto and try to produce from them a ballet with a more "Western" flavor. He had seen the Bolshoi performance in London a couple of years earlier. That production brought with it a history of difficulties and setbacks. In 1934, Prokofiev had begun working on the score and scenario for the Kirov theater, which subsequently backed down. The Bolshoi took over the commission in 1935, but they too broke the contract.[2] So although the three suites Prokofiev derived from the score were enjoying their due recognition in Russia's concert halls, the ballet *Romeo and Juliet* quietly had its début elsewhere, in Brno, Czechoslovakia, in 1938. Finally in 1940, the Kirov took on the challenge of performing the ballet that was received enthusiastically by the Leningrad public. In 1946 the Bolshoi revived it in Moscow, and went on to produce the immortalizing 1954 film version with Galina Ulanova in her original Kirov role as Juliet. As a result, the fame of Ulanova and of this ballet spread throughout the Western world. With the death of Stalin in 1953, the ensuing climate of political reform and the opening up of a dialogue with the West, the time was ripe for the Bolshoi's first ever tour outside the Soviet Union, which took them to London. It was that 1956 production, with the forty-six-year-old Ulanova still dancing her Juliet, that John Cranko had seen.

While, like others, he found the music inspiring, he saw the choreography as too heavily pantomimed, too formal and "academic" in its movement. He would take Prokofiev's music and write a new choreography. But he could not take the music without the libretto; they were indivisible, the multidisciplinary creative achievement of Prokofiev and his three collaborators: the theater director Serjei Radlov, choreographer Leonid Lavrovsky, and playwright Andrei Piotrovsky. As Cranko redesigned the bodies on the stage in reaction to what he had seen in London, little was he aware perhaps of how deep his debt was.

In an interview with a Venetian newspaper on the occasion of his premiere, Cranko explained that he wanted to give greater importance to dance movement than he had seen in the Russian choreography, that he wanted to accentuate the lyricism and the tragic moments of the young lovers' drama, and to bring the ballet narrative closer to the spirit of Shakespeare's text (*Gazzettino Sera* 1958, 3). Like many critics, he felt that the Soviet choreography laid too great an emphasis on the social conflict of the feuding families. It opened two of its three acts with long crowd scenes involving brawls and ended with an elaborate reconciliation scene. This was perfectly in keeping with the type of production of *Romeo and Juliet* being offered on the Soviet dramatic stage at the time when Prokofiev was writing his score in the mid-1930s and that still prevailed when the finished work was finally presented by the Kirov Ballet in 1940.[3] Shakespeare's Juliet became in the popular Soviet imagination something of a national heroine, for her courage to defy patriarchal authority, seen in perfect analogy with the modern revolutionary spirit. The reconciliation scene served to demonstrate that she had not died in vain. It also worked as a kind of political exemplum to encourage peace between the old and the new guard. Although Cranko's choreography is more corporeally expressive, freeing the body from the technical rigor of Russian-style dance movement, it is nonetheless mapped onto the same music score and libretto, with one important exception: Cranko eliminated the reconciliation scene and ended his narrative with Juliet's death.[4] However, in preserving the higher than average proportion of group scenes for a ballet, Cranko's choreography still draws a certain amount of attention away from Romeo's and Juliet's private drama as it focuses on social themes. Besides the street scenes with their brawls, Cranko's version also reproposes another very important group tableau: in this one, representing the Capulet feast, the ballet corps in heterosexual pairs performs the elegant "Cushion Dance," a sumptuous display of the authority of patriarchy, family wealth, conjugal coupling, and domestic rule. The music is grave, the movement in the performance space is complex and highly codified, the dancers' bodies are erect, their gestures rigidly prescribed. The function of this scene is very much like that of the baroque court dances where the aristocracy put on a display of its political authority. In the Italian postwar context of Cranko's work, Juliet's defiance of this authority could be read as a desire to break with traditional domestic mores strongly conditioned by the repressive official Catholicism.

The 1950s was a decade that witnessed radical changes in Italian society, beginning with mass migration from the countryside and the consequent explosion and diversification of the urban population. The postwar Economic Miracle was in full swing, with seductively attractive consumer goods beckoning at every turn. The incredibly cheap Fiat 500, launched in 1957, revolutionized people's lives, giving them the freedom to get out and about. The younger generation was becoming aware of alternative life styles, reflecting changes in social attitudes and norms (Forgacs 1996, 278–79). Domenico Modugno's "Volare" (To Fly), winner of the San Remo song festival in 1958, interpreted certain of their longings.[5] The Pill, marketed in 1956, although not available in pharmacies in Italy, symbolically represented a dream of pleasureful emancipation. Cinema, helped along by publicity billboards and wide-circulation illustrated magazines, played a vital role in substantiating emerging attitudes of longing and desire. It created icons of permissiveness like Brigitte Bardot, Elvis Presley, and Marlon Brando. Bardot's film début in *Et Dieu créa la femme* shares its anniversary with the pill; Elvis Presley, already known for his music, took to the screen in 1956, starring in *Love Me Tender*; and Marlon Brando's *On the Waterfront*, released in 1954, fixed in the popular imagination a new, more aggressive image of this already well-known actor. Italian cinema contributed its own myths: Sofia Loren, Marcello Mastroianni, and Anita Ekberg. Loren, already a well-established actress, became the focus of media attention when in 1957 she caused a scandal by marrying the divorced producer Carlo Ponte. Mastroianni and Ekberg owe their international fame to *La dolce vita*,[6] considered one of the most significant expressions of Italian culture at the end of the decade. It made Mastroianni the symbol of the Latin Lover and it made Ekberg, whose dip in the Trevi Fountain would become the "signature" scene of the film, the symbol of hedonism and freedom of expression in Italy (Gundle 1996, 310). Although these examples cover a wide spectrum of cultural situations, what they all have in common is their registering a focus on the individual in a changing society. It was becoming more and more difficult for the authority of church and family to have a strong hold over people's actions, thoughts, and aspirations. These were times for dreams—of self-satisfaction and the realization of personal objectives, outside the traditional social mores regarding courtship and marriage. Carla Fracci on the ballet stage was physically very different from the larger-than-life Ekbergs, Bardots, and Lorens of the cinema screen: in her stature and build, in her real physical presence before the audience, in the absence of wild scandals in her private life, she was much closer to her public. Those bosomy divas were a match for male fantasies; Carla Fracci could embody a young woman's dreams.

As for the ballet's portrayal of the strife between the two houses, representing another of its great themes, we have seen how politically charged it became in the Soviet reception. In the Italian context, it is not difficult to identify the sociopolitical parallels that would have made it meaningful. First of all, its historical origins can be traced back to the political tension in medieval Italy between the Guelfs and Ghibellines, supporters respectively of the pope and the Holy Roman Empire; since then, Italy has never been without its ideological divides, deriving from very strong local traditions, the cultural and economic dualism of North and South, deep family ties and strong political parties. In postwar, post-Fascist Italy, the tension between the "rival houses" easily finds any number of contemporary counterparts, in the antagonism between Catholics and non-Catholics, liberals and Marxists, conservatives and progressives, socialists and communists, monarchists and republicans (Martinelli, Chiesi, and Stefanizzi 1999, 6–26).

What becomes clear then is that Cranko's *Romeo and Juliet* "works" in this postwar context, in the sense that it offers both "vertical" markers (the generational conflict theme) and "horizontal" ones (the social conflict theme) with which its audience can construct meaningful analogies. However, the success of *Romeo and Juliet* as a ballet cannot be explained merely in sociopolitical terms. There are obviously artistic considerations to be taken into account as well, most of which were already determined by the Russian libretto and score. First of all, Prokofiev's music reveals the composer's revered attention toward Shakespeare's text. We can mention, for example, the first meeting between Romeo and Juliet at the Capulet feast. As we know, their speeches here construct a sonnet. Prokofiev portrays this scene musically with a madrigal, the sonnet's musical cousin that migrated to

England at the same time. During their second meeting, in the "balcony scene," we are presented with a piece of music based on Juliet's theme, then one on Romeo's, after which follow several bars where the two themes are interwoven, thus reflecting their solo speeches and the ensuing dialogue in Shakespeare's text. Mercutio's theme, on the other hand, is very erratic; it changes rapidly from one musical accent to another, and jumps abruptly from low to high notes and back again; the mood shifts from *allegro* to *scherzoso*, from boastful to quarrelsome. This same theme is used for his "death dance," only the tone is darker. The irony in his last words ("not so deep as a well, nor so wide as a church door") and the hatred in his malediction ("A plague on both your houses") echo clearly in the music. One example of an alteration by Prokofiev regards the second feud scene. The fateful fight that marks the turning point in the drama as well as the mathematical center of Shakespeare's text (Melchiori 1994, 212) is postponed in Prokofiev's composition. In this way, the musical score accentuates the tragic force this scene has in precipitating the ensuing events. Tybalt dies to fifteen slow inexorable beats of the kettle drum, which seem to pronounce the annihilation of all hope.

We know that Shakespeare fed his audience indicators of time in his characters' speeches, and this is especially so in *Romeo and Juliet* where the shifts from day to night and back to daytime are so important for the narrative and for the contextualizing of private and public. Orchestral music has its own conventions for indicating daytime—high-pitched instruments, treble keys, shorter and more rapid beats—as opposed to the use of lower pitched instruments, bass keys, longer and slower beats for nighttime. Prokofiev's attention to details about time is just one more way in which he demonstrated his fidelity to his source. The list of examples illustrating this could go on for several more pages, but I would like to move on now to ways the Elizabethan text adapts to more specifically performative conventions of ballet.

Shakespeare's dramatis personae for *Romeo and Juliet* offers a rich array of characters representing a wide variety of social conditions, from Friar Laurence to the Nurse to the servants and friends of both houses, from the Prince to the heads of household and their wives. The shift to ballet of this cast of characters was eased by the conventions of *ballet comique*, which tended to incorporate a wide range of characters from all walks of life. In Cranko's ballet, we have in addition gypsies and carnival performers in the street scenes. Their roles and dancing, following the conventions of ballet, are invested with the earthy elaborations of themes of erotic desire and defiance of social norms represented in the dialogues, for example, of Sampson and Gregory (which are not otherwise represented in the ballet), or in some of Mercutio's speeches.

The role of Romeo is cast onto the body of the *danseur noble*, who very strongly reflects the image of the dancing aristocrats of Europe's baroque courts from whom he descends; this can be seen in the shape and movement of his body (elongated, erect, privileging a well-turned ankle, neat and precise footwork, gracefully articulate arms, hands and fingers) and in his attire (booted foot, tights, close-fitting waistcoat, and full-sleeved blouse).

The role of Juliet is shaped along the lines of the Romantic ballet heroine with whom she shares an unhappy love story. Like Giselle, for example, she has fallen in love with the "wrong" man in defiance of the sociopolitical codes governing courtship and domestic affairs. Their deaths are indisputably personal tragedies; yet they also have a positive value as they indicate if not individual choice, at least the power to reject.[7]

Mercutio's choreography is a demanding one, just as his role is in Shakespeare, where his language gives vent to a frenetic mind. In both cases the performance calls for tremendous energy. Mercutio is an outsider, defying taboos in his thinking and likewise in his dancing. He is certainly not a representative of the status quo. In this sense, the dancing Mercutio finds his ballet roots in the "grotteschi" roles of court performances, where the aristocracy danced the noble roles and called in highly skilled professional dancers to perform transgressive, unnatural and sexually ambiguous ones.

Ballet, like other narrative genres, has its own tradition of villains, especially in the Romantic period. Tybalt with his sinister, destructive nature and his disregard for social codes (striking Mercutio under Romeo's arm) fits into this ballet mold; his movements are sharply accentuated and tend to close in upon him, his gaze is askew and cast downward. Rarely will he present himself in an expansive gesture; he is not at ease center stage.

Shakespeare's *Romeo and Juliet* is structured episodically, with twenty-four changes of scene. Ballet narrative by convention also proceeds episodically. The Russian libretto adopts this convention compressing its Elizabethan source into fourteen scenes. Shakespeare's drama was performed on a relatively unencumbered stage, which for ballet is a necessity. In danced versions of *Romeo and Juliet*, we find the same essential stage props we can account for in Shakespeare's time: masks, written notes, swords, knives, vials, etc., and most importantly a bed. Certain Elizabethan stage conventions regarding the actor's appearance also have counterparts in ballet: Juliet appears in a nightdress in her intimate scenes with Romeo. (In its sheer, soft adherence, it also serves in ballet to enhance the sensual quality of her choreography.) Ballet convention calls for the ballerina's hair to be pulled back tightly into a bun, but in these scenes, she wears it down, recalling another convention of the Elizabethan stage.

Of course there are many ways in which the ballet is different from the play. The logistics of ballet narrative obviously require the elimination of reported speech and reported action (hence on the one hand, for example, the physical presence of Rosaline on stage in the earlier scenes of the ballet, and, on the other, the elimination of Friar John and his undelivered message). They necessitate the simplification of the plot, the conflation of scenes and the elimination of secondary characters; they call for the employment of choruses—male and female—to establish social contexts and give an ethno-cultural sense of place, class, or gender; they call for the execution of pas de deux to express the heightened emotion in intimate relations, "variations" to provide multiple perspectives, and solos to communicate innermost sentiments. These are the precepts that informed the Russian libretto and choreography and they would later do the same for Cranko's production. When it comes to thematic subtleties however, Cranko does occasionally distance himself from his source. The Russian choice, mentioned earlier, to give more space to the choral scenes shifts the thematic accent away from the lovers. Cranko's choice (which became the "Western" solution, as confirmed, for example, in the well-known choreographies of Macmillan and Nureyev) to eliminate the reconciliation scene shifts it back to them again.

The original libretto was produced before we had fully recovered the complex nature of Shakespeare's text; before we had come to admit, among other things, how much it is concerned with sexual identity both male and female, and with the defying of sexual taboos. Yet in spite of this, when I see Cranko's ballet performed,[8] or for that matter any choreography danced to Prokofiev's music, I cannot help reading into it references to those themes we have come only recently to recognize. For example, although these ballets do not offer us a choreographic equivalent of Juliet's epithalamium speech, we can still see Juliet as "erotically fluent" when she dances with Romeo. There is no hesitation in her interaction with him, no uncertainty about questions of equilibrium between them, no shyness about his intimate grip as he lifts her. This happens because the dancer performing Juliet has acute knowledge and command of her body. Thanks to years of dedication to her art, and to intimate practice in partnering, the ballerina has achieved a "corporeal fluency" that can represent Juliet's physical desire. This analogy between role and dancer can be taken even further: Juliet in her self-determination, in her erotic awareness and in her opposition to patriarchal authority, is a defier of social and gender taboos. The history of ballet, as reconstructed in recent years by dance scholars using the tools of gender studies and cultural historicism, considers the lives of female dancers who have traditionally defied similar taboos: by violating dress codes, by exhibiting their bodies in public, by engaging in close physical contact with members of the opposite sex, etc. (see, for example, Foster 1996; Hanna 1988; Garafola 1997). Furthermore, ballet is a risky profession, where steady employment is not readily available, where it is difficult to make it to the top, where an accident can end a career and where in any case careers are normally brief. For this reason, many an aspiring young dancer has found herself, like Juliet, forced to act against parental authority in order to pursue her passion.

As for the figure of Romeo, here too we can find correspondences between dramatic role and ballet performer in the light of recent Shakespeare scholarship. Today we see in Romeo a study of male sexual identity. We see this in his fears of being effeminate, as he reveals in the fight scene after Mercutio's death ("O sweet Juliet, / They beauty hath made me effeminate," 3.1.113), and as he is described when he weeps his "womanish tears" in Friar Laurence's cell (3.2.109). Yet in the tomb scene he displays indubitable masculine energy in his decisiveness, in the vigor with which he forces open the gates to the tomb, in the boldness with which he faces his unknown foe. The male dancer by tradition is likewise often seen as effeminate. We should bear in mind that the popular convention of viewing male dancers as effeminate has its roots in those same attitudes found in Shakespeare's England regarding actors (for their emotional displays, for their cross-dressing), or members of the aristocracy (for their obsession with their bodies). But when the male dancer cuts through the air with his double and triple turns, flies across the stage with his grand jetés, or utterly dominates his partner in a lift, he demonstrates a power and an energy that, though graceful, is also indisputably virile. Thus the ballet role of Romeo provides its own performative and cultural frame of reference for querying male sexual ambiguity, in anticipation perhaps of developments in Shakespeare criticism.

We can say then that the roles of Romeo and Juliet in Cranko's ballet are a fairly faithful projection of Shakespeare's characters, and that, as with any other modern performance, are subjected to interpretation conditioned by the specific sociocultural context in which they are performed. It is also true that these roles, when they are performed in ballet, are further inspired by the personal and professional experience of the dancers themselves, and by the cultural history of their art. As for the ballet *Romeo and Juliet* as a whole, we have seen how certain conventions of that art combined with the cultural context in which it was presented to epitomize major themes present in the source text. Cranko's ballet worked against the backdrop of late 1950s Italy characterized by a new subjectivity and potential for desire. His choreography gave his dancers, in their solos, pas de deuxs, and choral pieces, the means to articulate the private and public tensions that define Shakespeare's drama.

Notes

1. Mario Pistoni danced Romeo. The performances, bringing together the orchestra of the Fenice and the ballet company of the Scala, were held at the open air Teatro Verde on the Island of S. Giorgio.

2. It is not clear to what extent these rejections were related to artistic rather than political issues. On the one hand, we have accounts by the prima ballerina and choreographer informing us that the dancers found the music too difficult to dance to, lacking the kind of clear, steady rhythm they were accustomed to. They also objected that the acting demands were outside their training and competence (Prokofiev [1959?], 224, 269). On the other hand, we know that in the wake of Kirov's assassination in 1934, the theater world suffered a purge of its avant-garde artists, including the director Serjei Radlov, one of Prokofiev's close collaborators.

3. According to Mikhail Morozov (1947, 49–52), in 1936 at the Moscow theater of the Revolution, Alexy Popov presented his innovative production of Shakespeare's *Romeo and Juliet*, in which he suppressed the idea of a lyrical drama or "tragedy of fate" in favor of "a social tragedy where the people of the new world, people imbued with humanistic ideas and feelings, Romeo and Juliet, were opposed by the ominous figures of the old world." Morozov also mentions a Georgian performance in 1940 that ends with a final curtain call revealing the gilt monumental statue of the young lovers "This finale ... never failed to provoke a great burst of enthusiasm among the young spectators."

4. This solution also has precedents on the dramatic stage, for example, in Peter Brook's 1947 production at Stratford.

5. According to legend, the song was inspired by a good bottle of Chianti and Chagall's paintings of people floating in the air. For those too young to remember, "Volare" became an international hit winning two Grammy awards including Song of the Year.

6. Filmed in 1959 and released a year later.

7. Interestingly for our purposes, a recent study of *Giselle* recognizes the ballet's debt to Shakespeare's drama (Banes 1998, 34). For us, then, *Giselle* can be seen as a "genetic" link, between our ballet and its narrative source.

8. There are no commercial videos available of Cranko's choreography. Today it is usually performed according to his revised version of 1962.

Jocza Savits: Organic Shakespeare for the Folk

Russell Jackson

JOCZA SAVITS USUALLY FIGURES IN ACCOUNTS OF THE DEVELOPment of Shakespearean staging as a pioneer of the return to (or revival of) Elizabethan theater forms. His achievements in Munich with the "Shakespeare Stage" are placed in the context of Ludwig Tieck's 1844 production of *A Midsummer Night's Dream* in Potsdam and Berlin, and the subsequent work of William Poel and Harley Granville-Barker (Hortmann 2001, 34–41; Kennedy 1993b, 35–37; Williams 1990, 185–90). Little attention has been paid to his aesthetic theories, which have largely been subsumed in depictions of him as pioneer of the movement toward "authenticity." In what follows, I hope to identify the ideological aspects of the "Shakespeare Stage" as they are evidenced in his voluminous writings. To this end, some attention must first be paid to this personal career, for Savits was first and foremost a practical theater worker.

Savits was born in 1847 in Török-Becse in Hungary, with Serbian nationality and Greek-Catholic religious affiliation. When he was nine his family moved to Vienna. Jocza received what Hans Durian, in his 1937 book-length study devoted to him, calls a "completely German" education. His early ambition was to become an architect, but he became an actor, and by 1867 he found himself in Weimar, whither he had gone in response to a summons from Franz Dingelstedt. Dingelstedt is an important and at the same time equivocal figure in the history of German-speaking Shakespeare production. He had argued eloquently that Shakespeare was best understood through performance, and had already staged enormously influential productions of previously unknown or unpopular plays during his tenure of posts in various cities—notably Weimar and Vienna. The productions toured, and were widely emulated, and Dingelstedt published his views and displayed his work as an adaptor in *Studien und Copien nach Shakespeare* (1858). His insistence that Shakespeare should be given faithfully and fully did not square with the heavily adapted acting versions he produced. Although he distanced himself in print from the English actor-manager's work, in scenic display Dingelstedt's productions in many respects resembled those of Charles Kean in London in the 1850s, and the simplifications and reordering of scenes he visited on the plays went even further than Kean's acting versions. Fifty years later Savits acknowledged his own—and the theater's—debt to Dingelstedt, and then proceeded to a devastating critique of his theories and methods.

When Franz Dingelstedt was appointed director of the Hofoper in Vienna he recommended Savits to the management of the Burgtheater, but the young actor failed to get the roles he hoped for and returned to Weimar in response to an offer from Grand-Duke Carl Alexander. With his wife, Luise Scharl, he became a mainstay of the comic repertoire in Weimar, and from 1875 onward he assumed responsibility for the staging of tragedies and "straight" plays, and undertook the training of actors, with particular attention to the training of the voice. "Precision of expression" was for him the most important and most immediately effective means of conveying the action, ideas and verbal style of a play. In 1884 he left Weimar to take up a three-year contract as artistic director of the theater in Mannheim, but after a year he left for Munich.

He was lured to the Bavarian capital at the instance of Carl, Baron von Perfall, the general manager (*Intendant*) of the court theaters, who was particularly impressed by a lecture he had given on the disadvantages of the "Meininger method"—that is, the advanced and carefully plotted realism with which historical plays (including those of Shakespeare) were staged by the company of the Meiningen Court Theatre. In 1889 an essay by the theater historian and critic Rudolph Genée caused a stir with its call for a simplified method of staging for Shakespeare's plays. In the same year, the fifth of his engagement as *Regisseur* in Munich, Savits, together with von Perfall and the chief machinist, Karl Lautenschläger, instigated a movement of theatrical reform in the city's theaters that was to preoccupy him until his retirement in 1906. A "Shakespeare Stage" was devised which could be installed in the Hoftheater, with a deep forestage built out over the orchestra pit, a "middle" platform reached by steps and framed by an architectural façade, and a third acting area beyond this. Although he gave von Perfall credit for the support and resources required for this undertaking, Savits insists in his own account of his life work that he took prime responsibility for the staging of all the plays for which this stage was used, struggling to defend the cause of nonscenic Shakespeare in the uncongenial context of a theater devoted to scenic display and in a city that proclaimed its preference for the painter's art—the *ausgeprochene Malerstadt* of Munich (Savits 1917, 25). Lautenschläger, who as machinist was responsible for the nuts and bolts of the stage, was not quite a kindred spirit: he is best remembered for his development of the turntable stage, and Savits is outspoken in his scorn for this device in his published works—although he attempts to give Lautenschläger at least some credit for the "theatre reform" they effected together.

Savits, who was appointed *Oberregisseur* in 1895, refused tempting offers from other theaters in order to stay in Munich and to follow through his plans, although the most important element of them—the "Shakespeare Stage"—did not function entirely according to his wishes. After the first production using it—*King Lear* in 1889—the stage was considerably modified, with the introduction of scenic elements that compromised its austerity but made it more acceptable to a public used to pictorial realism. His published works reflect not only his impatience with the methods of the theater of realistic illusion that he sought to displace, but also his disappointment with what he himself had been able to achieve. After his retirement in 1906 he devoted himself to writing, putting together the book that he hoped would broaden his influence. He also traveled to England. The first book-length study, *Von der Absicht des Dramas* (On the Aims of the Drama) was published in Bonn in 1908. By the end of the century's first decade Savits had encountered work by William Poel and Sir Sidney Lee: he cites Poel's essays in the 1917 book, and in 1911 he published a translation of Lee's article "Shakespeare on the Modern Stage" (first published in the *Westminster Review* in 1900 and reprinted in 1907). Poel had been propounding ideas and doing work that offered a parallel to those of Savits, but without anything like his resources.

Lee's essay, a critique of "modern" scenic production methods in Britain, lent further support to Savits: his translation is accompanied by a preface that amounts to a short statement of his own ideals. Savits died in 1915, and his second substantial volume of essays, *Shakespeare und die Bühne des Dramas* (Shakespeare and the Stage of the Drama) was published posthumously in Berlin in 1917. It includes plans for an improved "Shakespeare Stage," more radical in its architectural design than that he had been able to create in Munich.

It is important to bear in mind that Savits's theory—represented in these voluminous and often repetitive writings—followed several decades of practical experience, including fifteen years' work with the "Shakespeare Stage." One should also bear in mind that during his employment in Munich this highly regarded man of the theater was responsible for many productions other than those staged on the "Shakespeare Stage," both before and during its existence, and that he was a respected and sought-after actor and stage director. But he was hindered by the system obtaining in the theater, his subordination to the demands of star actors, and of the general manager's (von Perfall's) responsibility for offering a range of attractive entertainment. Savits enjoyed resources—the actors and technical staff of a lavishly endowed *Hoftheater*—available to none of his British counterparts, but he lacked the independence of such pioneers as William Poel, even if, unlike Poel, he had access to professional actors and staff and a grand theater to work in. I will describe aspects of some of Savits's productions in the last part of this paper, before that, I wish to look at some of the ideals that drove him, and the "realities" he strove against.

Savits's overall aim, which remained constant, is summed up in a statement published in a Munich newspaper, the *Neue Freie Volkszeitung*, in September 1916: "To make Shakespeare visible to the German people in all his greatness by means of productions according to the original"—and, he added, the Munich Shakespeare Stage was the arena in which this ideal was striven for.

Savits's notion of what "Shakespeare in all his greatness" might be can be traced to one source in particular—at least in the earliest stages of its formation. In 1867, during his engagement at Weimar, a diary entry records the resolution that his next intellectual task must be to become fully conversant with Shakespeare, specifically with the help of Gervinus's *Shakespeare Commentaries*. This enormously influential work, first published in German in 1849–50, was a systematic attempt to analyze the "moral" meaning (to use its Victorian translator's word) of Shakespeare's plays, which Gervinus identified by attending to the unified effects of poetic expression, plotting, and characterization. It distanced itself from the philological and antiquarian studies that preoccupied many English-speaking scholars, and in its English version (1863) was prefaced by F. J. Furnivall with a characteristically energetic account of the biographical method of reading Shakespeare. Gervinus had a political and social agenda, and a belief in the importance of Shakespeare's identity as a Teuton, that gave his work a particular appeal. Savits does not seem to have been much influenced by this notion—of Shakespeare as one of the great Germanic spirits—but it has a bearing on his sense of the "people" *for* whom Shakespeare ought to be staged, and *from* whom his Elizabethan theater derived its being.

For one thing, Savits insisted that, unlike that of Shakespeare's London, the theater as constituted in the city theaters of the late nineteenth century was not "popular," in the sense of being for or of the people, but rather was representative of a narrower group, "society"—*nicht volkstümlich sondern gesellschaftstümlich* (Savits 1908, 379). He regards the sophisticated, metropolitan and (mainly) foreign plays and the lavish productions they are given as incompatible with the simplicity and directness he associates with the German popular spirit. The words used acquired a sinister connotation in the subsequent decades of the twentieth century, and appeals to notions of a *Volksgeist* or national spirit, quite apart from their being outmoded in the writing of cultural history, have been contaminated by their appropriation in Nazi ideology. Savits (a steadfast supporter of a theater-workers' benevolent association) varies his use of words with *Volk* as their root between "popular" (*volkstümlich*) meaning "traditional" or "of the common people" to usages where the qualifying adjective "German" is understood. In the passage I have just referred to the adjectives used for the despised imported plays include a compound coinage *grossstädtlich-plutokratisch*, suggesting that not only are cities bad, but also money is too influential ("big-city-plutocratic drama"?). Nowhere does Savits engage in the kind of convoluted attempt to define the *Volk* that one finds in other writers—for example Richard Wagner. Unlike the composer, he was not a consciously cultural-political animal.

Savits's rejection of citified modern taste does not amount to a full-blown "back to the soil" impulse (although Savits was an enthusiast for open-air performances and wrote a book on them), or its more sinister Nazi derivative, "blood and earth" (*Blut und Boden*). Nevertheless, simplicity, directness of communication with the poet's mind, and the people's culture are often commingled in Savits's pronouncements. Later in the same section of his 1908 book he observes that "the less well-off, the broad stratum of the population, the lower middle classes [*kleine Bürger*] and workers with their families" are completely excluded from visiting the theater. This despite the fact that the theater "as a representation of life, and of persons in action, is not the institution of a special class in society, but is grounded on the common people—yes, on humanity in the widest sense—and consequently the general spiritual property of all, like light and air" (Savits 1908, 383). Moreover, it may even be that the poorest and least well provided for in society have the greatest claim to it. Thoughts of this kind, he goes on to say, guided him in the creation of the Munich "Shakespeare Stage"—but his desire to lower admission prices for performances was thwarted on administrative grounds.

Leadership also has its part to play. Earlier in the work, Savits suggests that the salvation of the drama in Germany lies in "a spiritually ambitious and elevated People whose will to demand Art has been aroused and cultivated by a few bold men, enthusiasts for art, who have achieved understanding and maturity" (Savits 1908, 67). Schiller, in his poem "Die Künstler" (1798), had famously entrusted responsibility for the moral worth of the people to artists:

> Der Menschheit Würde ist in eure Hand gegeben,
> Bewahret sie!
> Sie sinkt mit euch, mit euch wird sie sich heben.[1]

Unfortunately, the artist has been usurped in the theater by the *Theatermeister*, who "with his scenery, machinery and appliances has become the spiritual, financial and artistic fulcrum, around which the whole over-complicated machine of modern dramatic theater turns" (Savits 1908, 63). The overall aim is a simplification, ennobling and idealizing of the art of the theater (Savits 1908, 67), and Art herself is personified as a "healthy daughter of the people, in a simple dress that heightens her beauty" rather than a tawdry, coquettish baggage trying to hide her misshapen form in silks and satins (67–68). The contrast is repeatedly made between lavish scenic display—the *Dekorationsbühne* or *Ausstattungsbühne*— and the simple means required for plays where human action and poetic speech have pride of place. "The guiding principle must be, that the drama that is rich in action must always be poor in decoration, whereas the drama that is rich in decoration will always remain only poor in action" (Savits 1908, 362). Savits ranges engagingly from appeals to notions of national destiny or lofty ideals of art and thinking to simple, material consequences of this dominant idea. He argues that actors are spoilt by the provision of too many places to sit on the overfurnished stage, and that the simplified stage with its open platform is good for them because it gives nowhere to hide bad acting. (Actors, he notes, like the scenic stage with its frequent curtains—because they get more applause in the course of the evening!)

Savits lists, exhaustively, the obstacles that the dominance of the decorated stage puts in the way of true theatrical art. Rehearsal time is inadequate, especially where spoken drama has to share the same facilities as ballet and opera; it is impossible to achieve an ensemble in the context of tours by individual stars; the actors are forced to accommodate natural movement to the forced perspective of the scenic stage (a major complaint of enthusiasts of Shakespearean staging since Tieck in the first decades of the century); the clutter of scenery and furnishings impedes proper vocal production—on which Savits places great emphasis. More important than these and other practical objections—from experience accumulated through his years of work in Munich—is the damage done to the texts themselves in the name of the pictorial stage, which is in any case always a distraction from speech and action. Shakespeare, an inspired genius, chose to write for the popular theaters of his time (Savits 1908, 103). His works have an organic unity that is violated when they are cut and pasted to accommodate the demands for scenery: "it is to be remembered that in the last analysis every work of art, including the drama, is an organism, a unified whole, that is done to death when it is pulled to pieces" (Savits 1908, 396). As a young actor, Savits had already acquired this principle with reference to his own roles—he would diligently learn (not merely read) the lines from the original that had been cut out in the part he was given. Throughout his published writings, Savits emphasized the importance for the stage of what he calls "inner direction" [*innere Regie*]: the staging implicit in the texts, not so much in the directions added by editors (contemporary scholarship had alerted him to this pitfall), but by the action demanded by what is being said and done on stage. Only on the simple, open forestage and in front of the unvaried architectural façade of a truly Shakespearean stage would this inner direction be possible and the inner meaning and unity of the plays be apprehended. Musical interruptions of the plays—of which the by now routine subordination of *A Midsummer Night's Dream* to the performance of Mendelssohn's score was the worst example—would not be tolerated. The cutting of texts to suit the vanity of star actors was no more acceptable than alterations made for the scenic artists' or musicians' benefit.

The "Shakespeare Stage" designed and built for Munich, and erected for the first production, *King Lear*, in June 1889, had a deep, elliptical forestage and a "middle stage" formed by a platform under and behind a permanent architectural façade. There was no attempt to reproduce the wooden frame or tiring house of an Elizabethan theater, presumably because the stage was to be used for nonnaturalistic drama of all periods, including Molière and the German romantics. The traverse curtains that could be drawn across (not lowered) in front of the middle stage would allow entrances and exits to be separated from each other rather than overlap. There was no simple alternation of fore- and middle-stage: Savits allowed action to occupy the same space in successive scenes by using the curtain. In subsequent presentations, the stage was modified in ways that compromised with the audience's taste (and preference) for scenic locations. The *Wandeldekoration*, a movable panoramic backdrop placed behind the middle stage, was supplemented with and eventually supplanted by the use of scenic set pieces and backcloths in positions behind the middle stage and further back behind a third acting area. Another addition was an arch of foliage lowered to disguise the façade during open-air scenes (critics had complained of the absurdity of watching "heath" scenes when the solid architecture was still in place). The "Shakespeare Stage" was thus made to resemble the conventional scenic stage, and it seems that the element of stylization imposed by the platforms and forestage made it seem like an awkward adaptation of the scenic stage rather than a simplified stage that had been spoiled.

Relatively few of the productions on this stage were fully to Savits's liking, and he had to contend with opposition not merely from some sections of the press (he claims the public was more fully supportive) but from within the theater. Although he hoped to stage *Hamlet*, and drew up a full promptbook for it, the plan never came to fruition. Meanwhile, as stage-director-in-chief (*Oberregisseur*) he was also directing plays by Shakespeare and others on the scenic stage, with acting texts more or less adapted to it—including some by Dingelstedt—and using its resources as fully as ever. His promptbooks for Shakespeare and other productions on the pictorial stage are devised altogether in the Meininger tradition of complicated crowd scenes and illustrative business, much of it fresh and inventive in itself. (Hans Durian's 1937 monograph provides information derived from promptbooks then in the Deutsches Theatermuseum and the Prinz-Regenten-Theater: the following summary account derives from this work.)

The first production, *King Lear*, was that which most faithfully adhered to Savits's austere ideals. There were few properties on stage: a throne, two couches, and the stocks for Kent. In 1889 the *Wandeldekoration* indicated the location of scenes, but more conventional backdrops in two positions were used in the subsequent revivals of 1896 and 1900. The opening sequence exemplifies the pattern of movement throughout: after trumpet calls, the curtain goes up and Gloucester, Kent, and Edmund take the forestage. A curtain is drawn to reveal Lear and the court on the middle stage, and the daughters and their husbands enter from the side doors onto the forestage: they go up the steps onto the middle stage and arrange themselves on either side of the throne with the men on the left and the women on the right. After Lear's exit the curtain closes and the conclusion is played on the forestage. The curtain then draws again to reveal Edmund already on the middle stage, and he comes down onto the forestage to speak his soliloquy. During action on the forestage the upstage area is darkened and the back-scene is changed. In outdoor scenes the actors do not use the side doors of the middle stage but enter and exit from the back or using the side doors on the forestage.

The logic of this use of the different areas, which is common to all Savits's work on this stage, allows for some distinction between indoor and outdoor locations, and also allows a rapid succession of scenes, although the "discovery" of Edmund on the middle stage is redolent of the scenic theater. I have already mentioned the complaints about setting heath scenes in front of an architectural façade and the subsequent use of a "foliage arch" to mask it. Later productions made more concessions in this direction, on which Savits expressed his regret in the publications that appeared after his retirement. It has to be said, though, that most of the productions, although not "pure" in their stagecraft, seem to have been effective and an improvement on conventional pictorial stagings, even including Savits's own.

As we have seen, Savits's direction on the "Shakespeare Stage" was soon brought nearer to that of conventional productions of his time. In the history plays in particular the evidence of his stagecraft, invariably skillful as it is, does not often include effects that would only be possible on the "simplified" stage. The compromises Savits had to make when he was working after 1889 on the "normal" scenic stage of the *Hoftheater* are even more indicative of the tension between the two spheres of his employment there. A particularly interesting case is *Pericles*, where the complicated and realistic devices used by Possart for the shipwreck scene in 1882—with the deck and mast of the ship filling the center of the stage, moving on rockers in the customary fashion of realistic stagecraft—was used by Savits in 1888, but replaced in his second revival, in 1904, by a simpler staging where the lighting and sound effects of the storm were retained but the stage was not made to move (Durian 1937, 50). In his production of *The Merchant of Venice*, Savits was obliged to use an acting version devised by the leading actor, Possart, in 1880, and to set aside his own view of Shylock as a figure in a comic play, in favor of Possart's more solemn interpretation. The shadow cast by this tragic Shylock seems to have made it impossible for Savits to achieve the lighter comic effect he wanted in the final act (Durian 1937, 51–52).

In *Love's Labor's Lost* (1889) he was obliged to use a version published in 1887 by Rudolph Genée (the purist *fons et origo* of the "stage reform"—an irony not lost on the press). This squeezed the first three acts of the comedy into one and omitted the announcement of the French king's death in favor of the less momentous pretext of the princess's diplomatic mission as a reason for the year's delay. In any case, it seems that Savits was unable to achieve the lightness of touch he desired because he was obliged to use actors whose line of business was heroes. (The *Heldenfach* in the system of *Fächer*, or character types, that Savits despised.) In *Richard II* in 1885 he used Dingelstedt's version, with its watered-down poetry and rearranged text: in 1894 he was able to restore the lines to Schlegel's version, but was obliged by the management to keep to Dingelstedt's division of scenes and acts (Durian 1937, 53). In other history plays—for example the two parts of *Henry IV*—Savits consistently strove to restore portions missing or sequences reordered by earlier acting texts. Sometimes, as with the two parts of *Henry VI*, he adopted older acting texts: in this case, a version in two parts that used passages from *1 Henry VI* as a prologue to the events of the second part. In *Richard III* Possart himself appeared as Gloucester, and Savits was obliged to use Dingelstedt's version, which the actor was familiar with.

Overall, the record suggests that Savits's use of the "Shakespeare Stage" achieved some innovations and made some major compromises. Of his two books, that published in 1908 is an exposition—with sometimes excessive as well as extensive quotations from Lessing, Goethe, and others—of his arguments about the theater in general and Shakespeare in particular. The 1917 volume includes specific and lengthy analyses of the ideas and practice of Dingelstedt and others, with some analysis of the "spoken scenery" and "inner direction" to be discovered in Shakespeare's texts. As a commentator as well as practitioner, Savits had a career whose frustrations and achievements provide an intriguing parallel to the work of Poel and his adherents. Working in a different theatrical culture, and with a more systematic intellectual background, Savits illustrates other aspects of the meeting between Elizabethan stagecraft and nineteenth-century European scenography and theater architecture. William Poel, who had seen the 1890 *King Lear* and corresponded and met with Savits, could not altogether accept the kind of staging his colleague favored, but admired his energy and principles. The rapidity with which plays could be mounted was particularly impressive. Poel wrote after his death: "No English theatrical manager could say he has done in twelve years the work that Savits did in one year. While Tree had produced *Hamlet* or *Julius Caesar* and run it for 200 nights, Savits, in ... 25 weeks in Munich, had given 12 different plays of Shakespeare, and 125 other plays, mostly classics" (Poel 1929, 93).

Note

1. Translation: "The dignity of mankind is laid in your hands. Preserve it! It sinks with you; with you will it rise."

Unstopping Our Mouths: Shakespeare in Swiss-German *Mundart*

Sylvia Zysset

> Bänz: Und das es d Lüüt daa au verstönd, reded miir
> Natüürli nüd babylionisch oder—ee—latynieenisch,
> nä, mer macheds öppe so, win is de Schnabel gwachsen isch.
>
> Peter Quince: And to make sure people here understand it,
> of course we won't speak Babylion or—um—Latinalian,
> no, we'll do it just about the way our beaks are grown [i.e., in our own words].

INTRODUCTION

About a year ago I heard an interview on the Swiss radio with Bruce Myers, a South African actor, who has worked with the RSC and Peter Brook, and has performed Shakespeare's plays all over the world. He had come to Switzerland to conduct acting workshops with young people. Myers explained that Shakespeare could provide ideal material for those wanting to experiment playfully with their identities and learn more about themselves through acting. He described Shakespeare's characters as human in their imperfections, real rather than fictitious, and consequently stressed the necessity for people to act Shakespeare in their mother-tongue. Translations, he believed, had the great advantage of allowing plays to be adapted to specific places, times, and people(s), and so it was perfectly clear to him that in the German-speaking part of Switzerland Shakespeare should be performed in the Swiss-German dialect. I realized then that although Myers's contention sounded obvious, I had never witnessed a Swiss-German Shakespeare production, nor even heard of one existing. My curiosity was stirred: Surely such productions must exist?

Subsequent investigations revealed that they do exist, but that they had never been systematically collected or studied. Twenty-two translations of Shakespeare into various Swiss-German dialects have so far come to light, and thanks to the help of theater practitioners from the Swiss amateur theater scene I have by now managed to obtain thirteen of these texts, all of which are unpublished.[1] Not only has this number by far exceeded my expectations, the material has also proved both interesting and rewarding. Being used to the High-German—and therefore often quite literary—translations used in the Swiss professional theater, it was an unusual pleasure to experience Shakespeare in the language spoken by the German Swiss almost all the time, every day. Many of the productions and translations merit detailed analysis, and hopefully ongoing research into this area of Swiss Shakespeare performance will be possible. The scope of this paper allows only for a brief introduction. I would therefore like to focus on some more general aspects here. My chief concerns are: How do translations into a local dialect, a language that does not exist in a standardized written form, affect the way Shakespeare is experienced in performance? How did the groups adapt the plays to the place (geographical location and performance space), time, and people with and for whom they were performing? Can amateur performances in the local vernacular open up new perspectives and offer different insights into the meaning of Shakespeare's plays in various cultures?

Swiss Theater and the Question of Language

In order to understand the particular situation of Swiss-German Shakespeare it is necessary to give a short introduction into the country's theater history, a history intimately linked to the question of language. On reflection it appears bizarre that the principal theater language in the German-speaking part of the country should be High-German, also known as *Schriftdeutsch* ("written German," a term that describes its principal use in Switzerland), and not the *Mundart* ("dialect," or literally "way of the mouth") spoken by the German Swiss of all social backgrounds and ages most of the time; principal exceptions being during lessons, in official situations, and when conversing with, or in the presence of, Germans.[2] It is also striking that this state of affairs is simply accepted as a convention and not reflected on more prominently, particularly by the theater practitioners and critics who so often bemoan the population's flagging interest in professional theater. That this situation should have come about has to do with German Swiss theater history.[3]

History of German Swiss Theater

In the fifteenth and sixteenth centuries theater played an important part in Switzerland's cultural and social life. It provided a space where current social and political issues could be debated. Until about 1575 Swiss theater flourished, and due to a rich diversity of authors, plays, and theatrical forms the country was at times even at the forefront of European theatrical innovation. It must be emphasized, however, that while the whole population was involved as players and audiences, Swiss theater remained an entirely amateur activity. An important basis for this involvement and theatrical creativity was provided by a shared Swiss-German stage language—the pre-Lutheran *Oberdeutsche Schriftsprache*—used both in written and spoken form. In Switzerland it was interspersed with Swiss-German words, pronounced with regional inflections, and could therefore function as a significant identity-forging medium. However, the Reformation, Luther's Bible translation, and the spread of printed books gradually imposed a unified High-German written language, while the Counter-Reformation of the seventeenth century put an end to the country's rich theatrical activity. Foreign groups of professional actors began touring Swiss towns again in the eighteenth century, but there were still no professional Swiss actors. At the same time amateur folk-theater was reviving in Catholic areas, and people's confidence in their own language—Swiss-German—was again on the increase. It could perhaps be regarded as unfortunate for Swiss-German theater that the energy generated at this point did not suffice to create a common stage dialect with a standardized written form, although, as will be discussed below, nonstandardized oral languages can also be an advantage for the theater.

Swiss diplomats and tradesmen admired foreign baroque

court theaters and their repertoires on their travels, and consequently helped to introduce this tradition into Switzerland in the nineteenth century by founding the municipal theaters still in use today. The new repertoire called for professional actors and directors, and since these were not to be found in Switzerland they were recruited from Germany and Austria. They arrived, bringing their own language and a High-German repertoire with them, and in this coincidental fashion High-German became Switzerland's language of the professional theater.

> A defining decision had been made, which to the present day... separates the professional theater with its High-German "language of culture" from the amateur stages of popular theater, where dialect is spoken. If the new theaters were felt for a long time to be a foreign intrusion, only visited by the "better" upper classes, but regarded with distrust by the "common people" in whose culture they scarcely had roots—in some respects these reservations exist to this day—the reasons lie to a large extent in this linguistic division. (Schläpfer 1992, 33–34, my translation)

Professional theater in Switzerland has always had to fight the tough opposition of a deeply rooted and diverse amateur- and folk-theater scene, whose practitioners wondered why it was necessary to have theater "from the outside," when "theater is what we do" (Kotte 1994, 16, my translation).

Swiss-German on the Stage Today

Although there are a number of Swiss actors and directors working in the Swiss professional theaters today, Swiss-German is only rarely used there.[4] A lot more work needs to be done to investigate the effects that dialect can have on German Swiss audiences. In a recent production of Ibsen's *Enemy of the People* at Basel's *Stadttheater* a scene in which an actor suddenly addressed the audience in dialect regularly prompted not only strong feelings (positive and negative), but also made the audience feel less inhibited about calling out and interacting with the performance. Ruth Aders (1987, 75) points out that the German Swiss, often subconsciously, associate dialect with situations that promote interaction and discussion (in the pub, in the street) and High-German with situations requiring passive attention (school, formal lectures, news-programs on TV).[5] Surely in this country use of High-German must intensify a predisposition to be quiet and passive at the theater. Arguably it can also promote a feeling of detachment verging on disinterest toward what is happening on stage. Note, too, that German advertisements on Swiss TV are dubbed in dialect—particularly when they want to engage viewers emotionally rather than rationally—and that Swiss rock, pop, and rap singers use either dialect or English, hardly ever High-German. Yet High-German is still regarded almost unquestioningly as the language of culture ("high culture" in particular). Many German Swiss, including actors, harbor an inferiority complex and feel their High-German is not as good as that of their German neighbors.[6] In the two main Swiss acting academies speaking dialect is banned altogether (even outside of class), to ensure that at the end of their training Swiss actors can speak German without a trace of an accent betraying their origins and diminishing their chances of finding a job.

The reason why most people to whom I mention the subject *Mundart*-Shakespeare initially react with surprise, amusement, and incredulity may lie in the little-reflected-on identification of dialect—and dialect theater—with "low culture." It seems that some people even find the idea of Shakespeare in dialect a little blasphemous![7] As often when discussing *Mundart* it is surprising to realize how little we German Swiss reflect on our use of it and our emotions toward it. Even in personal conversations Shakespeare proved a useful point of departure, prompting more detailed reflection on personal attitudes to the Swiss and German languages and cultures.

Using Shakespeare to Celebrate and Explore Linguistic Situations

Before turning to the performances in Swiss-German I would like to mention two instances where Shakespeare performances were specifically used to reflect on particular linguistic situations in Switzerland. To celebrate the fiftieth anniversary of Rhaeto-Romance becoming Switzerland's fourth official language (spoken by 1 to 2 percent of the population), *Romeo e Giulietta* was performed in an amateur open-air production in Laax in 1988. It was presumably the first ever Rhaeto-Romance translation of the playwright's work.[8] In 1989 a German/French *Romeo and Juliet* was staged in the bilingual town of Fribourg: the Montagues spoke German, the Capulets French, and the Prince—symbol of authority—used the original English. The idea was to focus attention on conflicts between the Swiss-German- and the French-speaking communities in the town and to bridge the gap by having people from both language groups act together to a mixed audience. Ironically, while the project purported to address and replicate the linguistic conflicts existing in Fribourg, the German Swiss amateur actors were required to speak High-German. This may have been partly due to the conventions mentioned above, but was mainly a gesture toward making the proceedings more easily understandable for French-speaking fellow citizens, who may learn Standard-German but not Swiss-German at school.[9] As so often when Swiss amateur actors attempt "stage High-German" their only partial success was noted and criticized by reviewers. By contrast the reviews of the Shakespeare productions in Swiss-German, discussed below, almost consistently praised both the high quality of the acting (often describing it as easy, competent, and natural) and stressed the beauty of the language—frequently with a telling air of surprise.

Speaking about popular theater and his work with amateurs, Louis Naef, one of the most prominent professional directors of the Swiss amateur theater scene, stresses points reminiscent of those made by Bruce Myers: amateur actors remain essentially themselves, they bring their authenticity to the play, and through the part they are acting learn to communicate a part of their own life. Naef believes that this kind of theater work can be biographical and have an emancipating effect, because it helps actors to approach and explore their own identity and find the courage to be themselves.[10] Therefore he, too, emphasizes the importance of playwrights using dialect if they want to "help the people use their own mouths." Expression, he says, must come from inside. When questioned about translating classics into dialect Naef asserts that he is all for it: "If the play fits the environment and is adapted to the language of the players, every classic can be performed."

Shakespeare in Swiss-German

Bearing Naef's remarks in mind, how did the productions in Swiss-German adapt the plays to their specific performance contexts?

Choice of Plays

A large majority of amateur groups (most of them under professional or semiprofessional direction) decided to perform comedies. As some of the program leaflets suggest, this choice was probably intended to diminish their audiences' apprehensions regarding a "difficult," "classic" author. Frequently the programs stress that Shakespeare's theater was popular theater too, sometimes quoting from Robert Weimann's *Shakespeare und die Tradition des Volkstheaters* (1967). It is a pity that so many groups connected—or believed their audiences connected—the popular with the genre of comedy. However, putting on a Shakespeare play was generally perceived to be a risky and ambitious project and comedies obviously guaranteed the most success.[11] Given that most of these dialect performances seem to have been highly successful, one wonders whether playing it safe would be so necessary in the future. It would be interesting to compare this choice of plays with the RSC's "bums on seats"–selection for the main house in Stratford. Yet while *A Midsummer Night's Dream* predictably was the clear favorite, comedies were not the only genre performed. There have also been dialect productions of *Hamlet, Measure for Measure, Romeo and Juliet,* and *The Tempest*.[12] Often it was the youth theater groups who approached the more "difficult" plays, adapting them heavily and originally to suit their purposes: in terms of daring and refreshing disrespect toward the Bard they generally went the furthest.

Swiss (Re)settings

Most of the productions reset the plays in specific Swiss contexts, ranging in time from a medieval past to the youth-gangs of present-day Zurich. Dialect is often perceived to be something very local and there may frequently have been a feeling that it cannot be used to tell stories that are more universal, or clearly set outside of the country. This perception presumably had a strong influence on the choice of plays. Although some productions left their setting open or embraced clashes (a *Hamlet* set in Denmark but spoken in Swiss dialect), this remained the exception. Emil Bader transported his 1981 *Midsummer Night's Dream* from Athens to the castle and woods of medieval Wättischwyl (the old name for the town Wädenswil, where the production was staged in an inn). He replaced Theseus and Hyppolita with historically documented characters from the area's chivalrous past and the fairies by goblins known from local folktales. Swiss playwright Hansjörg Schneider remarked that seeing this production he felt he was able to understand every scene and sentence of the play for the first time: "I attribute this partly to the language, but also to the staging—they shamelessly played everything just as it is meant, free from the pressures which cause directors at the professional theaters to want to do things in a certain way for the first time" (Aders 1987, 87, my translation). The play's director, Franziska Kohlund, confirms that after seeing classic plays performed in dialect, school classes would often ask to study them at school: "That's an important role dialect theater can play. These young people felt they were being addressed directly; the *Dream* was much closer to them, because the actors were speaking their language" (Aders 1987, 89, my translation).

Many companies used inns or marquees as performance locations and served food and drink before or after the play. The Pieterlen *Dream* (1988) employed metatheatrical openness to diminish the distance between playgoers and actors, making the most of an inn that provided no backstage area. The audience was invited to arrive before the production started, was served soup and drinks by members of the company and watched the actors (often personal acquaintances or friends) getting dressed and made up. Breaking down the fourth wall obviously helped to overcome fears regarding a difficult classic text. Mario Barisi, member of the theater group, confirmed that many visitors later expressed their surprise at how well they had been able to understand Shakespeare. He also explained that the group had since performed a High-German *Twelfth Night*—due to working with a German director—but that this had been a more distanced and less popularly successful production. The *Dream* actors took on the translation themselves, dividing into groups (aristocrats, fairies, craftsmen) to work on their parts and create an individual style for the different sections of the play's society. During rehearsals they were then encouraged to change and adapt the translation until they felt comfortable speaking their lines. A point that would merit investigation is the way in which the makeup of a particular group (age, gender, etc.) affects the translation and adaptation of a Shakespeare play. In Pieterlen—as in other amateur productions—some parts were transformed from male to female. The 1996 *Dream* in Affoltern went furthest in involving the audience in the action. The playgoers started out in a marquee at the edge of a forest as guests at a rich local industrialist's (Theseus's) pre-wedding party. As the play progressed they were led into the woods where they encountered the craftsmen, fairies, and young lovers, before returning to the party in the marquee at the end. This modern *Dream* was particularly interested in focusing on the battle between the sexes, highlighting the subject in some improvised passages.

Evidence of improvisation in a number of the translations suggests that dialect can help amateur actors feel at home with Shakespeare's text, making it easier for them to play with it and adapt it to their needs. The youth theater groups repeatedly emphasized aspects of emotional and sexual violence in this way. Unfortunately space does not allow the discussion of other resettings here; a *Twelfth Night* set in the carnival atmosphere of a Swiss village in the 1920s and a *Romeo and Juliet* transferred to the youth gang culture of today's Zurich (both translations by playwright and director Paul Steinmann) would certainly merit detailed discussion.

Language

Five of the collected texts are successful Swiss-German translations into blank verse, and many of the prose texts also frequently approximate a five-beat rhythmic pattern. If the blank-verse meter seems ideally suited to the clause length of spoken English, it also appears to fit the Swiss-dialect quite naturally: Being an oral language *Mundart* often strings together fairly short main clauses, rather than employing complex sentence structures. Whereas many High-German Shakespeare translators are tempted to use more syntactically complicated literary language, it is dialect that ideally translates Shakespeare into a spoken language and emphasizes the oral characteristics of the text.[13] Swiss dialect is also strongly "verb-driven," another characteristic that would seem to make it ideal for drama.[14] The lack of standardized spellings and dictionaries appears similarly felicitous, enabling the language to stay open, flexible, and spontaneously inventive. It seems easier than in Standard German to create new words or add and drop syllables to fit the meter. A number of times I was unsure whether a word was an original creation of the translator's, or whether it had existed before (for example, *erchärndle*, "peel out the stone of a thing, situation"). The creativity possible when translating Shakespeare into dialect could even be compared to the linguistic situation in Elizabethan England, where language was not yet standardized and words were being incorporated into the language and newly created at high speed.

One of the most satisfying findings was the realization that Swiss dialects are capable of a wide range of stylistic levels. That there should be "differences of temperature" between regional dialects was to be expected, but that the language from one region could display such a wide range of tones was a surprise. While Emil Bader used a number of old-fashioned dialect words to re-create the atmosphere of sixteenth-century upper-class Zurich for his *Taming* (1978), the youth theater groups demonstrated that modern Swiss slang can be poetic, inventive, and erotically charged (for example, *Romeo and Juliet*, 1997, or *Zettels Traum*, based on the *Dream*, 1997). In one of the most impressive of all translations—*Was er wänd!* [Twelfth Night] (1995) from Glarus—Richard Wehrli created a high-flown and beautifully poetic language for Orsino, gave the comic characters vulgar but witty speeches (cleverly adapting the word games) and emphasized Malvolio's stiffness and status as an outsider by having him speak a diluted form of the dialect, his vocabulary tending toward High-German rather than regional expressions.

Conclusion

Mundart Shakespeare performances can have a number of advantages over High-German productions. The dialect not only helps to bring the plays and their text closer to the German Swiss by facilitating understanding, it arguably also involves the audience more directly and emotionally in the plays. A recurring statement from people witnessing such productions was: "I didn't think I would be able to understand Shakespeare so well."[15] Being allowed to "speak the way their beaks are grown" (that is, in their own words) helps amateur actors (and maybe also professional Swiss actors?) feel more at home with Shakespeare's text, and encourages them to improvise and adapt the plays to their own environments and needs. Experiencing a classic author in what is still widely regarded as a language unsuitable for "high culture" could even help some German-speaking Swiss look at their vernacular in a new light, perhaps with a higher regard. Shakespeare's texts generate Swiss-German translations that are poetic, immediate, and witty, and display surprising verbal creativity and range of tone. Hopefully the popular and critical success of *Mundart* Shakespeare performances will encourage more such translations and productions in the future; discovering them has certainly been an enriching experience.[16]

Notes

Epigraph from *Ein Sommernachtstraum (Mids. N.D.)*, 1.6., translated into Zurich dialect by Emil Bader (1980).

1. These are: *Der Widerspenstigen Zähmung (Tam. Shr.)*, 1978, *Ein Sommernachtstraum (Mids. N.D.)*, 1981, Freunde des Volkstheaters Wädenswil (Zurich), trans. Emil Bader; *Mass für Mass (Measure)*, 1980, Berner Heimatschutz-Theater (Berne), trans. Walter E. Meyer; *E Summernachtstroum (Mids. N.D.)*, 1988, Theatergruppe Galerie Pieterlen (Berne); *Was er wänd! (Twel. N)*, 1995, Theater Glarus (Glarus), trans. Richard Wehrli-Baumann; *Umfasnachtet oder Was ihr wollt (Twel. N.)*, 1996, Theatergesellschaft Villmergen (Aargau), trans. Peter Fischli and Paul Steinmann; *Ein Sommernachtstraum (Mids. N.D.)*, 1996, Aemtlerbühne Affoltern (Zurich), trans. Johannes Peyer; *Hamlet*, 1998, MTM-Theater Rothenburg (Lucerne), trans. Benedikt Troxler; *Romeo und Julia—eine Westside-Story (Rom. and Jul.)*, 1997, Jugendgruppe U21 (Zurich), trans. Paul Steinmann; *Zettels Traum (Mids. N.D.)*, 1997, Junges Theater Basel (Basel), trans. Kathrin Brülhart; *Sweet Hamlet (Haml.)*, 1999, Junges Theater Basel (Basel), trans. Sebastian Nübling and Daniel Wahl. *E Summernachtstraum oder E traumhafti Summernacht im Sihlwald (Mids. N.D.)*, 2000, Turbine Theater Langnau am Albis (Zurich), trans. Peter Niklaus Steiner.

2. The functional diglossia in the German speaking part of Switzerland is unique when compared to other German speaking areas: standard form and vernacular exist side by side and have clearly defined areas of use. Hardly any mixing occurs between the two forms, unlike in Germany and Austria, where a continuum between standard form and dialect is in operation. Except in a small number of particular situations that require High-German, dialect is the language spoken by everyone regardless of age, education, and social background. The differences between Swiss dialects and Standard German are considerable, making the dialect incomprehensible to most speakers of High-German (see Wyler 1997, 9–11).

3. The following information relies heavily on Schläpfer 1992, esp. 10–34.

4. The main Swiss acting academies concentrate on teaching their students Bühnendeutsch (stage High-German) and do not appear interested in providing speech training in the Swiss dialects (Aders 1987, 81).

5. Ruth Aders interviewed Swiss theater practitioners about the use of dialect and High-German on the Swiss professional stage. The responses were often surprisingly emotional and the interviewees frequently seemed to be reflecting on the subject for the first time.

6. "The Swiss don't want to speak like the Germans, and they can't—this has consequences for their relationship to Standard German. Most German Swiss feel inferior to Germans in situations where oral communication is necessary . . . even well-educated German Swiss have a command of written and very formal spoken German, but not of High-German as a colloquial means of everyday communication" (Wyler 1997, 15, my translation).

7. This calls to mind that a religious play in the early twentieth century was considered blasphemous because God spoke Swiss dialect. Compare Stephen Greenblatt's thoughts on the shock of hearing God's word in the English vernacular for the first time (Greenblatt 1984, 96).

8. *Romeo e Giulietta* translated into Rhaeto-Romance by Ursicin G. G. Derungs, first performed in Laax (Grisons), April 1988.

9. Thus the production brought to light another communication problem between the different language groups of Switzerland. The director and cotranslator of the project, Gian Gianotti, told me, however, that today he would be much more interested in exploring the use of Swiss-German on stage in such a production (interview, 23 October 2001).

10. Louis Naef in a recent publication that investigates the phenomenon of popular theater in Switzerland in all its diversity: Halter, Luginbühl, and Scagnet 2000, 13–14.

11. Paul Steinmann, translator of two of the vernacular productions and director of the Zurich *Romeo and Juliet*, commented on this aspect in an interview (18 October 2001): "People don't want to see tragedies at the popular theater anymore, unless the plot has some specific historical or topical link to the community for which it is being performed. Amateur theater groups are not subsidized and their choices have to be financially motivated. Youth theater groups can frequently be more daring in their choice of genre because they are subsidized and can rely on an audience consisting of 80 percent school parties."

12. The hit-list was as follows: *A Midsummer Night's Dream* (8), *Twelfth Night* (4), *The Taming of the Shrew* (2), *The Merry Wives of Windsor* (of Turgi and of Küssnacht) (2), *Hamlet* (2), one production each of *Romeo and Juliet*, *The Comedy of Errors*, *Much Ado about Nothing*, *Measure for Measure*, and *The Tempest*.

13. The least successful text in terms of language—the Rothenburg *Hamlet*—often appeared to have been literally translated from High-German into dialect, disregarding Mundart syntax and thus sounding unnatural and stilted. On this aspect compare Schmid 2000, 39.

14. On Shakespeare's practice of "verbing" see Crystal 1998, 20–21.

15. Paul Steinmann (interview, 18 October 2001) reported that the amateur actors from Villmergen's local theater group first reacted to the idea

of performing Shakespeare with more than a little doubt: "But that's literature, that's art, that doesn't have anything to do with what we do here!" But Steinmann translated the play into the local dialect and reset it in a village similar to Villmergen at carnival time. This allowed the actors and audiences to find a familiar frame of reference from which to enter into the play and appreciate the characters. Frequently heard reactions to the successful production were "We didn't know that Shakespeare was this funny, we always thought he was..."

16. In April 2001 the *Deutsche Shakespeare Gesellschaft* awarded a group of German students the Martin Lehnert Prize for their translation and production of *Much Ado about Nothing* in the vernacular *Plattdeutsch*. The play *Vell Jedöhns wääje nüss* was performed to great public success in a number of locations in and around Bonn, Germany.

IV
Instilling

National Identity and the Teaching of Shakespeare

Ruth Freifrau von Ledebur

> Shakespeare's message is the universal, timeless one, yet clad in the garments of his time. He is not just our poet, but the world's. Yet his roots are ours, his language is ours, his culture is ours.... For us all, roots are important: roots in our landscape, ... roots in our cultural and literary heritage.... Today's world is changing rapidly; too rapidly, sometimes, for the human psyche to adapt.... At the same time peoples all over the world remain as conscious as ever of their national and cultural identities.... Hanging onto our cultural roots is one way of preserving those identities, and indeed the stability of our civilization. (The Prince of Wales 1991)

THIS TEXT—AN EXTRACT FROM THE STRATFORD SHAKESPEARE Birthday Lecture 1991, held by the Prince of Wales—is loaded with ideas and stereotypes most teachers of Shakespeare all over Europe are familiar with from the very tradition of the subject they teach. They contain what is often called Shakespeare's philosophy, his creed or, more crudely, what the poet wants to teach us. Shakespeare is also part of our literary heritage; he is not to be uprooted from our national identity, lest we should lose the "stability of our civilization." Even the emphatic "he is ours" sounds pretty familiar, at least to German ears. The cultural security or hegemony that permeates this text came under heavy attack in the "culture war" that raged in Britain in the 1980s and '90s in and outside departments of English literature. At the very core of that ideological warfare, tied up with the introduction of the new National Curriculum, one meets with "Shakespeare" (mostly in quotation marks) together with various issues of pedagogy and of national identity. The belief in Shakespeare's formative powers over both individuals and the nation, which conservative academics shared with the Prince of Wales, is refuted by the opposite camp: "The deep entwinement of Shakespeare with a particular national culture is seldom straightforward even as it often takes the most traditional forms.... At moments of crisis rifts within this symbolic geography begin to open up and disconceal their complicity with forms of demonisation which are still pretty much engrained within the national psyche" (Joughin 1997b, 274).

According to Eric Hobsbawm, nations are constructed "from above," but they are also defined "from below" according to the interests, the hopes, and expectations that the people connect with the nation, the community they belong to. The identity of a nation is not something static; it is constantly being redefined in the course of the nation's history (Thadden 1991). National identities are constituted by convictions, by symbols, by collective memories. These compose the image that the collective community has created for itself, to recognize its members, and—at the same time—to discriminate "the other" as a nonmember of that community (Harth 1988).

When the unity of a national culture is being called in question, because two rival political and social systems are claiming their cultural heritage—as was the case with the two Germanys East and West—rifts within this symbolic geography open up and the darker sides of the national psyche are revealed. Since the German reunification in 1990, a controversial debate has been going on about various aspects of cultural memory and national identity. The question is being raised whether both states had developed their own national identity and how they had dealt with the traditions they had in common. In their cultural politics both states had recognized the importance of cultural continuity and legitimacy and, at the same time, of creating new, distinctive identities. In that competitive climate, the German classics and Shakespeare on stage, in schools, and in universities, played a decisive role.

The cover picture of an East German schoolbook allows us a first glimpse into this complicated matter. Published in 1987, it is the last volume in the series *English for You*, designated for the last school year before the *Abitur*, the German university entrance exam (Böse, Lademann, and Siebold 1987). The picture shows the monument of William Shakespeare in the Ilm Park in Weimar with a group of young tourists looking up at the Bard. Skimming through the book, you will not find any extract from Shakespeare's plays nor any text on his life and works but only the following reference to the poet: "The German Shakespeare Society has a long tradition and a firm place in the cultural life of our country. What are its aims and activities?" This exercise is part of the chapter "Taking care of foreign guests in the GDR" and is placed opposite the picture of the Goethe House in Weimar under the heading "Some aspects of cultural life in the GDR." The vocabulary for this unit includes "kulturelles Erbe erhalten/ bewahren: preserve cultural heritage" (Böse, Lademann, and Siebold 1987, 83). The message of the book's cover picture, then, reads as follows: You need not have studied any of Shakespeare's plays in English, but you ought to know about his prominent place in the German cultural heritage and about the merits of the Society dedicated to his name. In West Germany, in contrast, a high school student sitting for the *Abitur* would hardly have been expected to know anything about the existence of the Shakespeare Society, let alone about its aims and activities. But he or she would have studied one play by Shakespeare in the original language, whereas his or her peer in the East would have read two of his plays in a German translation.

The difference in the knowledge of Shakespeare of the average graduating student stems from the totally different school systems in East and West. Secondary education in the West continued along the traditional lines of segregating pupils according to their abilities into three different schools at the age of ten. The traditional Gymnasium, leading to university, with a total of thirteen years of schooling, was maintained, whereas in the East, all pupils attended the same type of school up to the age of sixteen. Two more years to take the *Abitur* followed, which amount to a total of twelve years. As to the teaching of Shakespeare in schools, the decision of most consequence, taken in the early fifties, was that in East Germany Russian should be the first foreign language to be taught in secondary schools, and not English as in West Germany. The political reasons for these decisions in both countries need not be explained. In the German Democratic Republic (GDR), English was as a rule introduced as the second foreign language. Language abilities became the main target of English classes; literature was almost completely cut out.[1]

In the West, English was being taught as the first foreign language in all secondary schools, in the Gymnasium for a total of nine years, and English literature remained an integral part of the syllabus. In East Germany, where Shakespeare was no longer part of the English syllabus, the authorities took care that he did not totally vanish from the educational scene. His works were made obligatory in the curriculum of German literature. In doing so, the authorities revived an old educational credo: in the traditional Gymnasium, Shakespeare was being taught in literature classes as part of the history of German literature and was honored for inseminating the classical German drama. Adhering to Goethe's model of *Weltliteratur*, Shakespeare was placed among the world's classics, which were all read in their appropriate translations. Thus, Shakespeare also served to propagate an educational assertion specific to the socialist identity, namely the teaching of world literature as part of the international socialist community. For Shakespeare, the schools favored the romantic translation of Schlegel-Tieck, which in itself had become a German classic (Habicht 1994a). It follows from this premise that the image of Shakespeare presented at the schools in East Germany, was that of the "third German classic," anchored deeply in the German cultural tradition (Bohlmann 1988).

Thus, the German curriculum for the Polytechnical High School (POS), which everybody attended up to the age of sixteen, decreed that one play of Shakespeare, namely *Macbeth*, must be read as part of the course on German literature (Bütow and Witting 1986, 170). In the *Erweiterte Oberschule* (EOS), leading to the *Abitur*, a second play, namely *Hamlet*, was made obligatory reading, again with the full embellishment of German literary and cultural history. Contrary to what happened in the West, each and every school-leaver in the GDR would have read at least one Shakespearean drama in a German translation.

As in East Germany, West German schools were also to preserve the German heritage. For a certain time after 1948, the English dramatist held his place in the German syllabus. To support this claim, a welcome model was found in a liberal and democratic curriculum of secondary education of the Weimar Republic, which had won general acclaim in the attempts to cleanse the educational system from Nazi indoctrination. These guidelines decreed that Shakespeare, like Goethe, Schiller, or Lessing, was a prerequisite for all secondary education and that no pupil should leave school without having become acquainted with Shakespeare (Küpper 1982, 108).

In safeguarding Shakespeare's position in the English syllabus of the West German Gymnasium, one also relied heavily on long-established cultural traditions. When, toward the end of the nineteenth century, the modern languages were finally incorporated into the classical type of the German grammar school, they could only face the dominance of the classical languages Latin and Greek by claiming that they, too, had to offer educative values superior to utilitarian language acquisition, namely "high-culture" literature. It goes without saying that in English classes Shakespeare was placed at the top of the list. Legend has it that from this ancient rivalry between the classical and the modern languages stems the time-honored preference for *Julius Caesar* in German classrooms, because this play could easily "prove" its value in a school dedicated to the teaching of Latin (Küpper 1982, 212).

For a while after 1948, Shakespeare's plays held their place in the curriculum of both German and English. When the accent shifted from the teaching of the history of literature to theme-centered projects on such topics as "Protest," "Youth Literature," or "War and Peace," Shakespeare gradually disappeared from the literature classes in German. As a result, only those students who attended a Gymnasium with English as their first foreign language, would have been taught at least one play by Shakespeare. After radical reforms in the West German school system, secondary school students were allowed to choose most of their four or five subjects for their final exams, which meant that they could also drop English altogether. At that stage, Shakespeare remained obligatory only in the curricula for English as a major subject (*Leistungskurs*) in all parts of the country. While the number of students to study Shakespeare at school steadily decreased, his singularity in the curriculum becomes even more conspicuous: with the general dislike of the literary canon, the lists of authors and their works whose reading was compulsory was either drastically reduced or totally abandoned. Hence, Goethe, Heine, or Brecht were read only when they were "relevant" to a particular political, ideological, or philosophical topic. In the English curriculum the one and only exception remains Shakespeare. In West German schools, the English poet had become a kind of lonely beacon of European literature.

Contrary to the East, the lack of a centrally organized school system in the West also led to a lack of ideological consent in matters relating to teaching. This does not, of course, imply that teaching in the West was void of any ideology. The official curricula as well as the teaching material and didactic literature on Shakespeare give evidence of their ideological bias. In the 1950s and '60s, Shakespeare's plays were regarded as the embodiment of universal and timeless truths—much as outlined by Prince Charles. Shakespeare's characters were praised for being models of mankind, the poet's understanding of fundamental human relationships was thought to be "eternally relevant" (The Prince of Wales 1991, 5).

As to the choice of plays, West German teachers followed yet another time-honored tradition: they taught either *Macbeth* or *Julius Caesar*, the former being the most frequently read. *Macbeth* served as a model for the eternal conflict between good and evil. Its other educational merits were seen in the fact that the play is comparatively short and has a clear structure and the spectacular marks of a thriller. Even the most recent school *Macbeth* on the German market, in a series with the misleading title *Discover*, is advertised along the same lines (Gocke and Stock 1999). No heed is being paid to the lonely cry of the critic: "Must it always be *Macbeth*?" in the wilderness of the profitable market (Glaap 1997). With the teaching of *Julius Caesar*, one could not neglect political and social matters. In the early years of the Federal Republic of Germany, the schools reflected a general tendency of the stage, namely to actualize the Roman play by alluding to the very recent experience of dictatorship in Germany. To keep the memory of the horrors of Nazism alive, and with it the political as well as the moral questions of guilt, responsibility, and atonement, had become part of the new cultural and national identity in West Germany and therefore also had its bearings on education.

With *Lear* and *Othello* as alternatives to the favorites *Macbeth* and *Julius Caesar*, the curricula gave clear preference to the tragic genre. Among the comedies, only *A Midsummer*

Night's Dream was popular in German classes as a play suitable for younger pupils. *The Merchant of Venice* was recommended mostly for the sake of the problems centered in Shylock. The histories were rarely read in school, from time to time *Richard III* or *Henry V* being mentioned as "suitable" plays.

Hamlet was the play most frequently suggested for the German literature classes in the West. The ideological premises for this choice were entirely different from those in the East. The play was meant to open the way to metaphysical speculations, the protagonist was turned into an existential hero for the students to model themselves on. Because of the rivalry with English classes, it was also argued that the philosophical contents and the complexity of the play made it too difficult an object to be dealt with in a foreign language.

The choice of *Hamlet* as *the* school play in East Germany has a rather complicated pedigree. *Hamlet* has become the prototype of the German assimilation of Shakespeare. "Hamlet ist Deutschland"—"Hamlet is Germany," the much-quoted title of Freiligrath's political poem hints at the epidemic "Hamlet-mania" in the history of German mentality. The GDR saw every reason to integrate *Hamlet* into the curriculum of the schools for future generations of a socialist society. In the schools, the play served as the model of the "history of emancipation" of mankind (Sorge 1992, 147). The other equally important argument for the choice of *Hamlet* relates to the Marxist aesthetic principle of mimesis. The drama does, of course, supply the key phrase "to hold a mirror up to nature" and thereby allows for a reading true to the teachings of socialist realism.

More conspicuously than in the West, *Hamlet* had become the paradigm of the East German Shakespeare reception in schools, academic discourse, and of course on stage. In fact, a celebrated production of *Hamlet* marked the reopening of the Deutsches Theater in Berlin in 1945, and soon became regarded as the cornerstone of a Marxist Shakespeare interpretation in the GDR. "Hamlet-Shakespeare was set up as a figurehead for a hoped-for emergent culture" (Hamburger 1998, 327). In the theater, more than in any other field, the play also became the focal point of cultural and political controversy. Two *Hamlet* productions, both from the quatercentenary celebrations of 1964, have become almost a legend in the stage history of the GDR. The production at Greifswald by Adolf Dresen (translation Maik Hamburger) came under censorship because of its subversive potential: "It questioned the validity of interpreting Shakespeare according to any ideological stencil" (Guntner 1998, 41). On the other hand, Hans-Dieter Mäde at Karl-Marx-Stadt presented Hamlet's ideals of mankind and of a humane society as a model for a utopia to be eventually realized by a socialist society. He thereby conformed with the then valid doctrines of Marxist aesthetics that were laid down as law by Alexander Abusch, the former Secretary of Culture in the GDR, at the Weimar conference of 1964. And it was this positive utopian model that was the guideline to the reading of *Hamlet* at school. The harmonious ideal of Renaissance man and the affinity between the heritage and the heir was made available for socialist pedagogy. It was "a bright mirror" that was held up to the school students, a mirror in which they were supposed to "see" their own future (Weimann 1992).

After the reunification, the supreme place that *Hamlet* had been accorded in the school curriculum was viewed with a certain nostalgia. When teachers and academics of the former GDR discussed the changes in the curricula at the Weimar conference in 1991, they lamented the fact that Shakespeare was no longer part of the courses in German literature. In retrospect, *Hamlet* served as a kind of icon of what had been lost irrevocably with the end of the GDR (Klotz 1992). The same almost ontological meaning was attached to Heiner Müller's production of *Hamlet* and *Hamlet-Maschine* in Berlin, which was completed only after the fall of the Berlin Wall (Pfister 1994; Hamburger 1998, 428–34).

Outside the schools, another cultural institution gained influence on the teaching of Shakespeare in both countries. With the split-up of the German Shakespeare Society into two separate German Shakespeare Societies East and West in 1963–64, it became clear that Weimar saw itself as the true "heir" of the cultural tradition of the nation also with regard to Shakespeare. Abusch's dogmatic speech, like the ruling against the Greifswald production and the official praise for Mäde's *Hamlet* were a warning against any subversion on stage as well is in schools, but also a heralding to the West of Germany where the true German cultural heritage of Shakespeare was being honored. The ideology of the GDR helped to strengthen that position. "A cultural way of life became synonymous with a socialist way of life.... The educated nation stood for the socialist nation" (Sorge 1998, 102). In the beginning, the Weimar Shakespeare Society saw its main objective in joining academics and theater practitioners in their common endeavors. It took yet another jubilee to officially welcome the teachers among their ranks. In 1979, the GDR celebrated its thirtieth anniversary, the motto of the Weimar conference was "Shakespeare-Reception and National Culture."[2] A party official, who—in his speech—linked Hamlet's question "What's Hecuba to him" (2.2), directly with the cultural heritage ("Was ist uns Hekuba? Wie halten wir es mit dem Erbe?"), deemed it essential for the cultural politics of the Shakespeare Society that teachers should voice their problems in the teaching of Shakespeare in the framework of the annual conferences (Schrader 1980). These were, of course, teachers of German literature classes, for whom the first "roundtable talk" was being arranged at the conference in 1979. There were two main issues to be "debated," which indicated the ideological bend of the meeting: "What are the ways and means of making Shakespeare's works more effective on the educative level? Which are the premises of historical and literary knowledge necessary for the reception of Shakespeare?" More practical matters, such as the translations to be used, or the choice of plays regulated by the curriculum, were also mentioned, and after a revision of the curriculum *Romeo and Juliet* was included as an alternative to *Macbeth* in class 9 (Klotz 1980, 189).

In the following year, the teachers' colloquium finds mention as "a new dimension in the work of the Shakespeare Society to further develop a socialist national culture." Carried out with the explicit permission and support of the Ministry of Education, the participants of the colloquium were reminded of the general guidelines of the Eighth Congress of Education, which emphasized the preservation of the cultural heritage and its "importance for our time" (Henning 1981, 223).

The Weimar Shakespeare Society clearly attached great importance to the academic as well as to the ideological training of the teachers. This is illustrated by the introductory lecture to the teaching of *Hamlet* (in 1983), which was allocated to Anselm Schlösser, one of the "grand old men" of orthodox Marxist Shakespeare criticism in the GDR (Schlösser 1984). In his lecture, Schlösser had a number of bones to pick: Jan Kott, the renegade, is refuted for his pessimistic, cyclical view of history, and a number of bourgeois critics, above all Wilson Knight, are castigated for their individualistic interpretations. Another heavy attack is launched against the teaching methods and relevant didactic publications of the Federal Republic of Germany (FRG), which propagate the abhorred *Hamlet* adaptations by Charles Marowitz, Tom Stoppard, or Heiner Müller, which "drape their nakedness with rags from Shakespeare's wardrobe." While these critical views were in line with the Party ideology, it must have come as a shock to Schlösser's audience that he also found fault with the official Study Helps (*Unterrichtshilfen*) on *Hamlet*. Their interpretations, such as presenting the experienced statesman Claudius as a positive character, obviously did not fit in with the then valid Marxist doctrines.[3] The image that Schlösser presents to the teachers and obviously expects them to present to their students, adheres to the "official" dogmatic interpretations propagated by Abusch and Mäde in 1964, almost twenty years earlier. Although the teachers' colloquia in the following years move away from a text-centered toward a theater-centered approach, *Hamlet* remains the focus of interest. Also in schools, the play is highly charged with the ongoing ideological debates. Teachers apparently had difficulties in extracting the play's essential humanism from "bits of the text" (Klotz 1987, 222).

A complete methodological reverse of the then well-established teachers' colloquium was effected in the three final years of the GDR. In 1987, instead of talking about *Hamlet* the Dresden Youth Theatre presented their "*Hamlet* Project," consisting of the play in Heiner Müller's translation and of a Danish adaptation for young schoolchildren, called *The Little Prince of Denmark*. The teachers were obviously fascinated by the young, active, rebellious, and clowning Hamlet (Klotz 1988, 300).

In the following year, 1988, Heiner Müller addressed the large audience of the Weimar conference for the first time and read, an act of significant ambiguity, his translation of the grave-diggers scene to them. That very scene was acted out with great success by secondary school students at the last teachers' colloquium in 1989 (Klotz 1990). In hindsight, the program of that year's conference looks slightly schizophrenic: three historical events of the cultural and national heritage were to be celebrated: the bicentenary of the

French Revolution, the fortieth anniversary of the GDR, and the commemoration of the revolutionary Thomas Müntzer (1489). They coincided, as it were, with the celebrations of the 125 years since the founding of the German Shakespeare Society and the "Renaissance" of the German Shakespeare tradition in the GDR since 1963–64. In the official speech of the minister of culture Shakespeare is heralded as the best example "for assimilating a foreign culture into our own identity" (Hoffmann 1990, 7).

As in East Germany, also in the West the German Shakespeare Society took measures to exercise influence over the teaching of Shakespeare in the schools. Here, too, these had a distinctly political flavor. When the school reforms of the 1970s began to destabilize the place of Shakespeare's works in the English curriculum, this could also lead to drastically reducing the numbers of English teachers needed for the teaching of Shakespeare. University teachers of English literature then realized that that might also endanger their prerogatives of training and qualifying these teachers. To draw attention to these matters, the West German Shakespeare Society held a seminar, "Shakespeare and the School Reform," at the annual conference in 1977. According to President Werner Habicht, who chaired the seminar, its aim was to "intensify the exchange between schools, universities, and theaters for the benefit of the teaching of Shakespeare and to coordinate the efforts of all three institutions."[4] After the 1977 meeting, special seminars for teachers became a regular item on the agenda of the West German Shakespeare conferences. Their overall purpose was to inform the teachers about current trends in national and international Shakespeare criticism rather than discussing down-to-earth classroom matters. Obviously, the teachers attending these seminars clamored for more nourishing instruction. So, from time to time, such topics as dramatic activities in the classroom, the use of films and TV programs, or so-called "didactic models" for single plays came under discussion. The seminars had a semiofficial status, as teachers were allowed to take time off for attending them.

Despite similarities in the organizational framework of the seminars run by the East and by the West German Shakespeare Society, their aims were different matters. In Weimar, the overall purpose was to give the teachers of German literature basic information on Shakespeare and to secure that his works were also appropriated under Marxist premises in the schools. In the West, the tendency was to assimilate the latest literary theories, preferably those coming from British and American sources, and thereby to enlarge the teachers' knowledge about the English historical and literary background of Shakespeare's plays. The fact that in the West the English original was taught at school and English was also the classroom language had directed the teachers' interest toward Shakespeare's "Englishness." Rather than linking him with the German cultural tradition, he was regarded as a poet who surpassed national boundaries. The tendency of the intelligentsia in the West to be suspicious of any overt nationalism and favor internationalism instead may have worked as a stimulus in this educational process.

With the reunification of the two German countries in 1990, the patterns, rules, and conventions developed over forty-five years in most areas of public life in the West had to be adopted in the East, despite their protest and attempts to maintain their own ways of life. Whether the two separate cultural identities generated by the different political and social systems have merged or still coexist remains an open question (Assmann and Frevert 1999). As regards the educational system, after heavy initial difficulties the Western model was, with only slight alterations, adopted in the East. Thus, the curricula of English in the so-called "new" Länder, established Shakespeare as an obligatory teaching subject,[5] whereas his works are no longer part of the curriculum of German literature classes.

Most of the publications on the teaching of Shakespeare published after 1990, carry on with the discussion that was familiar in the West, as if there were no newcomers on the scene. There are a few indications of unrest, as when the question of the "necessity" of teaching Shakespeare is being asked with a new urgency, as was the case at a conference on foreign language teaching at Halle in the East of Germany in 1990, when the provocative question was raised "*Macbeth* or McDonald's?" (Meyer 1991). The attempts to do away with Shakespeare yet again were, of course, abortive. Not only did the regulations of the official curricula prevent this but also the generally affirmative debate among teachers, which was carried on along the lines developed in the West with its preference for the Anglo-American tradition (Mosner 2000).

The predominance of British and American Shakespeare

criticism has always been noticed in the large body of didactic writings in the West. They disseminate the conviction that the poet's "Englishness" can best be transmitted in the classroom when following models set by the English speaking world. Among the courses tried out in English schools, the program of Rex Gibson's *Cambridge School Shakespeare* ranks among the most highly favored and has recently come under serious Teutonic criticism in an essay of more than twenty pages (Ullrich 2000).

In Britain, Shakespeare had become statutory with the National Curriculum (Aers and Whealer 1991). The "English" Shakespeare became a "sacred repository of national values, standards and identity" (Joughin 1997b, 274). The National Curriculum, as the critics see it, perpetuates the construct of Shakespeare as the perpetrator of eternal values and timeless truths, of great mysteries which transcend history. "Shakespeare" serves as an ideology that sustains the privileges of the ruling classes and cements the rift between high and low culture (Holderness and Murphy 1997). To the German outsider who is familiar with most of the clichés from home, the intensity of that conflict is baffling: it would be unheard of in Germany for academics to address a Party conference to voice their disagreement with some regulations concerning the teaching of Shakespeare at school, as happened in 1993 when five hundred academics sent a petition to the Conservative Party Conference "to oppose the government's policy that the study of Shakespeare be a mandatory part of the curriculum for students from an early age." Nor would German Shakespeare scholars regard Shakespeare for their own country and tradition "as of centrally strategic importance in the battleground formed by the intersection of education and politics" (Holderness and Murphy 1997, 20). In this respect, the problematic position Shakespeare holds in Britain's national identity is unique.

Considering the impact English Shakespeare criticism has on the German educational scene, it would be of interest to see whether British educators are aware of what happens to their national poet in the German classroom, even though—as a Finnish critic has put it—"the British people tend to be introspective in their Shakespeare tradition" (Sell 1993, 13). In print, there is some evidence of British transnational interest to be found in two articles in Rex Gibson's short-lived journal *Shakespeare and Schools*. Both tell us much about mutual prejudices that arise from the differences between the respective educational and cultural systems in Britain and Germany. While both British authors try to be fair to German enthusiasm, orderliness, and sincerity, they marvel at the institutional differences. The verdict "Facilities were far from perfect" results from the fact that in German schools there are no special drama studios to work in with students and no "drama classes" as in English schools (Lockeyer 1989). The title "Unser Shakespeare," of the second article sums up the strangeness the author experienced during a three-day seminar she gave on Rex Gibson's approach to teachers in Berlin. Everything strikes her as "typical" of the German approach: tables and chairs arranged formally to face the blackboard; teachers ferociously grabbing any printed material, eager to get solid information; and, most markedly, the insistence of the teachers on complying only with such activities as are closely linked to the text. Despite the British drama teacher's praise of the untiring attention of her German colleagues, it was not the internationalism of Shakespeare that had ruled the day but the attempts of a British teacher to come to terms with "Unser Shakespeare" (Redsell 1994).

There was yet another trace of "unser Shakespeare" in Rex Gibson's journal. Perhaps as an extra incitement to the readers, a cover puzzle appeared in several issues, representing various effigies of the Bard in the form of busts, pictures, or statues. The readers were asked to name the places—all over the world—where the images of Shakespeare were to be found. The solutions were published in the next issue with a commentary on the respective effigy: the numerous letters the editor received, and the almost equal number of correct answers. The cover picture of the autumn issue of 1990 showed the German Shakespeare Memorial in Weimar. In the next issue, the readers were informed that this puzzle had also drawn "dozens of responses." Among the many suggestions for the place of origin "Elsinore was a great favorite"—I presume because the Weimar figure has a skull and a fool's cockscomb at his feet— "But none," the editor continues ruefully, "identified it as the Shakespeare Statue in Weimar." To be fair to the English readers: at that time but few of them would have had a chance to travel to Weimar, to see the statue hidden in the Goethe park, or even—like Stanley Wells, then head of the

Shakespeare Institute in Stratford—to have his or her picture taken in front of the Weimar statue to be published in the Yearbook of the German Shakespeare Society.[6] Apparently, "Shakespeare discourses" operate differently in Britain and in Germany and also in the relevant professions. But that would be yet another aspect of the teaching of Shakespeare in Europe and—quite another story.

Notes

1. Some literary texts, such as short stories with a political or social tendency, were still on offer.

2. In his report on the conference, Henning (1980, 177) gives the official version. "Mit den Shakespeare-Tagen 1979 haben wir einen Beitrag zum 30. Jahrestag der Gründung unseres Staates leisten wollen. Die Tagungen der Deutschen Shakespeare-Gesellschaft gelten seit 1964 als kulturpolitische Höhepunkte im Leben unserer Republik" [With the Shakespeare Festival of 1979 we have made our contribution to the thirtieth anniversary of our German Democratic Republic. Since 1964, the annual conferences of the Deutsche Shakespeare Society have been recognized as cultural highlights in the life of our Republic.]

3. It is interesting to notice that in the following discussion one of the participants, grasping the political dynamite in Schlösser's criticsm of the study guide, came to its rescue by arguing that they contained no more than advice and stimuli for the teachers and were, anyway, under revision.

4. Habicht is quoted in the unpublished minutes of the seminar "Shakespeare und die reformierte Oberstufe," 17 April 1977.

5. Thus, the new curriculum of English for Thüringen, passed in 1990, does not name any specific play from the canon but decrees that due attention must be paid to the dramatic works of William Shakespeare. Most of the more recent syllabuses have similar regulations on Shakespeare; some of them are listed in the bibliography.

6. At the Shakespeare Conference 1991 in Weimar, Stanley Wells attended the annual ceremony at the Shakespeare Monument in the Ilm Park and delivered a short speech. It used to be the custom of the East German Shakespeare Society to invite a scholar from abroad to give this speech.

Undoing Nationalist Leanings in Teaching Shakespeare: Shakespeare and Eminescu

Madalina Nicolaescu

IN THE LATE 1990s BUCHAREST UNIVERSITY ADOPTED A MORE inclusive admission policy accepting larger numbers of students with a significantly lower qualification in English (British and American) literature than before. The resulting heterogeneity of students, whose training and attitudes to literature varied widely, has called for a rethinking of first-year courses. In my efforts to readjust and better tailor the Shakespeare course to the needs and background knowledge of my students, I designed a questionnaire that was given to students before the first lecture for two consecutive years (2000, 2001). The statements with the highest recurrence in the answers to the questionnaire indicated a surprisingly strong nationalist bias in their perception of the "Bard":

- Shakespeare is universal and hence our contemporary.
- Eminescu is Romania, Romania is Eminescu and, similarly, Shakespeare is England, England is Shakespeare; both poets embody the national spirit of their respective countries. The major difference between the two is the fact that Eminescu is little known abroad, a fact that derives from the small circulation of the Romanian language.
- We are interested in information on Shakespeare's poetry and his characters rather than in historical information about his age. We strongly dislike history as it deals with politics and conflicts.

The statement that identifies Eminescu with Romania can be traced back to a comparison made by Nichita Stanescu, a most celebrated contemporary poet, which was taken out of context and has been reprinted over and over again in schoolbooks as a definitive judgment on whatever poem by Eminescu is taught. One can easily infer that Eminescu is held up as an icon of our national culture, an embodiment of the Romanian spirit, and that the readings forged by our educational policies are largely nationalistic.[1] The feeble attempt at a revisionary approach that was launched in Eminescu scholarship a few years ago has not reached the textbooks as yet. (A similar iconoclastic rethinking of our national history, when included in a textbook for high school students, has caused fierce debates in parliament, where the proposal was advanced to publicly burn the respective textbook.)

The assimilation of Shakespeare with Eminescu is further indicative of the ways the dominant ideology encouraging nationalist views and beliefs has insinuated itself in the students' understanding of all canonical figures, Romanian or not. This is all the more shocking as Shakespeare used to enjoy a "privileged" position in Romanian school education, in a quite cosmopolitan cultural area that prided itself on preserving a safe distance from the aggressive invasion of nationalist discourses.

As the answers to the questionnaire suggest, teaching Shakespeare to first-year students has often meant undertaking a painstaking process of contesting nationalist attitudes, of deconstructing deeply set beliefs and visions, of undoing familiar practices employed in understanding high culture. This paper will investigate the causes behind many of the resistances I have encountered in promoting an alternative, radical approach to Shakespeare and it will also discuss some of the negotiations that could be considered when teaching revisionary Anglo-American approaches at university level.

Shakespeare in Romanian Secondary Schools

How is Shakespeare taught in Romanian secondary schools? There is the strong tradition of extolling the "bard" and the "golden age" he belonged to. Shakespeare is a universal genius whose work transcends time and place, and the Elizabethan period he lived in (no mention is ever made of the Jacobean one) is a beautifully harmonious one in which all previous conflicts had been resolved.

In a schoolbook issued in 1995, Shakespeare is described as "the greatest English poet and an undisputed world figure in literature"; he "was a great humanist," a "close observer of the people of his time"; he was "familiar with the traditions of English folklore and showed deep concern for his people" (Bunaciu and Focsaneanu 1995, 93). The major clichés of bardolatry combine with and reinforce residues of the dogmatic Marxist-Leninist approach to Shakespeare of the 1950s.

Just as antiquated is the approach to Shakespeare promoted in the commercially highly successful guides to English literature for the admission exams to the university, guides that were issued in the mid-1990s by two well-known university professors (Andrei Bantas and Pia Brinzeu) and that have been reedited and reprinted four times (Bantas, Clontea, and Brinzeu 1993, 2000). A collection of quotations extracted from histories of English Literature written mostly in the 1960s (Martin Day, David Daiches, as well as Legouis and Cazamian are particularly privileged) or culled from dictionaries of English literature manage to create a most strident version of bardolatry. Shakespeare is unparalleled in world literature since "the rare gifts which have been bestowed diversely on the greatest playwrights of all nations had merged and combined into the genius of Shakespeare" (66). His craftsmanship and genius are given a variety of essentializing and naturalizing definitions: he is "a child of nature," "vying with nature in creative power"; he reveals "an essential reality that has kept his plays vivid over three centuries" (67). The divine quality of his work and the mystery of his genius exert an irresistible spell upon us. Shakespeare is beyond rationality: "we submit to the poet's caprice without questioning" (73). Any critical distance to the plays, any interrogating move on behalf of the students would simply be sacrilegious.

Needless to add that there is no attempt at a historicized, contextualized understanding of Shakespeare's plays. They are presented in general and simplified terms: "the tragedies written between 1601 and 1608 are all pervaded with the same gloom: the world is pictured as full of evil forces" (Bantas, Clontea, and Brinzeu 1993, 2000, 65). The book does include a nuanced close reading of Antony's speech in *Julius*

Caesar. This could be looked upon as an example of high quality Romanian scholarship produced sometime in the late 1970s or early '80s. The meanings that are skillfully teased out from Antony's speech are not, however, located in either Shakespeare's or the Romanian reader's time but are left free-floating in a decontextualized, transhistorical space. The close reading does not in the least challenge the introductory presentation of Shakespeare as a universal and transcendent genius.

The third book I am going to discuss—*English My Love*—is the first of a new series of textbooks for high-school students issued under the influence of the courses on how to teach literature that the British Council organized in the 1990s. While the book reinforces the conventional view about the Elizabethan age—"Many people feel that the reign of Elizabeth I is the most glamorous, the most exciting period in English history. This is why it is called The Elizabethan Age or The Golden Age" (Balan et al. 1995, 92)—it does make an effort to include Shakespeare in some kind of context, albeit only a literary one. Short excerpts from Kyd, Marlowe, and Jonson are provided as a backdrop to Shakespeare. Apart from these excerpts the much trumpeted emphasis on context the new series of textbooks is supposed to introduce is basically decorative: it amounts to hardly more than beautiful pictures of Tudor castles, a painting of the Earl of Southampton or cursory information about the Shakespearean stage. Once again the student is supposed to be under a spell, to cherish and revere the bard and his age and never to question or doubt.

History in as far as it means struggle for power is not in evidence in the new textbook. Nor is there any difference between the historical past and our postcommunist present: the pastness of Shakespeare's age is largely a matter of costumes. The critical approach to the texts is just as traditional: most of the emphasis is placed on imagery (such as the imagery of light and darkness in *Romeo and Juliet*).

English My Love does introduce more fashionable concepts such as the one of identity but it tames it at the same time by including it under the heading of "themes." Juliet's difficult speech "What's in a name?" is dispatched with the following instruction: "Discuss with your partner the famous balcony scene and find the lines relevant to the *theme of identity*" (Balan et al. 1995, 159). No explanatory comment spells out either the novelty to Romanian students of such a concept or the contradictions inherent in the Shakespearean construction of identity.

Paradoxically the Shakespeare that students construct from the various textbooks does not differ in any essential way from the Eminescu they are taught in school. The two figures get conflated and the categories and attitudes that students are taught to apply to the Romanian national bard are transferred or displaced on the other "transnational" bard. Such approaches pave the way for more aggressive moves of appropriating or even co-opting Shakespeare to secure nationalism.

Romanian Traditions in Reading/Teaching Shakespeare

The declared commitment to a context-oriented teaching of literature in the recent textbooks testifies to a clear desire for change. The authors managed to introduce some change in the teeth of the persistent conservative thrust in the teaching of Shakespeare. What can account for the great gap between the classroom Shakespeare and the iconoclastic one of the theatrical performances, which for more than three decades have vied with each other in politicizing or, more recently, in deconstructing his plays?

One answer is that in socialist Romania, unlike in the former GDR, there was no close communication between theater people and academies, or schoolteachers (Weimann 1997; Pfister 1994). Consequently, critical approaches to Shakespeare did not receive any encouragement to establish the kind of challenging relations between past and present, between Shakespearian representations and problems of contemporary politics as was the case in the GDR. Romanian classrooms, whether in high schools or at universities, were not and still are not open to experimenting, but functioned mainly as what Althusser called ideological state apparatuses. Nor could schools indulge in the indirectness and allusive topicality of theaters. Their possibilities of "making meaning by Shakespearian texts" in provocative ways were very limited (Hawkes 1992).

Another answer to the question about the resistance to change in teaching Shakespeare is the rejection of anything that smacks of leftist, Marxist critical stances. More radical approaches such as those developed by cultural materialism, new historicism, or by feminist or postcolonialist theories have hardly had any currency in Romania. This attitude goes back to the 1960s and was initially understood as a way of resisting an oppressive dogmatic discourse on literature.

An important landmark in fashioning this "oppositional" approach to Shakespeare was the publication in 1964 of a collection of critical essays from all over the world. Tudor Vianu, a most prominent Romanian scholar, prefaced the book and also included an important essay "Umanitatea lui Shakespeare" [Shakespeare's humanism/humanity] (Vianu 1964). What Vianu set out to do was to counter the unrelenting dogmatism in the approaches to Shakespeare's "titanic" personalities, who were understood to prefigure and indirectly legitimate the socialist New Man. The comparison with Weimann's way of breaking through the straitjacket of this critical discourse seems to me quite apposite. Like Weimann, Vianu set out to resist the teleological continuity between past and present in the politics of reading Shakespeare of the early sixties and to introduce the possibility of discontinuity. Unlike Weimann, however, Vianu distrusted any solution that could be reached working from within the dominant ideological discourse (Weimann 1997); he tried to evade it and reestablish links with earlier traditions of critical thinking. He therefore insisted on preserving inviolate the *literary and moral value* of Shakespeare's texts, his basic humanism. Vianu tried to reassert what we nowadays call "the pastness of Shakespeare" by reconstructing the literary and moral context of Shakespeare's plays and by shifting the focus of criticism away from the sociopolitical context, which dogmatic Marxist criticism presented in a crude, reductionist way. (The official discourse abounded in simplifying discussions of the class struggle and of the emergence of bourgeois relations in Shakespeare's plays.) His strategy was therefore to evade the readings the oppressive sociopolitical context of his own time had imposed on Shakespeare and on literature in general and to generate different, covertly oppositional meanings.

Inevitably, Vianu's reassessment of Shakespeare's humanism did not reinforce the authority of the text against a reductive presentation of the context but also reintroduced the image of a transcendent, universal Shakespeare. Vianu fully acknowledged the geographical/synchronic and historical/

diachronic plurality of the Shakespeares that had been produced in the reception of the plays, all of them being more or less "conjunctural constructions." Against this "mobility" in the reading of Shakespeare, he asserts the transcendent value of "some ever self-same core" of his work, a core that continuously germinates new productions and that provides the links between past, present, and future constructions of the plays (Vianu 1964, 12).

Later Romanian scholars followed in his footsteps and developed sophisticated stylistic, semiotic, or pragmatic models to read Shakespeare, all of these models placing the act of reading at a safe remove from reality and from politics. The tradition of resistance against the intrusion of "ideology and politics" that was set up in the socialist period has lingered on, with politics and ideology still being defined as basically leftist or Marxist and therefore objectionable. (Conservative liberal discourses, the invasive discourses of the market are not as yet perceived as "ideology" in Romania, since they are being naturalized successfully.) Paradoxically, it is on the grounds of this very tradition of oppositional readings that attacks are launched against attempts at deconstructing the literary canon or at providing noncanonical readings of canonical texts. Leading scholars such as Mircea Martin use Harold Bloom's recent work on the canon and his derogatory comments on present Shakespearian scholarship to inveigle deconstructionism, feminism, multiculturalism, cultural materialism, and cultural studies (the latter operating with "an incredibly crude Marxism"). It is the *aesthetic value* of Shakespeare's work and other canonical texts that has to be rescued from such criticism (Martin 2001, 105–7).

The defensive mechanisms Vianu's followers have adopted to prevent the aesthetic world from getting contaminated with "dirty politics" has put a lid on the development of Shakespeare criticism. At the same time it has rendered these scholars ill equipped to devise proper discursive strategies against the encroachment of nationalist rhetoric. One can even detect an uncanny collusion between the stultifying and often outdated approaches to Shakespeare and the readings formulated from nationalist positions.

Historicizing Shakespeare

The benefits of teaching Shakespeare from a new historicist or a cultural materialist perspective in Romania do not need defending. One cannot emphasize enough the importance of the students' awareness and tolerance of difference and how the employment of such approaches counteracts the homogenizing discourses still prevailing in Romanian education. What also needs stressing, however, is the cultural specificity of Western oppositional readings of Shakespeare and the necessity for operating adjustments and negotiations when adopting these critical perspectives.

Of particular help to Romanian students are the bold, iconoclastic views such readings offer. Western radical theories could be referred to and aligned with local theatrical practices to provide incentives for a more provocative and explorative engagement with the Shakespearian text. This would make for the introduction of a discontinuity in the tradition of obedient veneration of canonized figures in classrooms. It would encourage Romanian students to believe in the possibility of introducing change by questioning established meanings and by generating new meanings.

Plays such as *Henry V* that appear to endorse triumphalist, nationalistic positions can provide interesting exercises in reading against the grain; an important goal to pursue in such readings is to stimulate the students' desire to question the discourses legitimizing heroic figures and to increase their awareness of the existence of alternatives to a given set of actions.

One of my favorite exercises is the investigation of the uses that the Archbishop of Canterbury and the king make of history in *Henry V*, act 1, scene 2.

The archbishop turns to history in order to legitimize Henry's claims for France. Recourse to history involves both archives and narratives of the past, such as the glorious feats performed by Henry's ancestors, Edward III and his son, the Black Prince. Like the divine design of nature referred to in the famous beehive metaphor, history is invoked as an authority: it provides the objective, hard-core truth upon which kings can build their policy. Under this guise—the play shows us—history legitimizes acts of violence that have dire consequences for the population.

In scene 2, the one who questions this use of the official discourse on the past is none other than the king himself. Anxious not to compromise his "image," Henry warns the archbishop to:

> ... take heed how you impawn our person
> How you awake our sleeping sword of war.

> We charge you in the name of God take heed,
> For never two such kingdoms did contend
> Without much fall of blood, whose guiltless drops
> Are everyone a woe, a sore complaint
> 'Gainst him whose wrongs gives edge unto the swords
> That makes such waste in brief mortality.
>
> (1.2. 21–28)

The king is, of course, shrewdly trying to shift the burden of responsibility on the archbishop, who assumes the position of the historiographer. The warning does, however, raise important questions and indirectly arrests the flow of action. It is admitted that the historiographer is fallible and that fatal errors are committed either in the research of the historical past or in the narratives in which the facts are presented. The absolute quality of the historical truth is thus seriously hedged in. Information on the debates around the adequacy of historical accounts in the Elizabethan period can indicate that the historical truth was not taken for granted in Shakespeare's time. Parallels can be established between Bale and of course Foxe, Hall, and Holinshed (Patterson 1995, 1996). Shakespeare's own "preposterous" reversal of the chronological ordering from Hall and Holinshed in *Henry V* should be emphasized (Parker 1996, 41–42). Contextual information thus lends weight to Henry's doubts about the impartiality and accuracy of the archbishop's reading of the archives: "And God forbid, my dear and faithful lord./ That you should fashion, wrest or bow your reading" (1.2.13–14).

The students could be encouraged to study the extent to which the play encourages a radical view of history, one that, according to Benjamin, can "blast open the continuum of history" (Benjamin 1968, 262). Henry's comment upon the effects of historiography projects a different version of the history of the wars between England and France, a version that no longer subscribes to the celebratory and jingoistic discourse Canterbury and Elly have been employing. Henry's warning suggests a vision of history that no longer endorses the perspective of the victors or of the "heroic" martial figures, as it foregrounds the wanton bloodshed and the sacrifice of innocent (common?) people that such military pursuits inevitably entail. Is Henry here ventriloquizing William and anticipating the latter's gruesome image of "all those legs and arms and heads chopped off in a battle [that] shall join together at the latter day and cry all" (4.1.124–25)?

The official discourse on history and on political and military action is therefore interrupted and challenged at the very center of authority. For a short moment the spectator can entertain the hope that Henry might opt for a different line of action, that there was an alternative to the historical events.

I think that Romanian students can benefit from lingering on such examples of fissures and contradictions in the dominant discourse. A new historicist reading of the lines quoted above would, of course, emphasize the fact that Henry is actually behaving like a Machiavellian prince who raises such subversive questions only to contain them later on. Henry may very well be just hypocritical in venting such fears or scruples, since the archbishop's ensuing demonstration of the legitimacy of the war against France is made on the king's request and is part of a bargain the archbishop made in order to save the property of the church. This line of argument is necessary in classroom readings of the play in order to demystify the aura around Henry V and to counter the assimilation of Henry with iconic heroes in Romanian history.

A reading along Stephen Greenblatt's line should also include the objections that cultural materialists have brought to this perspective, namely that it cancels out the possibility of resistance to power (Belsey 1991). These objections fully resonate with our anxiety in the face of the Romanian students' mistrust in the possibility of all oppositional action and their consequent disaffection with both politics and history. It follows that negotiations and adjustments to "local" requirements are necessary when employing new historicist and cultural materialist readings. These negotiations counter the potential tendency that Western radical readings may too easily impose themselves as the dominant global critical discourse on Shakespeare.

Note

1. According to some Romanian sociologists the dominant discourse in Romania is the "the national," ethnic one, which is a softer version of the nationalistic discourses that were employed in the nineteenth and first half of the twentieth century (Barbu 2000). Ceausescu's domination relied upon keeping strong nationalistic feelings alive and on invigorating certain types of nationalistic and chauvinistic discourses. They made up

much of the basic texture of the Romanian literature and Romanian history taught in schools. Romanian secondary education still abounds in residual elements of these heavily "national" and often even nationalistic discourses. Attempts at more radical changes have met with rabid resistance in all quarters of our society.

Children's Hours: Shakespeare, the Lambs, and French Education

Ruth Morse

> N'oubliez pas que Caliban est un paresseux et un négligent. Regardez autour de vous: la plupart de ceux que la vie condamne aujourd'hui aux besognes les plus pénibles étaient de petits fainéants sur les bancs où vous êtes assis.
>
> (Chaffurin and Delany 1929, ii)

> [Do not forget that Caliban is lazy and negligent. Look around you: most of those whom life condemns today to the most miserable jobs were little do-nothings on the benches where you were sitting.]

THIS SURPRISING PIECE OF CHARACTER CRITICISM, WITH ITS PRACtical application, comes from a school text, but not—or not quite—a text of *The Tempest*. It is part of the commentary from an edition of the Lambs' *Tales from Shakespeare*, aimed at teaching English to children in French Catholic private education. Its confident directiveness is now so alien as to be unrecognizable, whether as commentary, as an interpretation of plays in general, or this play and that character in specific. Yet there is nothing peculiar, even particular, about the moralizing approach as a way of educating children. That, after all, is part of what the Lambs opposed.

In one context, the distinctiveness of Shakespeare for French children highlights controversial arguments about *education* that are exaggerated almost into parody when the author concerned is—or appears to be—Shakespeare. In a second, equally controversial context, adaptation in translation (for schools or for private reading) throws into evident and obvious relief current questions about interpretation, appropriation, and control, and invites us to see them from another point of view. In the brief survey that follows I take "education" in the double sense of what children read at home, alone or with their parents, as well as what is thrust upon them at school. It is this latter point that may surprise, since the Lambs were recruited to teach English and morality. In what follows I shall explore aspects of the day's play if you were a French child coming to Shakespeare for the first time, not directly, but through the medium of Charles and Mary Lamb's *Tales*. My larger purpose is to open an area of research that involves a variety of topics usually taken in isolation. That France and Britain have different cultural traditions is obvious, but the fine grain of those differences can shed light on what anglophone readers and critics take for granted; that is, French Shakespeares offer alternative approaches to problems grown overfamiliar, and can offer correctives to current, insular, critical preoccupations. Thus Shakespeare for French children is exemplary for anglophone adults because of the number of issues it focuses. Not least of these is the claim of the "universal validity of literature" when the claims differ markedly between universes.[1]

Shakespeare for children is, if not exactly undiscovered country, certainly an outlying province in the cartography of Shakespeare scholarship. In the basement of the Folger Shakespeare Library, in Washington, D.C., there is a category of books shelved as "Sh. misc." Part of that catchall collection of "Shakespeare miscellaneous" is a series of versions of Shakespeare for children, in prose and verse, with illustrations and without. They are all in English. They are unlisted in Shakespeare bibliographies, ignored in Shakespeare studies and, with the honorable exception of the Lambs, largely unknown even in the annals of children's literature. Children's Shakespeare is equally absent from the burgeoning field of children's literature.[2] There is parallel neglect in studies of the history of Shakespeare in France, which extends to other European languages and countries.[3] Translations of the Lambs' *Tales*—not just for children, and not only into French—were always adaptations of Shakespeare. Many early translators had only rudimentary English, and some had none at all. They all lost the Lambs' clever creolization, with their embedded quotations. New editions relied upon previous ones whether or not they say so, and whether or not they criticize earlier efforts. All the adapters know what is best for the young.

Schools texts are set, and children's books are bought, by

adults, and when the Lambs' *Tales* were translated into French, they were often richly illustrated by artists noted for their work in other areas of book production. One aspect of the scholarly difficulties of tracing such publications can be indicated by a brief glance at those illustrations. Henri Morin, a well-known early-twentieth-century artist, actually revised his pictures for the translation of the Lambs' *Tales* by Téodor de Wyzewa, which appeared from 1914. As his illustrations show, Morin was clearly deeply engaged with the project, and changed his paintings in conception and size from edition to edition—but at this early stage of research it is impossible to say with certainty exactly how many states of de Wyzewa's book exist. The materiality of the book matters here, for the Lambs' *Tales* entered the children's books market with the *lettres de noblesse* that come from the status of a foreign classic, in books that were not cheap. The original illustrations (some were simply reproduced from preexisting engravings or paintings) are themselves criticism. Some of them mark a contrast to contemporary children's-book art on the other side of the Channel. They can be violent, sexually alert, and more influenced by the theater (especially the opera) than any illustrations since Rowe's in 1709. Above all, although Shakespeare's name, and the names of his characters, were known, his works were not.

It must be remembered that in Britain, the Lambs were already reacting to children's books' conventions of heavy moralizing and personification allegory, and to the books to which the young Jane Eyre took such exception in describing the offenses of the loathsome Mr. Brocklehurst, who "bored us with long lectures once a week, and with evening readings from books of his own inditing, about sudden deaths and judgements, which made us afraid to go to bed" (Brontë 1973, 124). We perhaps ought to be surprised, given the conservative pressures on publishing for children, to find that the Lambs championed stimulating the unformed imaginations of young minds, that they intended to inspire "very young children" (as the preface has it) to read Shakespeare for themselves, and that in their private letters about this project we can see their position as consistent with Charles's Shakespeare criticism for adults.[4]

Their preface has a remarkable emphasis on the pleasure to be anticipated in the reading; it does mention utility, but far less the forming of the young mind than contemporary educative moralizers might have done. This is not simply a contrast to Mr. Brocklehurst's monitory prose: it is a contrast to the received picture of the paterfamilias guiding a circle of listeners. In the same year in which the Bowdlers' famous *Family Shakespeare* was published, the Lambs were anticipating a new kind of family reading: what we might describe as a truncated family, in which the choice of what is read aloud is left to hypothetical older brothers, promising what need not be delivered. That is, uniquely, their preface proposes a degree of freedom, of unsupervised discovery, which emphasizes the children's own choice.

No one would wish to make the Lambs into libertines: they suppressed cruelty and explicit sexuality; they consistently omitted subplots; and they censored: Vienna is a more restrained city than we know, and there are no brothels in *Pericles*; Malvolio is not incarcerated in a dark room. As narrators, they sometimes take on the opinions of "good" characters within the plays. They interpret in period and in accordance with the kinds of character criticism with which they themselves grew up. They explain, for example, that Antonio's silence at the end of *The Tempest* was a sign of his being "filled ... with shame and remorse, that he wept and was unable to speak." That is, they may label, but they do not simply condemn. The last sentence of their preface hopes that the *Tales* will be "enrichers of the fancy, strengtheners of virtue, a withdrawing from all selfish and mercenary thoughts, a lesson of all sweet and honorable thoughts and actions, to teach courtesy, benignity, generosity, humanity: for of examples, teaching these virtues, his pages are full." After all, thinking that great literature will make its readers morally better is a long-lived fairy-tale that has perhaps not even yet died the death.

Correspondence reveals that in the English *Tales* Charles was responsible for the tragedies and, as he put it, the cuts, and the spelling; the long-invisible Mary did the rest. At first, publishing the tales separately, they sold rather slowly. In 1807, as is well known, they first appeared as a small collection, attributed to Charles only, as part of the Godwins' "Juvenile Library." Charles had meant the book to appear anonymously, and it should be remarked that Godwin, who took advantage of Charles's reputation, suppressed his own, hiding behind the name of his printer. Mary's name did not appear until 1838; she had, after all, stabbed her mother in a fit of madness. In France, where biography remained essential to literary history, the confident directiveness underlined the moral significance of the Lambs' family situation.

Much of this is well known. The Godwins were not the first publishers to offer such a book. Mary Godwin, who translated from the French, may have known J. B. Perrin's *Contes Moraux, amusants et instructifs, à l'usage de la jeunesse tirés des Tragédies de Shakespeare*, which was the first such collection, but one can only speculate.[5] The intention is to teach children French via Shakespeare. His book contains a summary and then a much longer narrativized reimagining of fifteen plays, not all of which we might categorize as "tragedy": *Hamlet, Coriolanus, Le Roi Lear, Romeo and Juliet, Othello, Macbeth, Julius Caesar, Marc-Antoine et Cléopatre, Jean sans Terre, Richard II, Henry IV, Henry V, Richard III, Cymbeline, Timon*. The overlap with the Lambs' selection is six plays.

Because there was public nervousness in Britain about such dangerously stimulating literature as fairy tales, with their apparently amoral violence, cruelty, and terror, Shakespeare offered an almost impregnable defense of the fancy, and adapters could themselves do some hiding behind the reputation (and also the very words) of the Bard. The Lambs smuggled considerable threatening imagery into their narratives. How could anyone oppose their stated intention to motivate children to read Shakespeare? Soon their twenty *Tales* were a success, as indeed they have continued to be. In almost two hundred years they have never been out of print. Those of us who come to the *Tales* cold, as it were, may find the narrator directive, but by comparison with the children's books of the time, the recounting is remarkably restrained.

Across the Channel, French Romantics—like Voltaire before them—seized Shakespeare not only as a great free spirit, but as a dramatist revolutionary before his time, and a stick with which to beat sterile academicism. Shakespeare thus had from the outset a political cachet that may escape the anglophone reader. Victor Hugo's *Cromwell* benefited from this vision of Shakespeare, and he wrote his book-length preface to Shakespeare partly to help his son, François-Victor, sell his new translations of the plays, translations advertised as complete and true to their original, that is, not adapted as Voltaire, and after him Ducis, had preferred. Perrin's pedagogic text seems to have sunk without trace. At the same time, the first French Lambs' *Tales* appeared—five years before Mary's death. Just as the Lambs interpreted their Shakespeare in period, so also do we find their work recycled in ways we can only too easily assimilate to our ideas of Romantic Shakespeare, but also to old-fashioned habits of presenting literature. So from the first French edition of 1842, we find an introduction specifically for French readers (by the industrious Philarète Chasles), lives of Shakespeare and of Charles Lamb (by the equally energetic Amédée Pichot, and recycled when the Shakespeare Gallery became a vogue, from 1844), placed before Alphonse Borghers's translation (all twenty tales), a habit that endured well after the Great War. Charles was the genius worthy to adapt the national poet. As for Mary, who did the bulk of the original work, she was *in statu pupillari*, a reduction that opened a new avenue for moral encouragement. It is a striking feature of the succession of editions that these frames, biographical and critical, often outweigh the *Tales* (seldom all twenty at a time), whether for home reading or for school study.

The Lambs' own preface aspired to introduce "very young children" to Shakespeare, and emphasized girls as their more-than-implied readers. In the spectrum of "translation," their version is neither (to use distinctions I have elaborated elsewhere) an accompaniment translation, to be used simultaneously with the original to aid the interpretation of a difficult text; nor is it a substitution translation intended to provide an equivalent for something too difficult to read (Morse 1991, chapter 4). It is a temporary expedient, intended to whet the appetite. For French readers, by contrast, the *accuracy* attributed to Charles justified the status of substitution: read this and you will know Shakespeare. There are three points to be noted here: first, the presupposition, not at all foreign to British experience, that "Shakespeare" is a text-to-be-read; second, his unfamiliarity either as a text-to-be-read or to-be-seen; and, third, the attitude toward foreign classics, which equated the story, that is, the plot alone, with the original. *All* early translations of Shakespeare into French struck upon the rock of the poetry, so very distant in language, metaphor, and vocabulary from anything acceptable on the French stage. The Lambs creolized Shakespeare, embedding quotation in their prose. Obviously, among many difficulties, no translation can mark the register shifts by which the Lambs incorporated the language of the plays.

The translations are also characterized by an approach that is less dramatized, less theatrical, less alert to what the metaphoric poetry conveys. Where the Lambs censored, the French translators, alas, followed them (*All's Well*'s "conversation," for example, which replaced the bed trick). Subplots that they suppressed remained suppressed. The Lambs, like many of their anglophone readers, could rely upon a degree of shared reference in their readers. Themselves steeped in Shakespeare, both in the theater and on the page, they proposed an aspiration to something similar in their juvenile audience.

Not only is it a striking feature of early European translations of Shakespeare that "translators" often knew little English and never had experience of early historical periods of English language or literature, but once translators could depend upon earlier translations it becomes almost impossible to divine how much original Shakespeare the adapters actually knew; how theatrical their experience might have been; or, consistent with publishing practice elsewhere, who had in fact made the translation. Nor is there necessarily "progress" where children's books are concerned (especially where old books are out of copyright). Over a century after that first, 1842, translation by Borghers, it reappeared and sold for over a decade in the 1960s and '70s in slightly updated editions that collected only ten or a dozen tales. It makes sense to refer to "tales" rather than "plays," because that is the thrust of the change from direct engagement with the theater to inherited prose narratives.[6] And, by a paradoxical historical irony, French translators of the Lambs began to reinsert in a framing prologue what the Lambs fought to banish: from the version introduced by Charles Simond, *Contes de Shakespeare Racontés aux Jeunes Gens* (1887, seven tales), we find once again the combination of censorship and explicit moralizing that earlier had so marked anglophone children's literature.

The impression that there is not perhaps a deep knowledge of the Lambs, or Shakespeare, or even, perhaps, English, is reinforced when one finds Charles referred to as a poet, or his audience characterized as ignorant even of Shakespeare's name, or Early Modern English as *less* difficult for modern anglophone readers than Ronsard would be to their French contemporaries. One reads farragoes of invention, as this contradictory élan from Téodor de Wyzewa's preface: "Shakespeare n'est directement accessible, dans son pays, ni au peuple, ni aux enfants; et cependant il n'y a personne qui n'aspire à le connaître, personne qui ne rêve de s'introduire dans l'intimité des figures imaginaires, plus célèbres à la fois et mieux aimées que celles des héros de l'histoire nationale: Desdémone et Ophélie, le jeune Hamlet et le vieux Lear."[7] As elsewhere throughout Europe and beyond, the characters have escaped their plays.

Thus far we have the Lambs in French. Perhaps the most interesting phenomenon, however, is the metamorphosis with which I began of the *Tales*, intended to give pleasure to and stimulate the imagination of children reading at home, into schools textbooks presented with all the commentary with which we are still familiar. As Perrin used Shakespeare to teach English children French, French teachers similarly recruited the Lambs to teach English. From 1885 we begin to find readers annotated by teachers of English, as well-known Paris Lycées respond to the Ministry's choice of texts for prestigious collège and lycée language classes (a much smaller number than would be the case today). Here, far more than in the books sold directly to the public, we find one of those changes of emphasis that transforms the work to be read. For now the biographical introduction calls our attention to Charles, who is credited with sacrificing his own happiness for the sake of his family, that is, in saving his mad sister from the attic. Mlle. Sohawan's search in the Bibliothèque Nationale unearthed no school edition that departed from this self-immolating artifact. So set a text did this become that she was delighted to find it translated *back* into English in a reader that collected "morceaux choisis" by Kipling, Longfellow, Wordsworth, Tennyson, and Kingsley, *Les Auteurs du Brevet Supérieur* (1909), a version that still held the (metaphorical) stage in the 1950s.

Shakespeare has ceded his place to the devoted Charles, and Mary's role in the *Tales* has altogether disappeared. Charles's sacrifice becomes a novel of its own, with a degree of overinterpretation that turns him into a self-denying celibate. In the context of French secondary education, there was nothing to suggest that these texts were not required of both sexes; and, of course, in the period, they would also have been Empire texts, with all that that implies. It struck me that there was a shift to infantilization that removed all initiative from the English *Tales*' original child readers, whom the Lambs had imagined in their preface as themselves deciding what to read, and what to read aloud. We had moved far from stimulating the desire of "very young children" to hear and see Shakespeare.

Schools texts are a sitting target, probably in all times and places. As recently as fifty years ago, the Lamb siblings shared praise for their accuracy, their fidelity to Shakespeare's language, and the superiority of their literary criticism. Above all, Charles was praised for his personal morality: family, duty, self-abnegation. One of the early French school adaptations implicitly regrets that the Lambs had not had French children in mind, since French children, with their ancestors the Gauls, would have better appreciated *Julius Caesar* than little English children could do. The Latin superiority of France is implicit here. So, I believe, is bedrock French Catholicism, however occult. We are fully in the epoch of the Jules Ferry reforms, with thousands of children of every race, color, creed, and national origin, reciting texts about "nos ancêtres les gaullois" in their thousands of schools, on the same day at the same time. The low point for liberating the fancy is perhaps reached as the schools text falls into the hands of the privately funded Alliance des Maisons d'Education Chrétienne (read "Catholic"), whose editions prune the *Tales* most severely. Mlle. Sohawon's own low point—if I may be permitted a pedagogic anecdote—came in the commentary on *The Tempest* with which I opened. Although this edition is exceptional in having Mary's name on the cover, my representations that at least it was universal and not racist cut no ice here, and it is hard to stomach its unthinking sexism and religiosity in this commentary on *Macbeth*:

> Vous comprendrez plus tard pourquoi Shakespeare a voulu que le sanguinaire tyran ait été poussé au premier assassinat par sa femme, qui s'était mis en tête d'être reine. Il y a, grâce a Dieu, peu de femmes aussi inhumaines que Lady Macbeth; mais il n'est pas mauvais que, garçons ou filles, vous sachiez de bonne heure de quelles sottises sont capables les homme faibles et quels châtiments attendent celles qui abusent de cette faiblesse: histoire vieille comme le monde, puisque ce fut pour s'être laissé mener par cette première femme que le premier homme fut chassé du Paradis. Et vous ne serez jamais fort en histoire si vous ne savez pas que beaucoup de massacres et de grandes

guerres ont eu surtout comme origine la vanité et la coquetterie féminines. (Chaffurin and Delany 1929, iii)[8]

Even the exercises in the back of the book tend toward teaching moral lessons: *Do you ever tell lies? Ought you to be ashamed of telling lies?* or offer the kinds of "give the indicative form of the following sentence" that we probably all remember, not to speak of paragraphs that attribute greater or less moral responsibility (Paulina or Camillo for devotion, Gertrude or Claudius for turpitude). Then as now, French education emphasizes mastery of the "oral" exercise, as well as correctness of response. There is no room for admitting that one sometimes tells lies, and many of the questions anticipate the right answer. Others, however, reach back precisely to the exercises of Roman rhetoric: "Was Leontes sufficiently punished for his causeless jealousy and cruelty?" or "Should Antigonus have disobeyed his sovereign's orders and, if so, what should he have done instead?"—with the double challenge of *comparatio* in a foreign language.

What conclusions can we, ought we, to draw from this brief survey? First and foremost there is the wonderful irony by which the Lambs' great attempt to free children from children's literature (in its moralizing guise) was reversed in both in translation and in schools. There is a corollary to this point, because the Lambs also loved the theater, and part of what they were doing incidentally defended the magical experience of seeing a play. For the Lambs, Shakespeare is a vibrant author, a vernacular classic who can be read and acted within a social and historical landscape informed by his presence. Shakespeare exists simultaneously here and elsewhere. It is sometimes hard to remember that plays went on needing such defense, though Jane Austen makes one toward the end of *Persuasion*, where she is critical of the Elliots' disdain for the theater (chapter 19). Thus, second, there is the striking shift from engagement with theatrical experience to a succession of adaptations of preexisting written narratives. This is a far cry from the amateur theatrical performance of *As You Like It* so lovingly described by Théophile Gautier in *Mlle de Maupin*, a romantic novel certainly not intended for "very young children."[9] It is also a far cry from the contemporary situation, in which Shakespeare is familiar from television, cinema, theater—and in which, in France, now, he belongs to the young.

In France, in French or English, the Lambs' prose narratives replace Shakespeare; the translations and adaptations imply that a prose narrative *represents* the core, the thing itself. This is part of the genre imperialism of reading texts through the novel. These adaptations, because they are translations, need not be treated with respect, and can be cut and commented upon with freedom. The *morceau choisi* approach to literature makes for touchstones, rather than shared theatrical experience, passages memorized for cultural mastery and display, quite like the school-day Latin thrown about by Restoration characters. In translation, poetry is—perhaps inevitably—displaced onto plot, and so, to a certain extent, is character, although biography and literary history perhaps supersede both; above all, literature is reduced to its moral. How un-Shakespearean, how un-Lamblike. But also how easy to be wise after the fact, and to condemn teachers who seem too Procrustean. It behooves us to remember that these *Tales* have been recycled because generations of translators and illustrators, publishers and pedants, saw that they were interesting to children.

Notes

Translations throughout mine unless otherwise indicated. The discovery of this aspect of school teaching of English through recycled Lamb belongs to a research student, Farzanah Sohawon, working last year on her Diplôme d'Etudes Approfondies under my supervision.

1. Even anti-Semitism cannot be taken as invariable, as translations of the Lambs' *The Merchant of Venice* make evident. The only study of this phenomenon known to me is Boika Sokolova's exploration of Bulgarian translations of "Shylock," first from a Russian translation of the Lambs' *Tales* (1881, date of Russian "original" not given). In considering attitudes to Jews via books for children, she contributes to larger debates upon education as an indicator of attitudes inculcated in schools. I am grateful to Dr. Sokolova for an offprint of this essay (Sokolova 1994).

2. But see the recent surveys by Isaac (2000) and Bottoms (1996, 2000, 2001) listed below. Dr. Bottoms is preparing a much-needed book on the subject.

3. Writing not *only* as someone who teaches in a French university, I note that there is undeclared contraband in this story: students continue to use the Lambs' narratives as cribs. This practice is not restricted to France.

4. Given the abundance of editions of the *Tales*, I shall refer to them by name rather than to a particular text. *The Letters* (1935) contain numerous references to the Shakespeare project.

5. Perrin was an émigré whose own preface mentions his availability as

a tutor. His book was published in London, by subscription (the alphabetical list that precedes it includes one Mrs. Garrick), in 1783. The copy in the Yorke collection (Yorke was one of the subscribers) in the University Library, Cambridge, has certainly been much read. The assertion of influence or emulation that one sometimes finds appears to be based on a misreading of Lucas's annotation (vol. 2, p. 9), e.g., in Riehl (1980, 60). I have found no evidence of its being republished in the same form, nor any evidence that either the Godwins or the Lambs owned a copy.

6. And, just as some of the children's adaptations show the influence of Gounod or Verdi, another question—perhaps unanswerable—that arises is whether some of the *Tales* had an afterlife in opera or theatrical programs.

7. "In his own country Shakespeare is not immediately accessible either to ordinary people or to children; however, there is nobody who does not want to know him, nobody who does not dream of getting close to these imaginary characters, at once more famous and more beloved than the heroes of national history: Desdemona and Ophelia, the young Hamlet and the aged Lear."

8. "You will understand later on why Shakespeare wanted his bloody tyrant to be pushed to his first murder by his wife, who got it into her head to be queen. Thank God, there are few women as inhuman as Lady Macbeth; but it is no bad thing for you, boys and girls, to learn early what stupidities weak men are capable of and what punishments await those who take advantage of their weakness: a history as old as the world, since it was because of allowing himself to be led by that first woman that the first man was expelled from Paradise. And you will never be good at history if you do not know that many massacres and great wars have had as their first motive female vanity and conceit." This is, of course, not far from Charles Lamb's own view of Lady Macbeth.

9. If I may add a final observation from my own pedagogic experience, in France, amateur theatricals, in the form of the school play, are very rare, and while the Lambs (as, indeed, I) would have taken for granted that all children produce plays (a part of English education actually required in the founding statutes of many grammar schools), in France that is not so.

Teaching Shakespeare: Indoctrination or Creativity?

Ros King

THE PROBLEM THAT BESET THOSE OF US WITH A PASSIONATE INTERest in Shakespeare in education in late 1980s Britain was that a sizable body of those teaching in universities had succumbed to the then fashionable idea that Shakespeare was a dead white male whose plays should be of no relevance and even less interest to ordinary white working-class kids, or to ethnic minority children of any class. This particular brand of class-consciousness was not, however, a problem confined to English studies. The London Borough of Hackney grabbed the headlines when it withdrew free instrumental music teaching from its schools on the grounds that playing the violin was a middle-class activity. Most other Education Authorities, of course, soon followed suit, but on the more usually philistine grounds of economy and utility. When the Conservative government launched the new National Curriculum in schools in September 1992, it was likewise with utility in mind: the need to turn out workers who could spell and add up. But the intellectual climate enabled it to claim the cultural high ground: the teaching and testing of Shakespeare at Key Stage 3 (fourteen-year-olds) was necessary to protect British culture from the ravages of "political correctness." A petition rejecting the compulsory canon of largely white male authors named in the curriculum orders circulated in university departments of English and was sent to the prime minister, John Major, who waved it gleefully during a speech to the House of Commons as proof of the degeneracy to which university intellectuals had sunk.

While the academics were advocating letting Shakespeare rest in peace, the Conservatives had long been trying to enlist him into their party. My blood runs cold when I see our national flag appropriated as a symbol for the National

Front, but it became inflamed when I heard "Once more unto the breach, dear friends, once more" quoted by the Chancellor of the Exchequer at a Tory party conference as a surefire, "patriotic" way of screwing the nation's courage to the support of yet another hike in interest rates. I likewise despaired when Shakespeare was used—as he was and still is used repeatedly—to promote a heritage nostalgia of warm beer and village greens (to quote John Major again) or in Lord Tebbit's reprehensible phrase, a kind of "cricket test for Englishness."

Both government and academics at that stage were, paradoxically, thus agreed that Shakespeare represented British establishment values. Both, in their different ways, were therefore guilty of the same basic faults in literary criticism: that a work of representational art is necessarily simply mimetic and therefore that it both reflects and disseminates a specific ethos. Margaret Thatcher herself had typified this approach when, on one occasion, she approvingly quoted Shakespeare as advising, "To thine own self be true." She did not appreciate that it was not Shakespeare who said those platitudinous words but Polonius, the prime minister of his particular play-world who, even at the moment that he uttered them, was contemplating an extraordinary act of duplicity: the surveillance of his son. This is hardly a felicitous quotation, one might think, for someone in her position as leader of a modern democracy. Even more dismayingly, no one on the opposition benches, or the universities, thought to point that out to her.

Shakespeare in British Schools: The 1980s and early 1990s

Despite the fact that attempts to broaden and decanonize the university curriculum had resulted in some university departments of English dropping Shakespeare from the compulsory syllabus, there was, at this period, an increasing amount of interest in school Shakespeare, encouraged by Rex Gibson's "Shakespeare in Schools Project" at the Cambridge Institute for Education, and numerous theater-in-education groups. Ironically, the steady decrease in public funding for the arts over this period had resulted in an increase in the number of small-scale theater companies who realized that they could scratch a living because teachers were desperate for their A-level and GCSE students to see live performances of the set texts, and experience the plays firsthand, *as plays*. This work, when it was done well, was capable of kindling sparks of interest, skill, and aptitude in pupils who may have previously been dismissed by their teachers as unacademic. Of course it was not always done well—but that was not the issue that the government was trying to address. They were not searching for a living, breathing, rough, disquieting Shakespeare, but a corralled, focused, controlled, and homeostatic body of material encountered only between the covers of a book, about which questions with definite, easily marked answers (to be filled in, in specially printed, forest loads of examination booklets), could be asked.

When it was first published, the National Curriculum divided children at Key Stage 3 into three ability ranges. The lowest group was deemed to be too stupid to be able to tackle Shakespeare at all. The middle group was to be exposed to a single great speech (Jacques's seven ages of man speech was touted). The top group would study one play in detail (chosen from among *Julius Caesar, Romeo and Juliet,* and *A Midsummer Night's Dream*).[1] This was to be Shakespeare as academic hurdle.

As a response to all this, I wrote an article that was published by *The Guardian* newspaper (6 October 1992), illustrated with a huge cartoon by Peter Clarke, which I hoped would be a call to arms.[2] The response, indeed, was such that I organized a series of conferences across the country that brought together teachers, leading theater practitioners, politicians and civil servants, and then wrote a report which was sent to Sir Ron Dearing, who had been given the task of modifying the national curriculum sufficiently to calm everything down (King 1993). The result in the end, although not everything that teachers had wanted, was certainly a good deal better than the government had initially tried to impose.

Shakespeare in the Classroom: An Undergraduate Course in English at Queen Mary

As a result of this experience, I devised a new kind of Shakespeare course to be taught in my own college of the

University of London that would involve ordinary undergraduate students of English (not teacher trainees) in going into local inner-city schools in order to teach a Shakespeare play. It was designed as an experiment in education, and planned according to the following principles:

   a. children younger than the government's target age-group of Key Stage 3 could enjoy (and benefit from) direct contact with the language and dramaturgy of Shakespeare;
   b. this enjoyment and benefit applied across the ability range and with children from all ethnic backgrounds;
   c. plays other than *Romeo and Juliet*, *A Midsummer Night's Dream*, and *Julius Caesar* might be of more relevance to the prepubescent but too-old-for-fairies age-group.

As far as my own students were concerned, the main pedagogical rationale was that one learns best by teaching someone else. In fact it was part of my thinking that all those involved in the project—schoolteachers, university students, school students, and myself—would all learn from one another.

The first partner school was a new coeducational comprehensive in Whitechapel, not far from the college. Whitechapel has been home to successive waves of immigrants since the sixteenth century and the school has a very wide racial mix. For some 70 percent of children, English is a second language. We were working with all seven classes of year 8, and I chose *King Lear* on the grounds that all the children would inevitably be experts in the parent-child relationship. I was also confident that they would enjoy the graphic nature of the storm, the bizarre imagination of the description of place on Dover cliff, the eye-gouging violence, and the bad language of the Kent/Oswald insult scene. I can confirm that these aspects are indeed perennial hits and that children involved in the project can often be heard playfully cussing each other in Shakespearean English in the playground! I have therefore returned to this text repeatedly over the years, despite brief forays into *Othello*, *The Tempest*, and *Richard III*—although the number of child characters and the violence in that play also go down very well. The course now runs in several local primary and secondary schools with children from years 6 to 8 (ten- to twelve-year-olds).

As far as the undergraduates are concerned, the course

falls into three parts. They spend the first five weeks studying the chosen play at their own level as university students of English literature, exploring techniques for introducing the play to younger students, and considering issues about education. For the next six weeks they work together in groups of two or three students to a class, teaching in one of the partner schools for up to two hours per week, with a further hour's troubleshooting session back in college. They receive a group mark (40 percent) for this work. For the school students, the course culminates in a presentation at the end of term in which each class shows the rest of the year group the work they have been doing. They act some short scenes and show some of the creative work—writing, artwork, and music—that they have made over those previous six weeks. The undergraduates then go away to reflect further on their experience and to write a theoretical and critical essay on some aspect of the arts in education. This essay carries an individual mark of 60 percent.

Over the years, however, it has become increasingly apparent that, although Shakespeare was the initial pretext for this course, teaching Shakespeare was not the only, or even the most important, thing any of us were doing. Countless modern professional productions and numerous articles on teaching Shakespeare have of course demonstrated that the plays lend themselves as vehicles for directly exploring real-life social problems. But I have become increasingly interested in the way in which the course impacts on the awareness and development of creativity amongst all those taking part.

In a series of books in the 1980s, the American clinical psychologist Howard Gardner, having observed the effects on his patients of massive damage to selected parts of the brain through stroke or trauma, suggested that intelligence, far from being a single quality of mind measurable by IQ, is manifested in seven distinct ways. Being intelligent in one of these areas does not mean that one is equally intelligent in them all. Gardner's seven "multiple intelligences" are: linguistic, logical-mathematical, musical, bodily-kinesthetic, spatial, interpersonal, intrapersonal.

One important implication of the concept of multiple intelligence is that we probably all learn in different ways. When, six or seven years ago, I gave the undergraduates on this course a standard learning preferences test, most of the class registered a preference for learning aurally (by listening to lectures) or visually (reading books). These are the learning preferences that are most likely to equip people to survive in a traditional academic system. More recently I have found that students are more likely to claim, at least in part, to learn kinesthetically, by needing to move about or use their bodies in some way while studying. My samples are too small to be statistically valid, but the suggestion that by increasing the numbers going to university we are not lowering standards but allowing students with different types of intelligence simply to be *recognized* as intelligent is attractive. It should also encourage us to rethink our teaching. Teaching styles that are sufficiently flexible to allow students with fundamentally different learning styles to flourish equally have yet to permeate far into any level of education.

Gardner's most recent book tentatively, and for me, less persuasively, adds three more to his list of seven intelligences (naturalist, spiritual, existential) but defines intelligence as "a biopsychological potential to process information that can be activated in a cultural setting to solve problems or create products that are of value in a culture" (Gardner 1999). This definition of intelligence as a capacity for *creating* something that is *valued* by others likewise has profound implications.

Shakespeare and Education for Creativity

Creativity now has a considerable bibliography in both psychology and business studies, while creativity in education, not just in arts subjects but right across the curriculum as an essential part of intellectual development, has been the subject of two important reports over the last two years in Britain (Harland 2000; Puttnam 2000). When I first started talking about fostering creativity with my students a few years ago, however, I was met with either blank looks, or disbelief. Most of them had not written fiction since their early teens and, except for some of those who enjoyed acting, they did not regard themselves as creative in the "arty" sense that informs the popular understanding of that word. They knew they were "academic"—they were, after all, at university—but they had real difficulty in thinking about their intelligence in terms of solving problems or creativity. This is perhaps hardly surprising. Their education for the previous ten years had been clearly mapped out for them in attainment targets, course guidelines, aims, objectives, and assessment criteria. The effect is that students have come to believe that success comes from doing exactly what their teachers want, no more and no less.

With the aim of getting these students to think objectively about their own learning in order to promote learning in the children in their classes (and of course with a dossier of aims, objectives, and guidelines on everything from classroom management to approaches to Shakespearean language), I have found that, both with regard to the understanding of Shakespeare's plays in general, and the particular task that my students take on in working together to teach Shakespeare in an inner-city environment, one of the most fruitful concepts to explore has been the connection between creativity and chaos.

Human social, intellectual, and psychological development in fact depends on unsettling encounters with novelty, change, or the unknown:

> As a species the "human" has a tendency to need to run up against a problem to be reflective, or to be what has been described as recursive, involved in a conscious or preconscious feedback loop with the environment, or self-referential... Utilizing this reflective, self-aware capacity, it is possible to produce internal and external symbols to understand, contain and describe experience. This act makes human beings quite different from other beings... The capacity for growth, psychologically and biologically, is symbiotically tied to one's relationship with the environment, meaning that to enact the self-referential process of producing a symbol it is necessary to encounter novelty. (Bütz 1997, 131–32)

Being thrown into a strange situation devoid of familiar landmarks and known patterns of behavior, as my students are when they suddenly become teachers themselves, is of course an alarming experience. The responsibility they feel to one another and to the thirty or so children in the class that they teach, combined with the apprehension, compels them to work hard to make sense of this new situation—much harder, they say, than they habitually work on other courses. But they are acutely conscious that no amount of preparation can cover every possibility for human interchange afforded by the gathering of thirty individual, boisterous young egos in a confined place. Compelled to be hardworking, and encouraged by the structure of the course to be self-referential and reflexive, they are well-organized beings who find themselves, metaphorically (even in the politest of classrooms), on the "edge of chaos":

> It will be ... wonderful if it proves true that complex adaptive systems evolve to a position somewhere in the ordered regime near the edge of chaos. Perhaps such a location on the axis, ordered and stable, but still flexible, will emerge as a kind of universal feature of complex adaptive systems in biology and beyond. (Kauffman 1996, 91)

Shakespearean Texts as Chaotic Systems

If, as is now being widely suggested, the nonlinear mathematics of chaos theory underpin change and development in the universe and even account for the inception, evolution, and maintenance of life itself, it need not surprise us that acute observers of human behavior will perceive such forces in operation even in advance of the discovery of the mathematics. That Shakespeare was such a person is evidenced by his ability to transform the often rather dull, culturally homeostatic stories of his sources into the plays that seem actively to invite constant, transformative reinterpretation across time and geographical space.

Shakespeare's work has been socially valued by successive generations, not because of some cultural hegemony that governments need to preserve, but because it is a genuinely creative symbol. Its precise expression—not its borrowed storyline but its particular use of language and juxtaposition of scene on scene and character on character—presents a complex web of psychosociological transactions. It is this complexity that makes the plays transferable from one age and society to another.

King Lear's multiple viewpoints, treating the Lear and Gloucester stories simultaneously and therefore reflexively, create intense images of the psychology of change and of the chaos that is unleashed both on the world and in the individual psyche as a result of fundamental breakdown in personal and social relationships. But while the drama of the story and its set pieces—the graphic symbols of the storm and of Lear's madness—engage the attention, it is the multiplicity of viewpoints in the construction of the text that encourages further multiple inputs of meaning from countless readers and viewers, encouraging them to be creative in the way they use the play to reflect on their own experiences. Very many plays from the Elizabethan and Jacobean periods (many more than are usually revived) can still make rather good dramatic entertainment in live performance, but comparatively few have this capacity for reinterpretation.

Terence Hawkes has famously argued that Shakespeare does not mean, we mean by Shakespeare (Hawkes 1992). His desire to demonstrate the instability and undecidability of the text and the autonomy of the critic/reader had a political application at the time he was writing, as we have seen. Analysis of seventeenth-, eighteenth-, and nineteenth-century adaptations of Shakespeare, however, show that they invariably close down the number of possible interpretations that spectators or readers can take from them. These versions may share the same basic story lines, and even preserve much of the language of their Shakespearean originals, but the alterations, intended to conform to particular social mores or abide by certain literary fashions or decorum, create a different ethos and so alter the meaning even of those Shakespearean words and passages that remain. This is not just a matter of changing tastes in much later historical cultures. While controversy still rages as to whether *The Taming of the Shrew* should be regarded as misogynist or as something more challenging, complex, and thoughtful, there is no doubt whatsoever that Fletcher's early seventeenth-century sequel, *The Woman's Prize or the Tamer Tamed*, though a sophisticated piece of writing and stagecraft, cannot be interpreted as other than a reinforcement of conventional gender relations. Thus if we are indeed able to mean by Shakespeare, or as I would prefer to put it, use Shakespeare as a source for our own creativity, it is only because the plays are written in such a particular way that they enable us to do so. If, as critics, we employ selective quotation, or, as teachers, teach answers where Shakespeare raises questions, we too close down those complex structures to the extent that those we are trying to instruct no longer have the space to construct their own meanings.

After the initial shock, students on this course find the concept of exploring their own creativity as critics exciting. In the brief three-minute essays that I regularly ask them to write and hand in anonymously at the end of classes, I recently got the following reactions to a session in which I had used the paradoxical, transformational image of a Möbius strip as a visual aid for thinking both about the relationship between the reader and the text and what faces them as they step out into the unknown:

> The Möbius strip idea will have to be at the forefront of my mind when doing lesson plans as it shows how I can turn the same topics "inside out" or see them from different angles to change the perception of the situation from the observer. This will make learning Shakespeare very interesting and unusual. (Student A)

> The image of the Möbius strip particularly struck me—the whole idea of the inside becoming the outside becoming the inside... The notion of the outside world of my experience, my thinking connecting and becoming part of the inside life of the play was especially powerful; where my experience is brought to bear on the detail of the play, and where the detail of the play affects and resonates into [sic] my experience. (Student B)

> The analogy of the Möbius strip is interesting in that it can be applied to this course. It not only symbolises our internal chaos at being thrust into an unknown situation but mirrors that of Lear, the storm etc. It is up to us as "teachers" to show the children that failure is OK it allows you to use your mind in a creative manner to help you succeed in the next task you decide to undertake. (Student C)

> How do we see this world? Is it an everlasting, ongoing intangible structure or something that needs destruction, chaos, and perhaps disaster? The idea of a Möbius strip has helped my thoughts to teaching [sic]. I was tempted to want everything to run to perfection without any hiccups or problems along [the] way. Of course this would be nice, very nice in fact, but in reality it is unlikely. It is a new experience, one which we cannot prejudge or guess what will happen. Problems will arise but we must use them to help us improve and get better. (Student D)

> *King Lear*, as it progresses, changes what you expect of it, right to the very end—it is itself quite chaotic. The chaos within the play itself can be capitalized upon to creative ends by encourag-

ing the children to think about what could happen or what doesn't happen, for example. (Student E)

Teachers of Shakespeare (at all levels) need a complex understanding of the way in which his precise choice of language and structural juxtaposition of scene with scene, character with character, works to create the spaces in which viewers and readers can construct differing points of view. My students are working at the interface between the historicism of the text, the presentism of their own experience and that of the children, plus their own and the children's varying abilities and preferential learning styles. For children at this stage of their schooling and development, the important thing is not for them to have passed their eyes over every word in the play, but to have examined and expressed what they think about the very real issues that the play raises. The necessity of choosing which parts of the play to study, and of accurately, concisely, and compellingly filling in the gaps in the story without imposing a narrow moral perspective, compels the undergraduates to develop a sophisticated approach to the criticism of the text and a considerable level of creativity, or problem solving, in all seven of Gardner's multiple intelligences.

As a pedagogical technique, the approach outlined here is not confined to English studies. Indeed similar learning in the community type courses exist in other subject areas. At postgraduate level, law students at the College of Law in London act as intercessors with prisoners, while medical schools across the country are increasingly including similar projects in their community health-care course programs. We intend that the insights gained from the Shakespeare in the Classroom research will inform aspects of the planned Centre of the Cell, an interactive biological science museum aimed at local children, that will be an integral part of the new medical school at Queen Mary. Perhaps, however, Möbius strip-like, with the inner becoming the outer, the salient point is the way in which direct interaction with the culture of our local community in connection with a Shakespeare play has enabled me and my students to understand more clearly what it is that we do when we encounter a real work of art, something carefully constructed not to confirm our social prejudices, but to bring us to the edge of chaos, and why that experience, fraught with the emotion of challenge, not packaged in predetermined examinable, moral certainties, is an essential part of all of our continuing education.

Notes

I am grateful to the Teaching and Learning Fund administered by the Higher Education Funding Council for England (HEFCE) for a research grant. I wish to thank my research assistant, Lilah Heilbronn, the successive generations of undergraduates who have undertaken the course, and our partner schools in Tower Hamlets.

1. These titles in fact bore a suspicious resemblance to the titles most commonly set for O-level, the old 16 plus national examinations, which many members of that government would themselves have sat in their youth.

2. In the cartoon accompanying this article, John Patten, secretary of state for education, as Henry V on horseback, mounts an assault on a hilltop village school, shouting, "Once more unto the breach dear friends, once more; Or close the wall up with our standard English dead!"

V
Rendering

Sexual Morality and Critical Traditions
Lloyd Davis

MUCH RECENT CRITICAL AND CULTURAL WORK ON AND WITH Shakespeare has aimed to radicalize his drama, contending that it stages deeply anxious desires and tensions or discontinuities in social-sexual relations and practices from the early modern period, or from later times when the plays have been interpreted and produced. Such readings often set themselves against supposedly orthodox constructions of Shakespeare's work. In doing so, they deploy and develop three key positions: the historicity of sexuality—that Shakespearean sexuality cannot be naturalized or eternalized in terms of heterosocial values; the volatility of desire—that Shakespearean desire is never fully unified or structured according to heterosexual origins and goals; the multiplicity of eroticism—that Shakespearean eroticism is not based on binary sexual difference but stages the tensions, conflicts, and pleasures in and between homoerotic and heteroerotic relations. Underlying these propositions are some of the main goals of historicist and cultural criticism: to locate the work of Shakespeare and contemporaries in complex historical and social contexts, and to avoid subsuming meanings, values, and practices they depict within later assumptions about gender and sexuality. The three points noted above aim to question and complicate normative ideas in order to reread texts and desires from the past.

This work's significance emerges to a large degree from its confrontation with the greater part of Shakespeare studies, which has consistently valorized his work. In his account of Shakespearean reinventions, Gary Taylor labels this latter effect "Shakesperotics," the enduring critical-cultural love for Shakespeare and his plays (Taylor 1989, 6). I would suggest that Shakesperotics is not only a general love affair with Shakespeare but in particular with Shakespearean love, that is, an idealized history that uses Shakespeare's work to stage and imagine conventional dramas of romance and desire. Michael Bristol observes a related kind of investment in Shakespeare as a major component of what he calls the humanist erotics of reading—a kind of disinterested love for the texts and genres that make up the literary tradition, which is then institutionalized through educational curricula, literary societies, scholarly and more general publications, special libraries and collections, and so on (Bristol 1990). Shakespeare's work exemplifies this tradition, signifying and ensuring its persistence into the present, a present that might have existed at any time from the late seventeenth century to now.

The humanist erotics that celebrates Shakespeare is an amalgam of personal, cultural, and historical desires. The discourse through which it is articulated is notable for its sexual and gendered terms, applied with ethical as much as aesthetic overtones. A rhetoric of sexual morality is used to evaluate and praise Shakespeare's plays, and on many occasions to disparage the work of other authors in comparison to Shakespeare, sometimes even to criticize Shakespeare himself. Critical discourse has never been completely dominated by this rhetoric; yet it regularly comes into play to draw distinctions not only between Shakespeare and other writers but also between critics and their approaches and positions. Images of deviant desire and identity are frequently introduced to characterize texts and critical positions and to justify their critique. This way of proceeding reflects the dialogical practice intrinsic to much literary criticism. Just as recent rereadings of Shakespeare's plays and significance are constituted to an important degree by disputing so-called humanist interpretations, the latter have always sought to consolidate themselves by insinuating the impropriety of language, characterization, and thematics that exist outside a privileged corpus of works and responses to them. In the British and European heritage of Shakespeare criticism, an improper but indispensable outside has sometimes been identified in the work of Shakespeare's contemporaries, such as Ben Jonson or Beaumont and Fletcher, and sometimes in that of European dramatists whose plays were based on contrasting aesthetic and cultural principles, Racine and Voltaire perhaps being the most notable. This comparative approach, proceeding from ideological as much as aesthetic motives, operates as critical topos whose influence has in many ways not waned.

Implicit in these kinds of judgments, some of which will be discussed later, is a kind of hypercanonization. Writers like Racine and Voltaire are acknowledged as great, often for the sake of delineating a strong national or European literary tradition. But once this status is granted they are relegated on the grounds of characters and style, whose limitations are often attributed to specific historical, national, or class conditions. Their inferior status testifies to Shakespeare's incomparability. Joel Fineman conceived the effect of such practices as part of "the historical hegemony of Shakespearean characterology" (Fineman 1989, 7). In pointing to the interrelation of history, institutionalization, cultural power, and subjectivity, Fineman's project drew attention to a conceptual fog that can seem to surround Shakespeare and other writers and that has built up through the tradition of Shakespeare criticism. He implies the lasting difficulty in not being circumscribed by the tradition's rhetoric and practices, though many commentators would not object to being so positioned but consent to it—the classic hegemonic effect. The corollary of this difficulty in separating critical positions from tradition is tradition's success in separating Shakespeare from other writers, a practice, as noted above, significantly realized through drawing ethical comparisons in which sexual and gender norms facilitate and justify the conclusions.

From the later seventeenth century, a critical rhetoric that significantly features tropes of love, desire, and ethics is used to discuss Shakespeare and other playwrights. The exact terms may vary but the value judgments that are being drawn converge in establishing Shakespeare's work as naturally superior. The tenor of the judgments usually acts as a means of elevating the discernment of the current age far above other periods, whether a preceding generation of readers or from the playwrights' time, and also above the views of rival groups within the critics' own societies or in other countries. This antagonistic dialogue can be traced through the British critical heritage, beginning prominently with John Dryden in the Restoration. In the context of European responses to Shakespeare it can also be explored in heated debates between critical positions motivated broadly by either neoclassical or Romantic concepts, and often involving allegiance and animosity to French or German cultural-political influence. In claims and counterclaims, seemingly based on aesthetic principle, national pride, or cultural tradition, the naturalized values of sexual morality play an important role in consolidating one position and undermining others. Two remarks from distinguished nineteenth-century commentaries illustrate the way in which moral opinion intertwines with critical judgment to define human nature, sexuality, and literary quality. The first comes from Chateaubriand's *Sketches of English Literature* (1801): "I do not believe that any writer ever looked deeper into human nature than Shakespeare" (LeWinter 1963, 74). By the beginning of the nineteenth century, the assumptions that a "deep" human nature exists and that "looking into" it is the aim of literary works seem like unquestionable critical common sense. In mid-century, in his frequently reprinted and translated *Shakespeare Commentaries* (first published in 1849), G. G. Gervinus writes, "This many-sidedness of love and its manifold bearings and effects upon human nature, Shakespeare alone, of all poets and of all ages, had depicted in its full extent" (Gervinus 1903, 152). Here "love" is seen as the epitome of human nature, and Shakespearean insight into it proves his exceptional status in the history of world literature. What are the stages in critical discourse that have led to a celebratory naturalized image of Shakespearean love?

The increasing use of sexual and moral tropes in European Shakespeare criticism in many ways complements the development of critical rhetoric in England in the seventeenth and eighteenth centuries. As noted, Dryden provides an early example of this trend. In the preface to his 1679 adaptation of *Troilus and Cressida*, he remarks, "*Shakespeare* generally moves more terror, and *Fletcher* more compassion: For the first had a more Masculine, a bolder and more fiery Genius; the Second a more soft and Womanish" (Vickers 1974, 1:255). Generic difference is put down to the gender orientation of the creative instincts. Dryden conceives masculinity in positive homosocial terms: "*Shakespeare* writ better betwixt man and man; *Fletcher*, betwixt man and woman: consequently, the one described friendship better; the other love: yet *Shakespeare* taught *Fletcher* to write love" (Vickers 1974, 1:266). A full depiction of love derives from understanding relationships between men. Platonic love combines with homosocial priority to explain the origins of successful characterization and interaction. Such conceptions are importantly related to European responses in a number of ways. First, as Eliane Cuvelier notes, some aspects of Voltaire's own influential praise and critique of Shakespeare derived from seventeenth- and eighteenth-century English attitudes (Cuvelier 1995, 30). European views are in dialogue with English ones, but it remains a two-way dialogue as Dirk Delabbastita and Lieven D'Hulst have underlined: in many ways, "English images of Shakespeare depend on interactions with Continental traditions" (Delabbastita and D'Hulst 1993, 21). Lessing and Herder had a significant influence on subsequent English critical commentaries (Habicht 1994b, 4). Even more strikingly, the impact of Voltaire's and similar responses are responsible not only for defenses of Shakespeare against neoclassical rigidity, such as that made by Dr. Johnson in the preface to his 1765 edition of the plays, but also for the English use of "taste" as a key critical term, less to criticize Shakespeare than his contemporaries. That is, Voltaire's judgmental stance is adopted and adapted to elevate Shakespeare. For example, late in the eighteenth century, Edmund Malone comments "with indignation on the tastelessness of the scholars of that age [the Restoration] in preferring Jonson to Shakespeare" (Vickers 1974, 6:534), while Nathan Drake is critical of early modern writing across the board. Shakespeare escapes only because he is *less* corrupt than his contemporaries: "We are now astonished at the miserable taste of our ancestors . . . Massinger, Beaumont and Fletcher have certainly many beauties, but I question whether they possess a single piece which a correct taste could endure without very great alteration, and they are loaded with such a mass of obscenity and vulgar buffoonery, that compared to them Shakespeare is chaste and decorous in the extreme" (Vickers 1974, 6:631). As Drake's terms suggest, the notion of taste is replete with sexual and moral values, which can in turn be read back into European critical texts.

In fact, one of the earliest recorded French responses to Shakespeare's work sounds the very note of sexualized taste, in Nicolas Clément's annotation to a copy of the Second Folio, held in the Royal Library prior to 1675: "This English poet has a beautiful imagination, his thoughts are natural, and his expression fine: but these good qualities are obscured by the filth which he introduces into his comedies"

(Haines 1925, 5). The loaded term "filth" reverberates with different kinds of censure, based on aesthetic taste in terms of refinement and culture, but also with sexual, moral, and class disapproval. Similar sensitivity to sexual morality and gender identity emerges in Voltaire's critical response to Shakespeare. In the *Discourse on Tragedy* (1731), addressed to Lord Bolingbroke in England, Voltaire comments, as had Ben Jonson, Milton, Dryden, and others, on Shakespeare's lack of education and natural genius, and notes the emotive "pleasure" and "delight" he himself gained from watching *Julius Caesar* when he was in England (LeWinter 1963, 34). As if sensitive to the ethical implications of such a response, he then goes on to provide a careful explanation of love and passion. A series of definitions of morally and artistically acceptable passion and a defense of French conventions and their implication for stable gender definitions are offered. Voltaire defends the "nation" against "having softened the drama by too much tenderness" (LeWinter 1963, 40), and imputes gender and emotive failings, perhaps a pathological flaw, to those who disagree: "To desire love in all tragedies seems to me an effeminate taste; to proscribe it always is quite unreasonable bad humor" (LeWinter 1963, 40). A notion of balanced masculine perspective, linked to proper Frenchness, underpins his stance. Those who deviate from this position fall into mere "gallantry," as do many French authors and characters, or "debauchery," as do English ones (LeWinter 1963, 41). Voltaire allows for romantic intensity, what he calls "truly tragic passion," residing in the tension between "weakness ... fought against by remorse" (LeWinter 1963, 41). The agonistic metaphor instills passion with heroism and nobility and holds it in ideal balance between masculine instinct and ethos.

Voltaire's much more negative attitude toward Shakespeare in the second half of the eighteenth century realizes his rhetoric's combative strain. He battles against other French critics who had started to praise and translate Shakespeare, especially Le Tourneur (Haines 1925, 59–62; Cuvelier 1995, 35–37), and he also responds to commercial and military tensions between France and England, the latter conceived "as both a literary and a military enemy" (Cuvelier 1995, 40). A complex mix of politics, patronage and status underpins Voltaire's stance and responses to it—Michael Dobson cites the nationalistic, religious metaphors used by Arthur Murray in reply to Voltaire in the 1750s (Dobson 1992, 7), and Werner Habicht notes that Voltaire was "xenophobically attacked" by German commentators (Habicht 1994b, 4). Nonetheless, Voltaire's aggressive metaphors and position imply a kind of masculinist rivalry, a battle to claim the role as the spokes*man* on cultural and literary matters, ranging from true dramatic style to true love. A related tone, wherein critical and philosophical discourse uses homosocial tension to draw key distinctions, can be heard in Hegel's reflections on Shakespeare in *The Philosophy of Fine Art*. Shakespeare's characterization has "complete virility and truth" (LeWinter 1963, 86), which "as a contrast to that exposition of vacillating and essentially self-divided characters, supplies us with the finest examples of essentially stable and consequential characters, who go to their doom precisely in virtue of this tenacious hold upon themselves and their ends" (LeWinter 1963, 89). Hegel's "essentially stable and consequential characters" embody a particular kind of masculine ethos, which distinguishes his position, as much as Shakespeare's plays, from the critical and creative responses of other German writers in the period. As Voltaire's preference shows, *Julius Caesar* is often central to this conception of controlled, resolved selfhood.

One of the main areas in Voltaire's remarks that Lessing disputes is the way love should be understood and dramatized. In the *Hamburg Dramaturgy*, he discounts Voltaire's ideas against the "living picture" of the "essence" of love in *Romeo and Juliet* and of jealousy in *Othello* (LeWinter 1963, 50). Lessing praises the detail and complexity of Shakespeare's versions. In comparison, "Voltaire perfectly understands the—so to speak—official language of love; that is to say the language and the tone love employs when it desires to express itself with caution and dignity" (LeWinter 1963, 50). Only Shakespeare depicts what is conceived as love's truly compelling power, which ultimately "succeeds in holding the post of sole tyrant of our desires and aversions" (LeWinter 1963, 50). Lessing rejects a notion of civilized or socialized passion and regards desire as central to identity and conduct. Such insight into general human psychology is a recurring theme in Goethe's praise of Shakespeare. In the earlier essay, "Shakespeare: A Tribute," written in 1771, he dismisses the offense Voltaire feels at Shakespeare's characters: "Nature! Nature! Nothing is so like Nature as Shakespeare's characters" (Goethe 1986, 165). The concept of general nature allows Goethe to write of his own response to Shakespeare as widely representative. His perceptions reveal traits that are intrinsic to everyone, "For we carry within us the seeds of the achievements we value in others" (Goethe 1986, 163). Shakespeare, perhaps Goethe too, stands for us all. In the later "Shakespeare Once Again," published in 1815, he is at pains to emphasize the "reality" of the world that Shakespeare represents, in order to affirm its literary, philosophical, and psychological value: "We experience the truth of life" in the plays (Goethe 1986, 167). As the discussion continues, we can see that Goethe does not, however, dismiss Voltaire out of hand, but aims to develop and correct the other's more limited conceptions, especially of the significance of desire and identity in Shakespeare's work. Tragic passion is no longer a battle poised between weakness and remorse; it has become the key motif of the "characteristically modern" individual, who is overpowered by "inner conflict" as moral obligation collides with desire (Goethe 1986, 170). In these terms, Goethe's reading of Shakespeare, and his deliberate revision of Voltaire's understanding of ethics and passion, provides an important step on the way to a Freudian conception of psychic volatility, and hence could be regarded as mediating the complex relationship between Freud and Shakespeare.

Sexual morality is used by Friedrich Schlegel to distinguish between Shakespeare and other English Renaissance writers. In so doing, he develops Malone's critique of Restoration opinions. Schlegel criticizes Beaumont and Fletcher for portraying "vulgar delight" and the "amusements of the populace" (Schlegel 1859, 464). In contrast, bawdiness in Shakespeare is linked to the intrinsic qualities of the character being depicted: "a man acts so because he is so. And what each man is, that Shakespeare reveals to us most immediately" (Schlegel 1859, 362). Dubious conduct here serves the greater ethical-literary goal of disclosing truth and depth of character. This kind of "inward devotion" is, according to Schlegel, lacking from Beaumont and Fletcher's work— "Their first object was effect" (Schlegel 1859, 468). Such a position clearly influenced Coleridge and other English critics. William Hazlitt significantly develops the idealization of profound identity through employing sexually and gender-based categories of value. Beaumont and Fletcher's poetry stimulates more than it gratifies, and leaves the mind in a certain sense exhausted and unsatisfied ... there is a too frequent mixture of voluptuous softness or effeminacy of character with horror in the subjects.... The tone of Shakespeare's writings is manly and bracing; theirs is at once insipid and meretricious.... They are not safe teachers of morality. (Hazlitt 1924, 250)

Masculinist rhetoric is embedded in critical judgment and an elitist heterosocial framework structures interpretation. Popular culture, femaleness, and femininity assume negative critical and moral value.

In this nineteenth-century mode of reading, Shakespeare's work is seen as revealing fundamental truths about human nature, from characters to readers. This type of perception was widely influential. In Italy, for example, there was a shift away from neoclassical concern about Shakespeare's work. The plays were "interpreted as paradigms of universal experience," along a "line linking author to spectator ... an almost unmediated contact between the writer's own passions and those of his characters, and between their feelings and those of the audience" (Locatelli 1999, 23, 32). By the mid-nineteenth century, the major German critics, Ulrici and Gervinus, aimed at correcting awestruck Romantic responses by disclosing "the aesthetic laws and the unifying ideas underlying his plays" (Habicht 1994b, 9). Notions of love and passion are central to their discussions. In *Shakespeare's Dramatic Art*, Ulrici regards *Romeo and Juliet* as exemplifying "that mysterious and yet indubitable interaction between the character of man and his destiny, by which the outer circumstances correspondingly answer to the inner tendency of the mind ... the fatal power of love, which has enslaved Romeo's whole being, is met by the external occasion" (Ulrici 1911, 1:388). In this view, love is one of the essential experiences that reveal the all-important "psychological truth of the character" (Ulrici 1911, 1:413). That truth might lead characters into conflict with their social world, as occurs in *Romeo and Juliet*, and in *Othello*, where "self-control gives way under the weight of impulses and passions" (Ulrici 1911, 1:424); or it can conclude in harmony, as in *All's Well that Ends Well*, where "that which is right and true prevails" (Ulrici 1911, 2:99). In this sense, Ulrici's conception of love recalls Goethe's distinction between desire and obligation. But Ulrici admires tragic passion ultimately because it testifies to the truth and power of social norms. The tragic lovers "have transgressed against the inviolable right of family, against the paternal authority from whose will the child cannot sever itself, without at the same time severing itself from the protecting bond of morality" (Ulrici 1911, 1:414). Ulrici identifies the highest form of love in betrothal and marriage, which he regards as "one of the fundamental props of human civilization, an indispensable condition of all morality ... the condition of all moral order in church and state" (Ulrici 1911, 1:424). Such comments make overt the ideological contexts in which the psychological and erotic "truth" of Shakespeare's texts is located.

In his *Shakespeare Commentaries*, Gervinus considers that Shakespeare "more or less exclusively represented the essence and nature of love" (Gervinus 1903, 151), and that *Romeo and Juliet* is "representative of all love-poetry" (Gervinus 1903, 208). He emphasizes the "twofold nature of love" in Shakespeare's work (Gervinus 1903, 157), its "ennobling" and "destroying power" (210), "its pure and its dangerous effects" (Gervinus 1903, 211). The effect of such intense representation remains didactic; the "moral spirit of Shakespeare's works" is conveyed "by living, acting impulses ... to develop in us that true self-love which strives to make the good and the beautiful its own" (Gervinus 1903, 888–89). The gap between Shakespeare and his work—that had frustrated Schiller in the late eighteenth century; "the poet could in Shakespeare never be seized" (LeWinter 1963, 71), he had felt—now becomes an ideal of personal detachment and control, the "property of perfect self-command" (Gervinus 1903, 892). Love does not merely stand at the emotive, artistic, and psychological center of Shakespeare's work but is crucial to its power to provide an ethical model of the kind of character that is or should be culturally valued and fostered for individuals.

The developing conception of love in Shakespeare's work interrelates notions of desire, gender, identity, and morality. Though Tolstoy famously condemns Shakespeare at the end of (and in response to) the century during which these ethical connections were most powerfully forged, his attack reiterates their terms. He does not specifically discuss Shakespearean love but moves directly to the works' moral effects. There is "no expression of character" and "no language of living individuals" in Shakespeare's plays (Le-

Winter 1963, 250), only an "immoral view" that "cannot possibly represent the teaching of life" (LeWinter 1963, 285). Shakespeare's standing is owing to the weakness and partiality of those who celebrate him: "free-minded individuals, not inoculated with Shakespeare worship, are no longer to be found in our Christian society" (LeWinter 1963, 246). Again, the nearly "unmediated contact" between author and reader is assumed, and the ethical flaws of the former are seen to have infected the latter. Tolstoy argues that Shakespeare's work and its reception exemplify the way that character, as a literary, ethical, and psychological concept, is on the verge of collapse.

In *Shakespeare's Perjured Eye*, Joel Fineman argued that the key to Shakespeare's effects on the history of literary-cultural identity in "his joining of particularized passion to particular person, of singularized characteristic to singular character," occurring in "a theater organized by a logic of personality—a theater of psycho-logic ... whose subjective intelligibility and authority have been uniformly remarked by the entire tradition of Shakespeare criticism" (Fineman 1986, 80). It is a large but significant claim, one which suggests that it is only ever possible to conceive of Shakespeare or *Shakespeares* through layers of scholarship that seek to trace their values and perceptions back to Shakespeare's text itself. What I have attempted in this paper is to explore some of the interrelated layers in the rhetoric of sexuality and gender, ethics and identity that have recurred in critical writing on Shakespeare over many years. Such analysis helps to disclose the motivations and effects through which the meanings of Shakespeare and the plays have been produced. It also helps to reveal the discursive struggle—the cultural, historical, ethical, and, in a way, sexual work that is constantly undertaken and reundertaken in the guise of literary criticism. Such work generates the singular author, character, or person, and also the complex relationships among authors, characters, and persons that underlie and inform the languages used to talk about Shakespeare.

King Lear: Kozintsev's Social Translation
David Margolies

SHAKESPEARE'S PLAYS, LIKE ANY WORKS THAT HAVE ENDURED the test of time, are read through the filter of later cultural perspectives. In England, since Shakespeare became part of university programs and a subject for examination in schools, the dominant view of *King Lear* has been that it is a family drama, a tragedy of old age and of selfishness. It is read as a book—a text complete in itself—severed from the complex of signifying practices in which it was created. Performance is often regarded as a secondary activity, as something that merely enlivens the lines or illustrates meaning. Treating the play as a book inevitably makes for distortion; it privileges extradramatic speculation about motive (a reading habit transferred thoughtlessly from novels) and focuses attention on the individual. Thus the subject of *King Lear* is usually presented as Lear's own tragedy, while *Hamlet*, even more clearly, is seen as Hamlet's personal psychological drama. Tradition has tied ideological values to some of the text so tightly that translation may be what is required to make a reinterpretation.[1]

In this paper I want first to look at Peter Brook's 1970 film of *King Lear* as an attempt to escape the traditional English limits of interpretation, which is only partially successful. Then I want to examine Grigori Kozintsev's *King Lear* (1970, released in 1971), which is "a deeply moving, deeply Russian view of the play, which, being Russian, throws a completely new and startlingly fresh light on many parts with which English audiences have become over familiar" (Mackintosh 1977, ix).

The image of a Shakespeare isolated from a real historical world lost its dominance (briefly) in the 1960s. In the wake of the events of 1968, disillusionment with the structure of society was widely expressed, and this was accompanied by sudden recognition of the ideological character of cultural production. A corresponding suspicion of literature arose—Literature, written with a capital "L" to identify the dubious role of canonical texts—and Shakespeare's value was subject to question.

An approach to Shakespeare that fitted with the rejection of high-culture dogma but was at the same time practicable and coherent was presented by Jan Kott's *Shakespeare Our Contemporary* (1964, English ed. 1965), which was powerfully influential.[2] Kott offered a relevance that was not merely political dogma tacked on to the plays but was found in the plays themselves. In a view of cultural production that was fundamentally (but not explicitly) Marxist, Kott interpreted drama in relation to the lived experience of society—the "basis" of social experience inevitably structured the "superstructure" of dramaturgical understanding.

Peter Brook wrote the introduction to the English edition of *Shakespeare Our Contemporary*, contrasting Kott's world of lived experience to that of the commentators on "Shakespeare's passions and his politics," critiques "hatched far from life by sheltered figures behind ivy-covered walls." Brook goes on to say that in England the problem is relating Shakespeare to our lives: "Our actors are skilled and sensitive, but they shy away from overlarge questions. Those young actors who are aware of the deadly issues at the moment at stake in the world tend to shy away from Shakespeare" (Brook 1991, x).

Possessed of the anger of '68 and the vision of Kott, Brook tackled *King Lear*. I did not see his stage production but in the film he rejects the sentimentalized *Lear* of old age and family relations and presents instead a world of violence, cruelty, and self-seeking. Brook cuts some lines, shifts and reassigns others in a way that reduces the play's demand for sympathy; he pictures a hostile society in a hostile nature (the sequence that epitomizes this is Lear driven out onto the heath where Regan's personal coldness is seconded by the icy wind that is suggested visually).

The lack of social feeling is emphasized throughout. Lear's hundred knights are as unruly as Goneril describes them. They not only jeer at Oswald, they pelt him with food and, following Lear's lead, they trash the great hall of the castle before they depart. Brook's use of gratuitous violence illustrates the nature of the world and the absence of fellow-feeling.

Edgar, successfully disguised as Poor Tom, is knocked down by a rock one of the soldiers throws at him for no reason other than his obvious madness, which the other soldiers find amusing. Oswald, in no production presented as better than a time-server and cowardly villain, here displays a memorable petty cruelty when he pulls off the boots of the stocked Kent, exposing his feet to the icy weather. The small gestures Shakespeare usually puts into the tragedies that might suggest the redemption of society Brook excises from the film. He curtails the protest of the servants when Cornwall goes to put out Gloucester's other eye and cuts out entirely the old tenant who tries to help the blinded Gloucester.

The most disturbing quality of the world Brook creates for Lear is the sense that it is normal—Goneril and Regan are viciously self-centered but appear as rational beings, discussing calmly the failings of the old king and what measures they must take. Regan, when Lear arrives at Gloucester's castle, speaks to him with soft-voiced reason while she strips him of the last elements of his dignity.

Brook's hostile world, however, remains background, against which the tragedy of an old man is played out. The camera individualizes Lear, lingering on Paul Scofield's face as he delivers his lines in a manner appropriate to the man rather than the king. The division of the kingdom speech has a naturalistic, private quality rather than any ceremonial character. Similarly with the speeches of Goneril and Regan: their only ceremonial aspect is that they are not entitled to speak until they hold the orb passed in turn to would-be speakers. The love-test seems impromptu, France is present but there is no Burgundy to give the potential of ceremony in choosing Cordelia's husband, customary civil qualities are gone. Even in scenes that are only semiofficial the private aspect dominates public speech, as when mad Lear's proverbial political truths lose their public quality by being whispered into the ear of blind Gloucester. Brook took *King Lear* as far as it could go within the limits of public acceptance: he made a forceful critique of contemporary society but retained the conventional individual focus of the tragedy. He stayed within the bounds of what the public would recognize as Shakespeare's play; to go beyond that point was to use Shakespeare's material for a new play, as did Edward Bond in *Lear* (1971) or, later, Howard Barker in his *Seven Lears* (1989).

However, translation allows a freedom to reinterpret what is still understood as Shakespeare's play. Grigori Kozintsev continued a strong European, especially Eastern European, tradition of using Shakespeare to speak other things through the plays, of using the plays as metaphors for political situations that under heavy censorship could not be approached directly, as he had done in his *Hamlet* of 1964.[3] In *Lear,* using much of the same material as Brook, he was able to translate into a context that gave a social meaning to what had been effectively suppressed by sentimentalization in anglophone culture. By altering the relation between the social background and the foregrounded tragedy, in effect changing the context, he manages to produce a significantly different emphasis that conveys a different meaning.[4]

The verbal translation Kozintsev uses is that of Pasternak (who also translated his *Hamlet*). Although the subtitles supplied with the film when it was released in the West are the English of Shakespeare, Pasternak rendered the text into modern Russian, making the play accessible in a way that it seldom is for anglophone audiences who find the archaism difficult and whose distance from the language generally makes them insensitive to differences in register and the attitudes such differences suggest. Kozintsev wrote that Pasternak thought Shakespeare's use of blank verse was a mechanism to speed up his composition, not an artistic enhancement, and even though he retains some of the couplets, the verse structure seems generally to have been abandoned.[5]

The significance of Kozintsev's film as a translation is less in its linguistic features than in the images he creates to realize the playtext. Alexander Anikst, discussing the role of the translator, said, "When a translator does his job, he doesn't translate words, he re-creates the images." He was referring not to images as the metaphors that appear like isolated jewels in the text but to the larger, defining images of the whole play. He went on to say, "we must not forget that there is a totality in works of art, and it is this totality which works upon us" (Anikst 1989, 54).

The question then is what *King Lear*'s larger images are. According to the Victorian heritage, they are family, old age, and sometimes power. For Brook, they are a hostile world— human indifference and cruelty and an inhospitable nature. Kozintsev draws on the collapse of a society based on collectivity and relations of mutuality and shows the intense development of individualistic behavior.[6]

Kozintsev's film begins with a striking postcredit sequence that, like other good film openings, gives a context to all that follows. He shows feet, rag-bound feet of the poor, trudging along a stony path. The feet are given particular prominence in that we only see the walking people from the waist down and the only sound provided by the sound track at this point is the shuffling of the feet and the creak of a wheelbarrow in which an ill child is being transported. Kozintsev gives us a full thirty seconds of this, after which he lets us see whole figures, and then two and a half minutes of the same peasants and homeless shown against the landscape, with shots varying from close-up to long views, with a solo voice added to the shuffling feet of the sound track. It emerges that they are making their way to Lear's castle to hear his abdication. The sequence suggests that the ultimate criterion of politics is the people, the anonymous masses ever present in the background of Kozintsev's film.

Kozintsev's landscape is as inhospitable as Brook's but, unlike Brook's, there are almost always people in it, groups of peasants or wandering beggars. Kott praised Peter Hall's *Hamlet* for its advance on the political naïveté of Olivier's because, he said, it offered a much better feeling for a totalitarian state. "I think, perhaps, he has learnt from the Russian school—that emphasis on the continual presence of other people, for instance, which Kozintsev pointed up in the latest Russian film *Hamlet*" (Kott 1991, 300). Even outside Dover when the blinded Gloucester and the mad Lear meet, where they are of course the focus of attention, there are people in the background going about their business, in this case picking herbs. They are anonymous and do not speak, but their presence is quite definite, and they are a reminder of the larger context of ordinary life in which the actions of the main characters have their consequences. Kozintsev wrote that the beggars must have prominence in the film not just because Edgar becomes one of them "but because one cannot portray the life of a king without portraying the life of his subjects" (Kozintsev 1977, 34).

The closing sequence, for which Shakespeare's text makes no provision, is of the royal bodies being born through the devastation of war, the fool kicked out of the way by one of the soldiers, and finally, people pouring water on the smoldering remains of their burned dwellings. The focus is moved from the high politics of the nobility to the suffering caused to the ordinary people.

What is for me the most striking sequence of the film is Kozintsev's treatment of the hovel in which Shakespeare has Lear take shelter from the storm. Traditionally, this is merely a building that offers enough space for Lear, the fool, Poor Tom, Kent, and the visiting Gloucester. In Brook's film it is not significantly different, and the interaction between Lear and Poor Tom has the character of personal exchange, in close focus with seldom anyone else in the frame. Kozintsev opens his sequences with Lear, outside the hovel, beginning his prayer. He then cuts to the face of Edgar/Tom, inside, who has heard courtly voices he recognizes and a close-up of whose face (clearly as Edgar rather than Poor Tom) shows a complex emotional response. Then the camera pulls back to reveal the homeless sheltering from the storm. Lear makes his prayer while looking at these wretched people, and it is inescapable that the misery he refers to in the prayer is understood to be their misery—real, material suffering, not an abstraction. The "poor naked wretches" whose "loop'd and window'd raggedness" cannot defend them against "seasons such as these," of whom he has taken too little care, are not a theoretical proposition; they are surrounding him. And Edgar/Tom's "unaccommodated man" is no longer just a particular case; it applies as well to the masses in the hovel.

The significance of anonymous mass is partly explained by Kozintsev's comments on Lear's relation to his hundred knights. Shakespeare, he said, did not give speech to any of the hundred, "neither names, words, nor character. Is this a coincidence? Of course it isn't. These are not people but a way of life. They are a whole, not individuals" (Kozintsev 1977, 170). He also offers a more theoretical explanation:

> At first we are confronted with the age-old problem out of the school textbook: a king and a train of a hundred men make altogether—a hundred and one men; when the train disappears there are a hundred and one minus a hundred: how many are left? The pupil answers without hesitation: one man. Shakespeare reaches a different result: one man is no longer a man. "Now thou art an 0 without a figure" the Fool tells Lear.
> One plus a hundred = a king. A king minus a hundred (train)

= 0. The measure is very much less than a man. A new measure is introduced: Poor Tom is a bare, forked animal, and nothing more. Nothing. An 0 without a figure. (Kozintsev 1977, 182–83)

Man (as opposed to the bare, forked animal) and the king are social beings; individuals gain meaningful identity only as part of a social whole. The wolf-child is *homo ferus*, not *homo sapiens*. "*Lear* is not only the drama of a particular group of people who are linked by the plot, but also a stream of history" (Kozintsev 1977, 117). The character is not a unique individual but a type, used in the case of Poor Tom to represent the collective voice of homeless poverty: "If the words are only Edgar's, they are superfluous; if they contain images of the unjust life, then they are not only essential but are worth their weight in gold" (Kozintsev 1977, 117).

Kozintsev changes—makes social—the criteria by which actions are judged. For example, Edgar's transformation into Poor Tom in Brook's rendering is an idea that comes to him as he is fleeing and in isolation. Kozintsev, on the other hand, has the exhausted Edgar see the chanting beggars and transform himself to join them. For Brook, Edgar simply takes on a disguise; for Kozintsev, he conceals himself by becoming part of a group of which no notice is taken. The difference is slight but the implications are significant: Brook presents Edgar's transformation as individual suffering, whereas Kozintsev sees it as the misery of a class whose suffering Edgar highlights:

> Many voices have merged into one voice; Poor Tom is the leader of the chorus. The poverty-stricken hovels groan, the unharvested fields lament, the great highways beg for alms, the homeless and outcasts tramp along them—where can they shelter, who can feed them? (Kozintsev 1977, 197)

The peasants and homeless are the ideological core and touchstone of Kozintsev's film.

Kozintsev has translated Shakespeare with images that draw on a heritage that valorizes social being and gives priority to values of collectivity. Working within a Soviet ideological emphasis on the masses, he is making explicit attitudes that are already implicit in the play, and that would have been accessible to any audience that experienced the social changes at the beginning of the seventeenth century.

Such a reading had in effect been expunged from English Shakespeare. Kozintsev by translating was able to render visually the excluded themes and regenerate the play. And he goes beyond the play as a document to understand it as something that presents a moral imperative to the audience:

> Shakespearean characters demand an answering call. Lear's call, "O, you are men of stones" is not unanswered.
> Who does he expect an answering call, a reply from? From everyone. Does that mean from all who enter the stage? No, rather from those who are in the audience. And not literally from those who that same day bought a ticket and came to see the play, but from all those who continue to live; from those who will come in the future; from those who understand; those who are not made of stone. (Kozintsev 1977, 184–85)

Notes

1. The simplest example of this is probably Hamlet's hawk and handsaw remark to Rosencrantz and Guildenstern: "I am but mad north-northwest; when / the wind is southerly I know a hawk from a handsaw" (2.2.373–75). The usual English understanding of this is that Hamlet makes a subtle distinction in falconry. Schlegel-Tieck follow this sense in their German translation, rendering it as "Tauben und Dohlen." But Heiner Müller's modern version gives it as "Hacken und Säge," drawing the distinction in popular terms of workman's tools, which gives the exchange a very different ideological cast. Distinguishing Shakespeare's plasterer's hawk from the carpenter's handsaw is also more consistent with Elizabethan forms of popular expression.

2. It was reprinted in 1965 and republished in a revised edition and a paperback in 1967, which was reprinted another six times.

3. I am indebted to Zdeněk Stříbrný's splendid *Shakespeare and Eastern Europe* for an understanding of the long tradition of using Shakespeare as a political platform.

4. Kozintsev records in *King Lear: The Space of Tragedy* some of his correspondence with Brook relating to the progress of their films. Brook wrote to Kozintsev in 1969: "I am sure from what I understand of your intentions we are both trying to tell the same story. But with very different means within very different cultures" (241).

5. "Pasternak considered that Shakespeare's genius was most evident in his prose, that his verse was often overloaded with metaphors, and too complex. He thought that the flow of unrhymed blank verse was no more than a method of speed writing: the poet was forced to hurry and this was the most convenient shorthand for his thoughts and feelings" (Kozintsev 1977, 51).

Alexander Anikst said that Pasternak's idea was not to translate but to re-create, and thus he used modern language. Theaters switched to his translation because they were in the language used by ordinary people (Anikst 1989, 45).

6. In *Monsters of the Deep: Social Dissolution in Shakespeare's Tragedies*, I argue that this concern with individualism dominates the development of Shakespeare's tragedies.

The Shakespearean Sound in Translation
Alexander Shurbanov

CALIBAN'S ISLAND IS "FULL OF NOISES, SOUNDS AND SWEET AIRS, that give delight, and hurt not," and so is the poetic work of his creator. These very noises, sounds, and sweet airs, constituting the chief magic of Shakespeare's drama, are the hardest and therefore the last of its components to find its way into translation. Such is the evidence of its reception in my national culture and I have reasons to believe that the situation is similar in other countries too. Boris Pasternak says that "Translators are used to reproduce the sense rather than the tone of an utterance, yet what does matter above all is the tone" (Pasternak 1961, 215).

Let me begin the survey of the problem with an observation made by Winifred Nowottny in her book *The Language Poets Use*:

> Features of sound and spelling can emphasize meaning, as when Shakespeare, remarking in *Henry V* (4.2.43) that the exhausted and ill-equipped army on the eve of Agincourt is a travesty of the well-found army that set out, writes,
> 	Big Mars seems bankrupt in their beggar'd host
> —calling in alliteration's aid and that of a sound-change through the alliterating words to make emphasis fall on the contrast between "Big" and "beggar'd," a contrast which adds to the impact and meaning of "bankrupt." One relation of sound-effect and meaning has been briefly but clearly characterised by Empson: "I think myself its most important mode of action is to connect two words by similarity of sound so that you are made to think of their possible connections." (Nowottny 1962, 5)

This type of formalist assessment has been out of fashion for so long that it may strike some of us as archaic, and, certainly, when it comes to drama in particular, it is absurd to consider spelling together with sound as part of an intentional stylistic scheme. It would hardly be acceptable at any time to think of Shakespeare, or of any dramatist for that matter, as making remarks in his own person rather than giving one of the characters a cue of such and such a kind. But, all that granted, sound patterns of the said type are so frequent in Shakespeare and they are so far from the automatically decorative vignettes of Lyly's Euphuism that we cannot dismiss them as casual and conventional.

Nowottny's study of Shakespeare's uses of alliteration includes cases in which it generates an ironical reversal of avowed meaning as, for instance, in Berowne's speech in *Love's Labor's Lost* (3.1.180–88):

> This whimpled, whining, purblind, wayward boy;
> This senior-junior, giant dwarf, Dan Cupid;
> *R*egent of love-*r*hymes, lord of folded arms,
> The anointed *s*overeign of *s*ighs and groans,
> *L*iege of all *l*oiterers and malcontents,
> Dread *p*rince of *p*lackets, *k*ing of *c*odpieces,
> Sole imperator and great general
> Of trotting paritors: O my little heart![1]

The bathetic debunking of Cupid in this series of identically structured *of* phrases is reinforced by the sound pattern that gives them sanction. In other cases such pairing-off of related words can underline the metaphorical effect of their coming together:

> And this our life, exempt from public haunt,
> Finds *t*ongues in *t*rees, *b*ooks in the running *b*rooks,
> Serm*ons* in *st*ones, and good in everything.
> (*A.Y.L.*, 2.1.15–17)

Alliteration can also express the vehemence of passion, held in check yet threatening to erupt any minute, as in Mark Antony's famous funeral orations (*Julius Caesar*, 3.2)—

> O judgment, thou art fled to *b*rutish *b*easts

(the adjective subtly undermining Brutus's popularity by suggesting—again through similarity of sound—that his nature is evil), or already rumbling, as in King Lear's indignant reply to Regan with its elaborate and effective interlacement of several recurrent consonants and vowels—

> O! reason *n*ot the *n*eed; our *b*asest *b*eggars
> Are in the *p*oorest thing *sup*erfluous.
> Allow *n*ot *n*ature *m*ore than *n*ature *n*eeds,
> *M*an's life is cheap as *b*east's.
>
> (*Lear*, 2.4.266–69)

If you deprive such speeches of their phonetic orchestration the power of the utterance will be sadly—sometimes even fatally—reduced.

But we must not forget that ever since the Alliterative Revival—perhaps even since the Old English period—alliteration has been a deeply ingrained principle of text construction in English, informing set-phrases, rhetorical figures, titles and headings, etc. Even when all sense is gone, alliteration seems to persist, as in so much nonsense verse or, to come back to our material, in Hamlet's inscrutable formula:

> *M*arry, this is *m*iching *m*alicho. It *m*eans *m*ischief.
>
> (*Haml.*, 3.2.135)

Most European languages, however, have no such tradition and seldom expect so much from alliteration. It would therefore be unproductive to repeat or imitate the original sound patterning in translation, for in its new linguo-cultural context this would not necessarily have the same effect. The "general ear" of the new audience may not be inured to alliteration in the same way as the English ear has been through a long training. Even the phonetic system of its language, characterized for instance by less tense consonants, may be less propitious to such developments. Working under these constraints, what should a sensitive translator do to ensure the preservation of quality?

The Bulgarian experience shows that until recently the problem was not apparent or urgent and the pervasive presence of this device in the original was almost completely ignored. It was only in the 1970s that a major poet, Valeri Petrov, resolved to devote more than a decade of his literary career to the translation of the complete Shakespeare canon, attempted an adequate re-creation of his prototype's stylistic intricacy. This feat was hailed by a spurt of new theater productions. Petrov's forte was in the scope of comedy where he managed to achieve something similar to Shakespeare's youthful exuberance, spirited playfulness, and linguistic ingenuity. As far as alliteration is concerned, he chose to transmute some of that into rhymes, which seemed to him a more acceptable device in Bulgarian verse. Berowne's Dan Cupid speech is a good example of this strategy.

Rhyme is, of course, a device akin to alliteration, and its impact on the audience can be seen as analogous, although the end-result is an undeniable stylistic impoverishment, a collapsing of two techniques into one and an ultimate reduction of the number of tools one operates with. Also, the finer underscoring of semantic links within the line is thus replaced by a general increase of euphony or playfulness. These functional losses, I am afraid, may be unavoidable. What would perhaps be more dangerous is the employment of the same method in the translation of the tragedies. The multiplication of rhymed verse there would compromise the sober tone of the genre. Such damage has unfortunately been done to some parts of the plays. Petrov, however, has generally refrained from drastically reducing the predominance of the blank verse and has striven to either reproduce some of the original alliterative schemes or relinquish them without any attempt at compensation.

As for rhyming itself, Shakespeare's ways of using it are no less subtle and varied. We are all aware of the punctuating effect of the closing couplets at the end of an important speech or episode. There are also the series of rhymed couplets, quatrains, sextains and other, more elaborate stanzaic forms, emerging unexpectedly like phonetic crystals forming in the midst of what appears to be a fairly amorphous linguistic medium and drawing attention to themselves. The most striking achievement of this kind is the sonnet enveloping the first meeting of Romeo and Juliet (1.5.92–105). A play that is particularly rich in such lyrical patterning is *Love's Labor's Lost*. Large tracts of dialogue in this comedy tend to turn into ingenious games of allegedly improvised versification. A conscientious translator would hardly bypass such structures. And European languages as a rule will offer little resistance to their reproduction. Naturally, in most cases this will mean greater concision imposed by the uninflatable prosodic form and, more often than not, some loss of semantic detail.

The really important question in the last analysis is how much of this painstaking work is worth the candle. Even if we assume that the theater director gets interested in those textual vagaries—which is not very often the case these days—will he/she make a point of highlighting them on the stage and will this be noticed and appreciated by an audience that has largely unlearned to apprehend poetry as an oral art?

What the audience cannot help sensing are the schemes of lexical repetition that foreground certain words and phrases often turning their phonetic shell into something like an alarum bell. It is important that the translator does not skip even a single link in such chains, for they can easily disintegrate and lose their cumulative effect. The expressive and rhetorical value of anadiplosis, as in Hamlet's rebuke of his mother, should be quite obvious:

> ... for at your age
> The heyday in the blood is tame, it's humble,
> And waits upon the *judgment*, and what *judgment*
> Would step from this to this?
> (*Haml.*, 3.4.68–71)

Such instances are usually recognized by translators. Emotionally loaded refrains of the following kind are also generally done justice to:

> *Return to her?* and fifty men dismiss'd?
> No, rather I'll abjure all roofs and choose
> To wage against the enmity o'th'air;
> To be a comrade with the wolf and owl,
> Necessity's sharp pinch! *Return with her?*
> Why, the hot-blooded France, that dowerless took
> Our youngest born, I could as well be brought
> To knee his throne, and squire-like, pension beg
> To keep base life afoot. *Return with her?*
> Persuade me rather to be slave and sumpter
> To this detested groom ...
> (*Lear*, 2.4.209–19)

Problems start arising when such refrains are less regular and may appear rather diffuse and therefore optional, as for example in Mark Antony's funeral speech where he plays cleverly on the words "ambition/ambitious" and "honorable men," charging them with more and more irony at every new turn. The multiple repetition of "banished/banishment" in a number of passionate speeches uttered by Romeo and Juliet in 3.2 and 3.3 is also essential but seldom retained in its entirety. Key words punctuating a play from beginning to end and sharpening its thematic focus, such as "nature" in *King Lear* or "love" in *Julius Caesar* with their cognates, are even less often reproduced with the same insistence.

Some emphatic repetitions seem fairly unimportant and translators are tempted to dispense with them in order to keep the rhythmic compactness of an important utterance in conditions where most of the original monosyllabic words have to become polysyllabic in the new language. As a result, anguished cries of the following kind can lose much of their impetus:

Blow, winds, and crack your cheeks! rage, blow!
(*Lear*, 3.2.1)

Macbeth's sigh of despair in "*Out, out,* brief candle!" (*Macbeth*, 5.5.23) is likely to be halved for the same reason and with similar consequences. And even Hamlet, whose knack of repeating words is generally respected, will seldom be granted the luxury of saying: "O that this *too too* sullied flesh would melt." (*Hamlet*, 1.2.129) with the same exasperation. The otherwise admirable rule of economy in translation can in such cases prove counterproductive. To be fair, however, we should not blame such stylistic losses wholly on the translators' indiscretion. The prosodic constraints they are compelled to work under should always be taken into account. But it remains nonetheless true that a tonal change of the said kind affects the makeup of both character and situation.

Lexical repetition, phonetic schematization, and syntactic parallelism are the distinctive features of proverbs, aphorisms, and wordplay, which abound in Shakespeare's texts. These are often almost impossible to salvage in the passage to another language because of their inimitable imagery but a good translator should make the effort by approximating both their content and their form, because their absence would seriously impair the overall effect of a play by flattening its tone and dulling its movement. Both the characters and the action would also be deprived of their verve. Malapropisms in particular contribute a good deal to humorous characterization and to the lighthearted mood of the comedies. Near identity of sound between two words or phrases of radically different meaning is at the root of this device. A lot of ingenuity is needed on the part of the translator to find a similar pair within the same semantic group in his/her own language. Valeri Petrov's admirable care for the re-creation of all these classes of figures in their corporal intactness has helped him reveal much of the fascinating atmosphere of the romantic comedies that was sadly dimmed in earlier translations.

∞

The patterning of the text of poetic drama, of course, goes deeper than the phonetic and lexical levels. Since most of it is written in verse, the prosodic features of this medium are important to consider. Though the history of Shakespearean reception almost invariably starts with the conversion of all poetry into prose, most European languages have eventually opted for a restoration of the original verse form. It is hardly necessary to argue that the specific prosodic structuring of the text chosen by the author carries no less relevant information than does the already discussed linguistic one. There are, obviously, languages and cultures that are compelled by ingrained traditions and specificities to avoid verse translation partly or altogether. Japanese, I understand, cannot tolerate a poetic text that would run longer than a few lines and, consequently, renders the bulk of the play in prose. With French and Italian it seems to be a matter of choice, again sanctified by tradition.

Bulgarian passed from prose to verse renditions in the early years of the twentieth century and since then has embraced this approach as the only legitimate one. It must be made clear from the very beginning that by the end of the nineteenth century iambic pentameter had been established as a staple metric form of modern Bulgarian poetry and this fortunate coincidence with the Shakespearean setup, no doubt, facilitated the process. The prosodic foundation of poetic translation could thus be deemed identical with that of the original. However, there were some significant differences in the treatment of this foundation in the two languages and they were bound to bring about some changes of the texts' characteristic "sound."

If, for brevity's sake, we risk an oversimplification, it may be said that while the English combination of the tonic and syllabic principles has always traditionally privileged the former, the Bulgarian one has leaned more heavily onto the latter. These preferences are historically explicable in each case. As a result, English versification can indulge in a wide variety of metrical irregularities such as anacruses, internal pauses, insertion of extra unstressed syllables, foot substitution, variation of line lengths, etc. As long as the number of stresses in each line remains stable, the flow of the text is felt as sufficiently smooth. This situation encourages a good deal of rhythmic variety—liberties that are, unfortunately, inadmissible in Bulgarian with its stronger syllabic leanings. Any excessive deviation from the metrically regularized ten- or eleven-syllable line would lead to cacophony here. The standardization of Shakespeare's protean prosody is therefore inescapable in any translation. And this tendency is only reinforced by the translators' natural gravitation toward a recognized norm making it nearly absolute. To further complicate the problem, hypometric lines are hard to keep shorter in the new version if you can for once render the full meaning of the author's text in a regular five-foot unit in spite of the much longer words you have to deal with in your own language.

Nevertheless, there are ways of breaking away from the literary monotony that such extreme regularization is apt to breed. Lyubomir Ognyanov, who translated a dozen Shakespeare plays in the 1950s, hit upon an interesting method of imitating the English original's internal variation of the poetic line. He started treating syllables that are usually slurred in normal speech as of no metrical value. The method was applied especially in cases where two or more vowels came together and could be elided, though not in such cases only. Since, in order to scan, Bulgarian verse usually treats every vowel as a separate syllable irrespective of its accentual prominence, this invasion of conversational informality into its domain created interesting and vitalizing tensions. A number of prosodic units started functioning as fractional quantities, thus problematizing the meter without seriously disrupting it. Some Bulgarian words proved capable of being treated as longer or shorter entities depending on current metric requirements—rather like Shakespeare's "heaven/heav'n," "th(e)," "dev(i)l," "ev(i)l," "spir(i)t," "treach(e)ry," "mirac(u)lous," "diff(e)rence," etc. Regrettably, Ognyanov's example has so far had few followers, but this fact does not make it any less significant.

Another way of breaking the monotony of metrical speech is the use of enjambments puncturing the self-contained existence of the poetic line. Shakespeare's utilization of this device, especially in his mature plays, is quite extensive. One of Macbeth's famous soliloquies enjambs nineteen of its twenty-eight lines, developing long passages without a single end-stopped unit:

> If it were done, when 'tis done, then *'twere well*
> It were done quickly: *if th'assassination*
> Could trammel up the consequence, *and catch*
> With his surcease success; *that but this blow*
> Might be the be-all and the end-all—*here*,
> But here, upon this bank and shoal of time,
> We'd jump the life to come.—*But in these cases*,
> We still have judgment here; *that we but teach*
> Bloody instructions, which, being taught, *return*
> To plague th'inventor: *this even-handed Justice*
> *Commends th'ingredience of our poison'd chalice*
> To our own lips. He's here in double trust:
> First, as I am his kinsman and his subject,
> Strong both against the deed; then, *as his host*,
> Who should against his murtherer shut the door,
> Not bear the knife myself. Besides, *this Duncan*
> Hath borne his faculties so meek, *hath been*
> So clear in his great office, *that his virtues*
> Will plead like angels, trumpet-tongued, *against*
> The deep damnation of his taking-off;
> *And Pity, like a naked new-born babe*,
> Striding the blast, or heaven's Cherubins, *hors'd*
> Upon the sightless couriers of the air,
> Shall blow the horrid deed in every eye,
> That tears shall drown the wind.—*I have no spur*
> To prick the sides of my intent, but, *only*
> Vaulting ambition, which o'erleaps itself
> And falls on th'other—

Most Bulgarian poetry of the "Golden Age" (late nineteenth to early twentieth century) was written in predominantly end-stopped lines and its models of aesthetic excellence have persistently influenced the recreation of foreign masterpieces, including Shakespeare's drama. A daring exception to this rule was attempted in 1919 by the brilliant young poet, translator, and critic Geo Milev, who produced a version of *Hamlet* unsurpassed to the present day. His inspired translation is quite free when it comes to rendering details of imagery and argument but the overall tonality of the original is masterfully preserved and that feat owes not a little to the frequent employment of enjambments and variation of line length. If Milev errs in anything it is in neglecting Shakespeare's rule to end even an enjambed line on a semantically pivotal word, thus reinforcing the pause while obliterating it. His enjambments are sometimes logically unjustifiable but almost always noticeable, if only because of their unexpected abruptness. Valeri Petrov, who is the next important translator to employ the device systematically, although not so frequently, on the contrary, makes the transitions too smooth and deprives the line of its strength by merging it into long verse paragraphs in which the complexity of syntax stifles the poetic rhythm to a dangerous extent.

The problems of metrical exigencies bring us face to face with the question of medium. The verse organization of Shakespeare's poetic drama is both apparent and unobtrusive, radically relaxed by techniques of the kind we have just examined. Metrical irregularities and enjambments create the necessary conditions for actual conversational intonations to enter more or less unchanged the domain of ictus and become naturalized in it. The breadth of register and the possibility of all sorts of effective combinations are truly stunning. This makes the transition from verse to prose and back to verse again easy and sufficiently smooth though not imperceptible.

The prose itself is immensely flexible, capable of passing from the intonations of everyday to a rhetorically structured form that brings us quite close to the effects of poetry. It is doubtful whether the audience can readily notice that Brutus's funeral speech in *Julius Caesar* (3.2) is in prose while Mark Antony's is in verse, though its appeal to reason rather than emotion does distinguish the former from the latter tonally. Hamlet's Picoesque monologue in 2.2 ("I have of late, but wherefore I know not, lost all my mirth") is nearly as poetic in its vision and structure as any of his verse soliloquies. Much of his dialogue with the gravediggers in 5.1, however, is not raised above a casual verbal exchange. A translator should be mindful of these differences and try to employ the full scale of tones crossing the boundaries between the various compartments of the text without unnecessary jolts yet not obliviously.

The question of how inserted songs should be translated would call for a special study. Are we obliged to observe the original prosodic scheme of the piece? Should it be composed so that it is sung to its original tune if that is known? Or can we have another tune in mind? It is not very often that international theater directors opt for authentic Elizabethan music scores.

Treading the thin line between the casual and the formal we touched upon a little while ago, one must strike a difficult balance. There are some renditions in which the prosodic organization of the text is inadmissibly relaxed, but the more frequent danger is that of approaching a stilted literary style that may be quite impressive on the printed page yet lack all vitality on the stage. It must be remembered that, as a rule, Shakespeare's dramatic dialogue is not a series of orations but a lively verbal interaction with a strong phatic coloring, a language of gestures often combined with physical action and conscious of it. When we come to the monologic utterances, perhaps the only type that is not vigorously dramatic is what Manfred Pfister calls "informative soliloquies" (Pfister 1988, 136). All other classes, both actional and nonactional, are immersed in the dynamics of becoming rather than in the repose of being. In the words of Una Ellis-Fermor, they present "the image of a mind as yet in chaos, not of the resultant that we shall find when the forces have come into equilibrium" (Ellis-Fermor 1980, 33).

Such a mental state presupposes the lack of smooth and consistent argument, frequent interruption in the flow of speech, illogical switching from one idea to another, broken and elliptic sentences, exclamations, and questions left without an answer, etc. A good illustration can be found in Hamlet's first soliloquy in 1.2 ("O that this too too sullied flesh would melt"). The task of the translator is to retain the excited, segmented, and jerky intonational pattern of such utterances. However, translation, as a reproductive act based on text assessment and therefore having a more strongly ratiocinative character than original creation, tends to exert an additional disciplining influence on its material, increasing the elements of order on both its logical and its tonal level. This reduces the emotional amplitude of the utterance and curtails its expressive potential.

Similar discretion is required in the process of differentiating individual voices in the plays. As Ben Jonson observes,

"Language most shows a man: speak that I may see thee ... No glass renders a man's form, or likeness, so true as his speech" (*Timber, or Discoveries*). The intonations of Hamlet and Claudius are radically different and when you learn to recognize them you will be able to probe into the depths of each character. The prince's sparing and thoughtfully ironical use of words is contrasted with his uncle's impersonal formal orations. Polonius's way of speaking with its confused verbosity is also psychologically determined and similarly opposed to Hamlet's. A comedy like *As You Like It* can be no less varied in terms of intonation. Here Rosalind's playful irony revealing her unusual independence of mind and her heart's capacity for sympathy sparkles against the much dimmer, though far from uniform background of Orlando's romantic rhetoric, Silvius's soft sentimentality, Jaques' melancholy bitterness and Touchstone's hollow quibbles. We do not need to be told that Macbeth and his wife speak in two markedly different ways suggesting an essential inner disparity, and so do Othello and Iago, Cordelia and her two elder sisters, Richard II and Henry Bolingbroke. A translator insensitive to such fine modulations in the uses of language can level out the differences and reduce the wealth of individuality that is the chief glory of Shakespeare's dramatic world. A degree of leveling seems to be an inevitable corollary of all but the most brilliant translations.

Besides being differentiated by their inimitable idiolects, characters in Shakespeare are grouped together by the sociolects they represent. Aristocrats speak in their distinctive way, which is opposed to that of the uneducated and uncultured clowns. Though these distinctions are usually carefully preserved in translation, the traditional intolerance of Bulgarian belles-lettres to foul language has until recently tended to narrow the gap between the two levels by elevating the lower one. The theater, on the other hand, has for the last couple of decades headed in the opposite direction collapsing the higher level into the lower for fear that the former would sound affected. Both kinds of tonal unification are unfortunate because they rob the plays of their scope of representation encoded in a variety of tone.

A good translator should also be able to discern and find a way of transposing a whole set of parodies and pastiches that Shakespeare creates to expose the extravagances of language as it is used in specific areas of social life. Here we should include the ironic portraits of the theater in *Hamlet*, *A Midsummer Night's Dream*, and *Love's Labor's Lost*; the no less sophisticated representation of the law-court jargon in *The Merchant of Venice* and *King Lear*; the speech mannerisms of characters like Don Armado, Holofernes, Osric, and others. In translation these aberrations of normal communication ought to be related to models recognizable in the new cultural environment yet retaining their correspondence with the historically defined conventions Shakespeare had in mind—a rather daunting task, particularly where similar models are not available.

∞

A third group of problems in the acoustic organization of the reproduced texts deals with a number of aspects that are largely unencoded in the prosodic and phonetic structures but pervade the text and contribute not a little to the way a play "sounds." One of these is the translator's perennial dilemma whether to adhere to an absolutely modern language or to signal the "oldness" of the original. It is true that the re-creation of the text is undertaken for the sake of today's audiences and it would be absurd to encumber them with an archaic linguistic product—after all Shakespeare wrote his drama for his contemporaries and sustained it in their current accents. Translation, understandably, tends to emulate this communicational setup and update the plays in linguistic terms. This, however, should be done very cautiously, for an extreme modernization of diction—including the latest slang coinages—would predetermine one specific approach in theater production, that of the modern-dress type, and would necessarily preclude any alternative to it as incompatible with the sound of the text. A certain amount of quaintness—less than that experienced by the English-language audience in its exposure to the unrevised original—would only help us retain a sense of distance from the story, a patina that is an asset rather than a liability when we deal with art.

The drawback of this attractively balanced position is that it tends to discourage translators from experimenting with the hidden potentials of their language and thus prevents them from rendering one of Shakespeare's most striking features, his linguistic creativity. As a matter of fact, this aspect of the poet's work has, with time, become less visible to a public used to thinking of him as eternally present in all language from its inception. It has also been played down by the majority of translators, who do not feel confident enough to bring their own innovations into the target language. A striking exception to this rule in the Bulgarian history of Shakespearean reception is again Valeri Petrov, whose inexhaustible inventiveness in his play with words and sounds is amply manifested both in his translations and in his own works. An even more recent translator, Spas Nikolov, has shown a similar willingness to emulate Shakespeare's linguistic acumen, but has, sadly, failed to show the same good taste and so his texts often take on a frivolously extravagant tone that is at odds with both character and atmosphere. In such cases one appreciates the reticence of his less confident colleagues.

Another important equilibrium translators are called upon to cultivate is that between the foreign and the familiar notes in their work. There is a constant temptation to discover native parallels to details in the fictional world of the original. Such discoveries come naturally and they constitute one of the chiefest emotional rewards in the act of translation. But the gratification may be delusive. For the parallelism between two very different cultures is for the most part superficial and it is very easy to unwittingly create an entirely new picture along these lines. The most serious danger for an inexperienced Bulgarian translator is to slip into a colorful Balkan setup replacing the West European one of the original. In order to avoid this thorough naturalization of the material, an approach typical of the early phase of the reception history, it is perhaps wise to retain in the new text some early modern English realia in spite of their foreignness. Here we may wish to include knightly accoutrements, weaponry, social ranks, political and religious institutions, popular customs, etc. It might, for instance, be preferable to carry over into the translation such aristocratic titles as "prince," "earl," "duke," "baron," and the like, as well as addresses of the kind of "sir," "madam," "my lord," "my lady" as pointers to a British setting rather than replacing all these with local pseudo-equivalents and thus completely erasing the difference between here and there. Even topical references, with all their undeniable opacity for an audience far removed in space and time, should not be lightly jettisoned.

The practice of Bulgarian translation shows a good deal of latitude in dealing with such matters. It is, as usual, best to take the middle road. A case in point is the group of telltale names of humorous personages in the comedies. In the past they were not infrequently left in their original form—like all other personal names. The ironical labels attached by the author to some of his personages were consequently lost. It was thanks to Valeri Petrov that the meaningfulness of these names was finally done full justice to. His work demonstrates how cultural distance can be retained in spite of the acculturation that the text is obliged to undergo in any translation. Thus Speed is turned into *Skok* (Jump or Skip), Dull into *Pun* (Log), Costard into *Kratun* (Gourd/Pate), Sir Toby Belch into Sir Toby *Hluts* (Hiccup), Sir Andrew Aguecheek into Sir Andrew *Chikchirik* (Chirrup), etc. The principle seems to be that the Bulgarian name should disclose the respective personage's nature in a way as suggestive as—though not necessarily identical to—that of the English one. The deviation from full equivalence is necessitated by the exigency to make the new name sound not as a Bulgarian nickname but as a dually oriented lexicosemantic unit, conveying a clear, albeit often figurative, meaning for the new audience while at the same time resembling what sounds like a typical English name to it. For the most part the desired effect is achieved by choosing short, preferably monosyllabic, words containing consonant clusters or other characteristics denoting "Englishness."

An even more complicated case of "foreignness" is presented by plays with a non-English setting. The Italian stories are especially problematic. The original text has a strong tendency to anglicize names, titles, addresses, and details of the environment, thus subduing most of the strangeness of other places and drawing them closer to home. As a result we get such family names as Capulet and Montague or such personal ones as Tybalt, Balthasar, Peter, Gregory, Friar Lawrence, and Friar John, or such place names as Freetown, all associated with Verona. Ognyanov introduces most of this English linguistic coloring of the Italian scene into his translation, but Petrov feels obliged to purge it away from his version. Consequently, his names are by and large restored to what is supposed to be their authentic form: Capuletti, Montechi (the respective "ladies" becoming "signoras"), Pietro, Gregorio, Lorenzo, and Giovanni, leaving only a few unrevised. Freetown, of course, resumes its much more sonorous appellation of Villafranca, and Romeo is seen by Benvolio to walk dejectedly "underneath the grove of fig trees" rather than the original "sycamore," an emendation apparently aimed at reinforcing the southernness of the setting. Petrov's strategy in *The Merchant of Venice* is very much the same. Here the Duke of Venice becomes the Doge of Venice, the Marquis of Monferrat is transformed into Monferrato, Launcelot Gobbo turns into Lancilotto Gobbo, and his mother Margery into Margarita, while Belmont is duly restored to Belmonte.

This thorough re-Italianization of the material is now accepted as the only sensible solution of the problem, but it may be argued that it erases an important feature of Shakespeare's text, that is, the partial naturalization of an imported story. If we decide to pay more attention to this peculiarity of the original, we shall have to grapple with another difficult problem: does the author's approach prompt us to similarly naturalize the play in each of our own languages and cultures or would we be more faithful to his work if we retained its anglicized Italianness along the lines preferred by Ognyanov? The answer to this conundrum is not at all apparent.

It is perhaps even less easy to deal with instances of other languages spoken in the plays or of other nationals speaking English with their characteristic accents. *Henry V* is particularly rich in such linguistic inserts: the King's conversation with the French princess in her own language, on the one hand, and the various ways in which English was spoken on the British Isles as demonstrated by Fluellen, Macmorris, and Jamy. (Even tougher problems are faced by the translators of the Spanish passages in Ben Jonson's *The Alchemist* or Lacy's Dutch approximations in Dekker's *The Shoemaker's Holiday*.) As these alternative ways of speaking in each case have to be related to the default language of the play, its translation has to orchestrate the whole polyphonic composition anew by preserving the meaningful distances between central and peripheral ways of speaking without transferring the whole scene into another geographical region. Petrov's translation occasionally slips into an acoustic suggestion that Fluellen is something like a German national trying to speak Bulgarian, Jamy reminds you of a Serb, and Macmorris must have a speech defect. Such unplanned effects are unfortunate but they are probably impossible to fully avoid unless the translator is willing to obliterate the whole spectrum of phonetic variants exhibited by the original.

The tendency to cultivate an element of foreignness in translation can affect even the more strictly codified levels of the language. Some translators, for instance, believe that the predominance of masculine line endings in English verse creates a special sound and should therefore be imitated at all costs. In certain languages, especially the more heavily inflected ones, such configuration is very difficult to achieve and would anyway have an unnatural ring. Traditional Bulgarian verse usually alternates masculine and feminine endings and any exclusion of the one or the other kind would sound strange.

Another characteristic of the English language that is particularly noticeable to the translator of poetry is the striking brevity of its words and phrases. To take for example a line considered earlier,

Blow, winds, and crack your cheeks! rage, blow!—

it consists of monosyllables only and this makes its adequate translation a formidable task in most other languages. In such cases Valeri Petrov was induced to coin new words—especially abstract nouns—shorter than the existing ones in order to pack more of the original meaning into the available prosodic space. Thus, with the help of Shakespeare, a peculiarity of the English language has managed to penetrate so deeply into Bulgarian as to mold some of its morphology.

The length of the utterance should, by the way, be closely considered in all its aspects when we deal with a dramatic text. In order to sound right, the way it normally does in Shakespeare—not as a literary exposition but as verbal action—its units should be speakable and expressive of a concrete state of mind. Any overambitious attempt to cram all possible nuances of the original message into its new form can easily result in unpronounceable monstrosities and a serious slackening of the text's rhythmic sinews. The very bulk of inflated texts makes it difficult to stage them. A recent survey of the latest Shakespearean translations in Balkan countries conducted by the Belgrade colleague Vujadin Milanovič shows that *Macbeth*'s total of 1,963 lines has risen to 2,265 in Albanian; 2,410 in Bulgarian; 2,045 in Croatian; 2,220 in Greek and 2,754 in Serbian—an average increase of almost 20 percent coming up to 40 in one case (Milanovič 1996). This picture can probably be taken as representative of the situation in all Europe and, possibly, the world. Translators who really care for the reproduction not just of the sense of Shakespeare's poetic drama but of its characteristic sound too, must privilege selection over thoroughness as the guiding principle of their work.

Lastly, we should not beguile ourselves that as translators we are absolutely free to choose the method we believe in and employ it in its pristine form. Our hands and our minds, our languages themselves are tightly bound to long traditions and new fads that cannot be defied—we have to negotiate our every move with these broad elements in which and through which we function, winning some and losing some.

The Bulgarian tradition of translating and presenting poetic drama was from the very first dominated by the French and German neoclassical exemplars and Shakespeare continues to be markedly disciplined by this aesthetic habit. Consequently, he is made more formally rhetorical than he really is. The text frequently acquires a certain independence from the action on the stage and at times is recited. This was, anyway, the norm in the past. From the late 1950s a countercurrent that tried to play down the poetic character and the verse form of the dramas, foregrounding the "naturalness" of their language, started making itself noticeable in the theater. The modern trend, especially since Peter Brook's tour of Eastern Europe in the 1970s, has been that of the "physical theater," which relies on the effects of mise-en-scène and largely dispenses with the text as a complex fabric of meaningful sound.

This virtual erasure of the text has, fortunately, been counteracted by the new, highly artistic re-creation of Shakespeare's plays I have referred to more than once, Valeri Petrov's rendition. It reveals to the sensitive ear the rich interpretative potentials that their language offers, making it impossible to ignore this language completely. All this comes to show that, far from being a mere handmaid to the theater, translation can sometimes give it shape and direction. In order to do so, it has to render not just the outline of physical and verbal action but its vibrating tissue of "noises, sounds and sweet airs, that give delight, and hurt not."

Note

1. All emphases here and in later quotations are added.

Translation and Performance
Alessandro Serpieri

A FEW YEARS AGO I WAS INVITED BY STANLEY WELLS TO STRATford to organize and run a seminar on "Shakespeare in Translation" based on three main issues: (1) aspects of the history of Shakespearean translation into various languages; (2) theories of dramatic translation; (3) the actual experience of translating Shakespeare into French, Italian, Spanish, and other languages.

Apart from the different opinions regarding the problem of rendering Shakespeare's iambic pentameter in other languages, the overall discussion revealed an interesting convergence of both theoretical and practical approaches. This common view witnessed a radical change in contemporary critical sensibility, connected with the recent developments of dramatology as a specific method for tackling texts that at some stage are destined to abandon their literary, that is, written, status. Most of the participants,[1] if not all, agreed on the following crucial points:

a. dramatic translation must take into account the nonlinguistic codes embedded in dramatic language. Dramatology, considered as a semiotic approach oriented to grasp the theatrical event as a whole, can offer important keys to locate the theatrical route *within* the dramatic text: in fact drama is both voice and action in space, and any translation should first of all be faithful to the performative aspect of speech;
b. whenever possible, a certain amount of literalness in Shakespeare translation proves to be not only more faithful to the literariness of the text, but also more functional to its theatrical implications than any kind of explanation or expansion of meaning;
c. the original semantics and rhetoric should be saved even when this means slightly forcing, overstretching, the semantic import of the target language;
d. rhythm (which is part of the prosodic pattern, but is also

strictly related to syntax and rhetoric) is no less important than semantics. The question of free choice as regards a codified or an uncodified meter in the target language text was, however, left unsolved.

I will here try to go briefly into the issues just sketched. Let us start from dramatology, which investigates the specific features of a language in which other nonlinguistic (theatrical) codes are embedded. Following the Aristotelian distinction between narration (*diegesis*) and drama (*mimesis*), we may all agree that diegesis is self-sufficient in its textuality; it privileges the utterance (*enoncé*) over the act of utterance (*énonciation*); it does not need a pragmatic context to which to refer; it is shaped according to a temporal axis mostly based on the past; it is able to move easily from one temporal and spatial level to another. Dramatic mimesis, on the other hand, is institutionally tied to the speaking process (*énonciation*); it requires a pragmatic context, which is virtual on the page and actualized on the stage; its temporal axis is always based on the present; its space is that of *deixis*.

As Pirandello put it, theater is essentially "spoken action." Drama in fact expounds a story through a dynamic progression of intersecting speech acts and corresponding actions. Speech acts articulate along deictic and performative segments connected with a pragmatic context, and implement the joints of the story. In a word, it is language *in situation* that inscribes in itself the nonverbal or, more precisely, the implicitly lexicalized messages of its referential and pragmatic context. Meaning in drama seems to depend primarily upon deixis, the referential axis that regulates speech acts: even rhetoric, just as grammar and syntax, is related to deixis. In fact it subsumes and sorts out the meanings vehicled by the images, by the linguistic modes (prose, poetry), by rhythm, by the different discursive styles of the characters, by proxemic relations, by the kinesics of movement, etc. Moreover, the speech act as a situated message, while necessarily referential, must at the same time *perform* something on the stage. A dramatic speech act is never a simply locutionary act: in Austin's terms, it is rather *illocutionary* (that is, having the task of informing, ordering, warning, undertaking, etc.) and/or *perlocutionary* (that is, bringing about or achieving something by saying words) (Austin 1962). And that is not all. As has been noted, even the imperative and the interrogative forms have a performative quality in drama, since they express command or uncertainty, and therefore turn out to be *acts* of commanding or interrogating. We can go even further and consider as intrinsically performative: syntax, style, rhythm, and meter, as stylistic features of characters in action/situation.

Thus dramatic performativity unfolds itself within deixis and constitutes the core of a genre, which represents an action (the original Greek sense of *drama*) through the speech acts of characters talking and moving on deictic tracks within ostensive and spatial relations. On both the performative and the deictic levels dramatic language conveys most, if not all, of the codified and conventional stage signs that contribute to the overall, multimedia theatrical performance: intonation, mimic, gestures, proxemics, kinetics etc. (what Brecht altogether defined as *Gestus*).

Accordingly, the semiological unit of dramatic language seems to be a complex sign or, better, a band of sign relations to be identified within the speaker's deictic-performative action. This amounts to an oriented enunciation that cannot be considered as a bit of information, an image or a narrative microsequence, but rather as an indexical and pragmatic utterance on the stage (but already *inscribed* within drama). Characters speak in many ways: they ask, answer, imply, simulate, declare, allude, narrate, anticipate further acts, presume, pretend, command, etc., and in so doing they address each other, or refer to objects, or parts of the stage, or to the audience. Therefore, we can divide the seemingly incessant flow of their speeches into several units according to the characters' deictic-performative orientations, which correspond to the shifting of their spatial and locutionary attitudes.

Translation should try to follow as closely as possible this complex—both linguistic and semiotic—track. I will soon go back to the specific features of dramatic language. But first I would like to dwell briefly on the literary richness and complexity of Shakespeare's texts, a literariness that should never be overlooked by regarding his plays like mere scripts for the stage, pretexts for acting. The extraordinary linguistic and thematic richness of his plays offers textual evidence of a highly imaginative mind caught within the dramatic contradictions of a turbulent age. In translating Shakespeare one must be aware that what needs to be rendered is not only the play of characters and of actions, but also the interplay of cultural codes and modes of perception whose conflict mirrored on stage the struggle between different cultural paradigms. In fact it was an age that was questioning its own historical heritage, and opening the way to new, unstable cognitive, axiological, and ideological parameters. Reality was becoming manifold, uncertain, and relative: it was, metaphorically speaking, a stage endowed with numerous wings, showing a prismatic play of multiple points of view. Every aspect of the world was liable to be newly recoded, and it is in such a vertiginous scenario that we must locate the enormous *energy* of Shakespeare's language, which dramatically hybridizes world pictures, styles, ideologies, perceptions. Language itself underwent a sort of radical shake-up, which Shakespeare's inventiveness took to its extreme, producing hybrid registers and styles, a flurry of new words—especially compounds—and stretching the syntactical potentialities beyond the limits of what was conventional or generally accepted. As many critics have noticed, Shakespeare had an extraordinary ability to activate the various different senses of almost every word, and unexpectedly to either put them together or set them one against the other. There followed a dramatic concert of meanings sometimes difficult to disentangle, especially when a number of contrasting semantic perspectives are opened up.

As a result, the translator has not only to face linguistic, but also epistemological problems, because he must bring about a *similar* cognitive and imaginative turbulence. But, after all, in spite of the sometimes insuperable difficulties, Shakespeare's plays are still very much alive just because they continue to transmit a rich idea of how an elusive world can be refracted through a complex and "myriad-minded" perspective.

The translator must therefore deal with the multileveled energy of his texts in order to keep them vital and communicative also to a modern, non-English reader. More specifically, he or she has to render in the target language the *energy* of dramatic speech, which is virtual on the page, while showing all its pragmatic significance on the multicoded stage. The multifaceted energy of Shakespearean drama can be briefly sketched as follows:

1. It springs from the complex representation of a rapidly changing world.

2. It is linked to the theatrical *space*, any enunciation being related to the speaker, to other characters, to objects (real or imaginary), and to the audience. Besides language, the performance thus involves mimic, gestures, movements, etc.
3. It has to do with the theatrical *time*, the "here and now" in which the speech acts absorb both past and future, pushing forward the "continuous present" of drama.

Any dramatic translation will consequently be both interlinguistic and intersemiotic since it must take into account the stage devices embedded in the original text. I will start with a few simple examples of deixis. In *Hamlet* 2.2, Polonius expounds to the king and queen his theory of the cause of the prince's madness, and, when asked if he is quite sure of it, he peremptorily puts his life at stake: "Take this from this if this be otherwise."[2] His play on three *this*es (the first two referential, the third anaphorical) belongs to his rhetorical attitude, while being at the same time a stage figure that should not be paraphrased in translation, for instance with something like "Cut off this head from this trunk if this which I have been telling you comes out not to be true." Similarly, Macbeth's phrase on entering the stage for the first time as a king (3.1), "To be thus is nothing / But to be safely thus,"[3] is an extraordinarily elliptic meditation on the precariousness of his new rank. Macbeth is here marked by the signs of royalty (a crown on his head, maybe a scepter in his hand), and the double deictic *thus* is distributed in the figure of parallelism reinforced by strong accents: this both shows the rank of Macbeth and immediately points to its vanity. In this case, too, the translated text should not paraphrase, unravel, the theatrical ellipsis.

The stage track inscribed in drama is not always so evident. Let us take for example *Hamlet* 3.4.220, where the prince leaves his mother and addresses the dead Polonius with grim irony: "Come, sir to draw toward an end with you." The primary linguistic meaning is "to finish with you," but the phrase at the same time activates, on the theatrical level, a secondary meaning that has to do with the interpretation of the verb *to draw* as to pull, to haul. While uttering these words, Hamlet is in fact tugging away the corpse. Dramatic language shelters an intersemiotic play, as is confirmed by the following scene (4.1), where Gertrude answers the question of the king about the movements of Hamlet. Where is he gone? "To *draw apart* the body he hath kill'd." In my translation I tried to render the two meanings expressed by the verbal phrase, pointing both to the semantic level and to the action proper: "Venite, signore, per *tirare* fin in fondo il discorso con voi."

We noticed that the performativity of drama articulates along deictic orientations related to the various ways in which characters move and address each other. The asides make this point particularly evident because characters suddenly change their referential axis, shifting from an interlocutor to another or to the audience. However, deictic orientations contained in dramatic speeches are always dynamically at work, even in soliloquies. I will briefly refer to one of Macbeth's many monologues in 2.1. Let us see some of its segments:

> Is *this* a dagger which *I* see before *me*,
> The handle toward *my* hand? | Come, let *me* clutch *thee*. |
> *I* have *thee* not, and yet *I* see *thee* still. |
> Art *thou* not, fatal vision, sensible
> To feeling as to sight? Or art *thou* but
> A dagger of the mind, a false creation
> Proceeding from the heat-oppressèd brain? |
> *I* see *thee* yet, in form as palpable |
> As *this* which now *I* draw. |
> *Thou* marshall'st *me* the way that *I* was going,
> And such an instrument *I* was to use. |
> *Mine* eyes are made the fools o'th' other senses,
> Or else worth all the rest. | *I* see *thee* still,
> And on *thy* blade and dudgeon gouts of blood,
> Which was not so before. | There's no *such* thing.
> It is the bloody business which informs
> *Thus* to *mine* eyes . . .[4]
>
> (ll. 34–50, my italics)

First, Macbeth has the vision of an imaginary dagger in the air, whose status he tries to certify by the evidence of the deictic *this* and by describing its position in space: the handle offered to his hand is an icon prompting him to the deed he is going to perform. Then, Macbeth addresses directly the object with an accompanying gesture, and his mimic frustration is likewise inscribed in his language. Questions about the status of the dagger then arise in his mind, but soon he changes his meditative attitude and asserts the preternatural "reality" of the visionary object by comparing it with the solid evidence of his own dagger, which now he draws. At this point he has ascertained the symbolic function of the dagger in the air, but his sensibility has split down through the diverging of sight and touch: the noble sight is being made the fool of the baser touch—and the disarrangement of the perceptive hierarchy comes thus to mirror the upheaval of the political hierarchy that his action is going to produce. The vision not only persists, but develops in time, now showing gouts of blood that point to a murder already performed. Macbeth is horrified at this, but soon afterward he denies reality to his vision. Alternatively, throughout these lines, he adheres to the possible reality of his vision and detaches himself from it. The soliloquy goes on, but the first part is sufficient to show the paramount importance of deictics and deictic orientations in drama, whose faithful translation is therefore imperative.

If dramatic language always moves and performs, syntax, as a consequence, must be one of the main vehicles of performativity. Drama is in its own nature pluridiscursive and pluristylistic, such a plurality being entrusted first of all to the linguistic modes of different characters who speak—and therefore act—according to their peculiar roles and functions. Consequently, the translator must avoid homologating them at a syntactical level, because it is here—as well as through grammar, lexicon, style, rhetoric, and even rhythm and meter—that the characters deploy their attitudes and tactics together with their axiological and ideological assumptions. The *tactics* through which they argue seem to me first of all syntactical: they organize their speeches in a way that at the same time characterizes them, making them act in and through language, and lends rhythm to their stage movements. Speech acts mean, beyond and above their semantics, according to their syntagmatic expression.

Let us see, for instance, in *Hamlet* 1.2, the first long speech of the king, which at the same time characterizes him as a subtle and suspicious character, and deploys his indirect and machiavellian strategy:

> Though yet of Hamlet our dear brother's death
> The memory be green, and that it us befitted
> To bear our hearts in grief, and our whole kingdom
> To be contracted in one brow of woe,

> Yet so far hath discretion fought with nature
> That we with wisest sorrow think on him
> Together with remembrance of ourselves.
> Therefore our sometime sister, now our queen,
> Th'imperial jointress of this warlike state,
> Have we as 'twere, with a defeated joy,
> With an auspicious and a dropping eye,
> With mirth in funeral and with dirge in marriage,
> In equal scale weighing delight and dole,
> Taken to wife. Nor have we herein barr'd
> Your better wisdoms, which have freely gone
> With this affair along. For all, our thanks ...[5]

This speech shapes itself—through its convolutions, parallelisms, oxymora, suspension—as the utterance of an illegitimate king who is looking for the legitimization of his newly grasped power. His opening sentence runs through seven lines, showing his concern in both *remembering* and arguing the necessity of *forgetting* the past legitimate king. His second sentence develops through seven more lines: note the oxymora, the parentheses, and the suspension of the verbal function. His syntax is a subtle net of semantic balances aiming at obtaining consensus. This intent comes to the fore in the following three lines, where he addresses the notables of the kingdom for the support they have given him for his coronation and marriage, and flatteringly gives them credit of *better wisdoms*. Up to this point he has made a speech of domestic policy. Now he can pass to foreign policy, and informs the court of what they already know ("Now follows that you know young Fortinbras"). Here he spins a sentence of nine lines followed by another of thirteen. His strategic procedures are much more important than what he actually says. The translator therefore should not disentangle the passage by using shorter sentences and giving them a less convoluted manner.

Convolution is typical also of the rhetorical and pedagogical syntax of Polonius. Let us look at just one example from his speech to Laertes in 1.3:

> ... Beware
> Of entrance to a quarrel, *but* being in,
> Bear't that th'opposed may beware of thee.
> Give every man thy ear, *but* few thy voice;
> Take each man's censure, *but* reserve thy judgement.[6]

Quite different, of course, is the syntax of Hamlet, extremely varied according to his interlocutors (or to himself as interlocutor in the soliloquies). At times it is fragmentary, but it can also be high-sounding, or mimetic, or parodistic, or even destructive: in a word, it appears centerless, as Hamlet is, the discursive production of a hero always exploring language without being able to discover either the foundations of being or the strategy of existing.

To sum up, one can safely claim that syntax is essential to performance on the stage. But of course syntax is just one component of dramatic language, coterminous with style, rhetoric, rhythm, and meter. One can think for example of the decisive importance of the syntactical *and* the rhetorical components in relation to the stage action of characters such as Iago and Othello. Iago's language develops through disjunctive, suspensive, and negative clauses; Othello's mainly through expanded and assertive constructs. Accordingly, the rhetoric of Iago exploits the rhetorical figures of irony and litotes, whereas that of Othello often moves around hyperbole.

Of no less performative relevance are figures such as antanaclasis (for instance in *Richard III*), and, generally speaking, all the figures of speech (or *schemata* in Greek) that contribute to both the meaning and the rhythm of dramatical exchanges: the figures of repetition (anaphora, epiphora, etc.) and the figures related to order (anastrophe, hyperbaton, isocolon, etc.). Brian Vickers put it very clearly:

> Modern criticism has rediscovered the tropes extremely well . . . but the figures have yet to be generally accepted . . . The figures sometimes involve changes of meaning, but they are primarily concerned with *the shape or physical structure* of language, the placing of words in certain *syntactical* positions, their repetition in varying patterns (to make an analogy with music, tropes exist in a vertical plane, like pitch or harmony; the figures exist in a horizontal plane, like rhythm or other stress-devices). (Vickers 1971, 86–87, my italics)

Dramatic exchanges may pivot on such figures throughout a whole scene, as we can see in the verbal duel of Richard and Lady Anne (*Richard III*, 1.2.68–86). A brief selection may be sufficient to show how speeches rebound from one character to another:

Richard: Lady, you know no rules of charity,
   Which renders good for bad, blessings for curses.
Anne: Villain, thou know'st no law of God nor man.
   No beast so fierce but knows some touch of pity.
Richard: But I know none, and therefore am no beast.
Anne: O wonderful, when devils tell the truth!
Richard: More wonderful, when angels are so angry.
   Vouchsafe, divine perfection of a woman,
   Of these supposèd crimes to give me leave
   By circumstance but to acquit myself.
Anne: Vouchsafe, diffused infection of a man,
   Of these known evils but to give me leave
   By circumstance t' accuse thy cursèd self.
Richard: Fairer than tongue can name thee, let me have
   Some patient leisure to excuse myself.
Anne: Fouler than heart can think thee, thou canst make
   No excuse current but to hang thyself.
Richard: By such despair I should accuse myself.
Anne: And by despairing shalt thou stand excused.[7]

The duel goes on through the figures of anaphora (with change of value: positive-negative, negative-positive: ll. 68–70, 74–75, 75–78, 81–83), epiphora, parison and isocolon (almost everywhere), chiasmus distributed in two different speeches (ll. 71–72), etc. Translation should devote particular attention to such rhetorical texture, which marks the rhythm of exchanges.

Rhythm is a highly performative vehicle in drama. It has been defined as a measured *flow* (the original Greek meaning of the word) of accents or beats according to particular patterns that may or may not establish a regular meter. Grammar, syntax, and style run side by side through rhythm. In drama, and particularly in poetic drama such as Shakespeare's for the most part is, rhythm and meter do make *voices act*. The question is: how can translation render the original sound? In search for impossible equivalencies, it has to deal with the different body and skin of the words of another language, starting from the morphological and phonological levels. Then it has to arrange these new bodies and skins, all of them endowed with different sounds and lengths, within rhythmical and possibly metrical measures. An impossible, and at the same time inevitable, task. Which raises a preliminary and unavoidable question: should the original meter be rendered in a regular meter of the target language? In other words, should rhythm be formally reorganized in a regular recurrence of durations and stresses? The question of course is open to debate, but my opinion is that translating blank verse into a regular meter (which in Italian would be the hendecasyllable) may after all *betray* the sound, the music, and the distribution of meaning of the Shakespearean line. My preliminary choice was therefore to stick to rhythm rather than to meter, since fidelity to rhythm may better render the syntactical and rhetorical levels that especially contribute to the performativity of speeches. If we go back to the king's first speech in *Hamlet*, we may easily see how, though regular, the blank verse overflows its measure with frequent enjambments and therefore does not seem here to *perform* what is rather entrusted to the overall rhythm and syntax.

The case of songs, such as Feste's or Ariel's or Autolycus's, is to be dealt with in a different manner, because they exhibit a distinctive music (together, sometimes, with a music proper that was supposed to accompany words), and have an intrinsic performative quality. I have always tried to render songs through a more or less regular meter and through rhymes. The case of rhyming couplets is also different when they have *more* than the historically conventional function of closing a scene, or a semi-scene, and may therefore sound rather clumsy in the framework of quite different contemporary conventions. See for instance the abundant use of couplets in the first and third scene of *Richard II*, where they appear as the very form through which the ceremony of the challenge between Bolingbroke and Mowbray—secretly involving the king himself—deploys its false incidents and rituals. The king pretends to act as a neutral judge of the dispute, but he is in fact the real accused. His defense relies on a false ceremony in which he asserts impartiality and at the same time stresses his royal role, thus minimizing his parentage with Bolingbroke. The exchanges in this false ceremony often articulate in couplets, where rhymes sometimes rebound from one character to another and always regulate both their attitudes and their movements. Here meter and rhyme may have to be reproduced in translation. Meter is equally functional in many other cases, such as the exchanges between Romeo and Juliet at their first encounter. But otherwise plain blank verse may, in my opinion, be sacrificed to the advantage of rhythm, syntax, and rhetoric.

Translation has to cope with the large overall questions of syntax, rhetoric, style, rhythm, and meter. But at the same time it must face the microstructures of single overdetermined words, of cultural units, of linguistic knots, of local or intratextual isotopies or pluriisotopies, of semantic fields and synonymic clusters, and of textual cruces.

Here I can give only a sketchy survey of some of these problems. I will start from the denotation and connotation conveyed by a single lexeme. For example, in *Hamlet*, 2.2.174, when Polonius asks the distracted prince: "Do you know me, my lord?" and receives this disconcerting answer: "Excellent well, you are a fishmonger." The denotative sense of the word is of course a seller of fish, while the connotative is "pander," an oblique charge to Polonius (in Q1 it is clearly a charge for having used Ophelia as a bait for confession, since this exchange comes *after* the Nunnery scene in which Hamlet, at a certain point, has clearly become aware of the trap laid against him; in Q2/F this charge appears less perspicuous). The Italian translations usually miss the connotation, while I tried to render it relying on intonation and suspension in order to transmit the idea of Polonius's *selling* not just fish but his daughter: "Eccellentemente: siete un venditore, di pesce."

Lexemes may also be cultural units, which translation must consider whether to transmit according to their historical value or not. *Titus Andronicus*, 3.2.12, where the desperate Titus thus addresses the poor, disfigured, and defaced Lavinia offers a good example: "Thou map of woe, that thus dost talk in signs." How should one render the word *map*? Commentators usually actualize the meaning: Maxwell (Arden edition), for instance, glosses it as "image, embodiment." Italian translators far too often follow this reading adopting words ranging from image (*immagine*) to figure (*figura*). I decided to stick to the original: "Tu mappa di dolore, che così parli per segni." The word *map* was at that time particularly rich with meanings, being as it was at the center of various cultural codes: technical-cartographic, mercantile and commercial, adventurous and fantastic. In literary texts it revealed a great imaginative suggestion: see John Donne for example, but also Shakespeare's *Twelfth Night*, 3.2.79–81, where Maria, referring to the beguiled Malvolio, who is reading the forged letter, says: "He does smile his face into more lines than are in the new map with the augmentation of the

Indies." In Titus's speech, *map* is particularly pregnant, since it agrees with the metaphorical exchange between microcosm and macrocosm so recurrent in the whole play, and it perfectly adheres to the verbal function *talk in signs*: the defaced Lavinia can only talk in signs in order to reveal her story in the same way as contemporary maps talked in signs about known and unknown lands.

Isotopies—in a very rough definition, lines of meaning mainly entrusted to grammar and semantics—may be explicit or implicit. Often metaphorical, they always should be pinpointed and rendered in translation. To give just one example, see *Macbeth*, 5.2.12–25, where Caithness and Angus discuss the situation of the desperate Macbeth under siege and point to his state of mind:

> *Caithness*: Great Dunsinane he strongly fortifies.
> Some say he's mad ... But for certain
> He cannot *buckle* his distempered cause
> Within the *belt* of rule.
> *Angus*: ... Now does he feel his title
> *Hang loose* about him, like a giant's *robe*
> Upon a dwarfish thief.
> *Menteith*: Who then shall blame
> His pestered senses to recoil and start,
> When all that is within him does condemn
> Itself for being there?[8] (my italics)

The clothing metaphor becomes immediately evident when, from *buckle/belt* (he cannot any longer dominate/constrain his *distempered cause*—an overdetermined clause: his uncontrollable passion, his mental sickness; his now indocile followers—to obey him) we pass *to hang loose* and *robe*. The clothing paradigm had established itself in 1.3.107–8: "Why do you *dress* me / In *borrowed robes*?" he had asked Angus, who greeted him with the title of Thane of Cawdor, and afterward in the same scene Banquo had thus commented the event: "New honours come upon him, / Like our strange *garments*, cleave not to their mould / But with the aid of use" (ll. 142–44). Much more secret is the metaphorical isotopy at l. 23, "His pestered senses to recoil and start," where a *bellum intestinum* is hinted at: Macbeth is now unable to dominate his senses, and his very personality splits down, the metaphor being that of his vital functions as fettered horses that recoil and start, refusing to stay calm in a stable.

His *starting* like a frightened horse had already been noted, in the ghost of Banquo scene, by Lady Macbeth who reproved him for "these flaws and *starts*" (3.4.62)—and she used the same verb in her later sleepwalking scene "you mar all with this *starting*" (5.1). A translation should keep track of all these occurrences and employ, though at a distance, the same words.

But when different metaphorical isotopies knit together in a single passage the task of translation gets much more difficult, and sometimes impossible. Let's take just one example, from *Hamlet*, 1.3.126–31, where Polonius dissuades Ophelia from continuing her relationship with the prince:

> Do not believe his vows; for they are brokers
> Not of that dye which their investments show,
> But mere implorators of unholy suits,
> Breathing like sanctified and pious bawds
> The better to beguile.[9]

In his typical syntax and semantics, he here conveys several lines of meaning, hardly graspable by any audience. The pluriisotopy springs from the initial *brokers*, which, as has been noted by Nigel Alexander (in his Macmillan edition), "maybe of three kinds and Polonius unites all three functions in this complex series of images: (a) dealers in finance who are not of the true color or appearance (dye) which their authorizing documents (investments) indicate but simply solicitors for improper requests who talk as if their proposals were holy and religious in order to deceive their victims; (b) go-betweens in matters of love who are not of the kind of men claimed by the garments they have borrowed (from the church) but simply makers of lewd and immoral suggestions who talk the language of marriage vows in order to deceive their victims, (c) dealers in old clothes—though this meaning is less fully worked out." And Nigel Alexander concludes: "Hamlet is thus a shady financier, a pander who promises marriage, and an old clothes man." The three isotopies, developing from the three different agents, continually overlap, so that all key words sound ambiguous, open to more than one meaning. Thus Polonius manages to convey an ambiguous image of Hamlet, false wooer of Ophelia. This image springs especially from his ingenious use of the following terms: *investments* 'financial documents, garments of go-betweens, secondhand clothes,' *implorators* 'solicitors, entreaters,' *unholy suits* 'profane procedures, improper mediations,' *bonds* 'contractual obligations, marriage vows, warranties.' Here we are really past the limit of translatableness. Theater directors know it very well and usually cut passages like this.

I will now come to paradigms, synonyms, and matrix-words. However different in their language and style the characters of a play may be, the semantics of a text offers paradigms that are typical not only of a character, but also of the entire work. See for example in *Hamlet* the paradigms or semantic fields of *sickness, flesh, ear, weapon, prison, madness*. These semantic fields produce synonymic constellations that throughout the action exhibit an open or secret internal hierarchy.

Let's take the paradigm of *madness* in Hamlet. It may be strictly madness (of the seventy-one occurrences in the canon twenty-two appear in this play); but it is also "transformation," "distemper," "lunacy," "affliction of his love," "wildness," "melancholy" (for Claudius); "lunacy," "ecstasy of love" (for Polonius); "ecstasy" (for Ophelia), etc. The translator has to find the right synonyms for a semantic field that operates through attenuation and through the questioning of the real state of Hamlet, who, in his turn, defines it as an "antic disposition."

Rendering matrix-words is of crucial importance since they act in the textual economy not so much as lexical units but as keys of a semantic system. And this is a very difficult task for the translator who must approximate at the same time the synonymic cluster and its internal hierarchy. Let us look at just one example from *Titus Andronicus*, 2.3, the scene in the forest where, following the plan of Aaron, Martius and Quintus plunge into a horrible pit or hole. It is one of the most symbolically strong and overdetermined horrific paradigms of this tragedy. The pit or hole is a tomb (l. 228: "monument"; l. 240: "grave") and an infernal cave (l. 236: "Cocytus"), and it is defined by synonyms ("pit," "hole," "hollow," "den") oscillating at the connotative level from the mortuary to the sexual meaning. It is, implicitly or explicitly, a mouth that sucks or breathes (l. 224: "blood-drinking pit"; l. 236: "Cocytus misty mouth") or eats (l. 235: "devouring"; l. 239: "swallowing"). It is also the womb of an enormous beast (l. 229: "ragged entrails"), and finally, at the culmination of all this alarming symbolism, it is a uterus or a vagina that swallows and buries instead of procreating (l. 239: "swallowing womb"). Mouth, tomb, womb (womb-tomb), the horrid pit or hole (l. 193: the "loathsome pit," so it is initially defined by Aaron), it is therefore the place of a double terror: terror of death and of sex as death. In the synonymic field, the lexeme *pit* appears to be hierarchically privileged, since it is the first to occur with the most perturbing qualifications. It is a highly frequent lexeme in this drama (ten occurrences, and all of them in this scene, on a total of twenty in the entire canon). Looking at the canon, one discovers that *pit* finds in *King Lear* (4.6.128–29) a very strong overdetermination as the final monstrous image of female sex ("There's hell, there's darkness, there is the sulphurous *pit*—burning, scalding, stench, consumption!"). The hierarchy of this synonymic field seems to be established both textually and macrotextually with the dominance of *pit*. Accordingly, in my translation I opted for *buco* as the matrix-word, and then for *buca, fossa, tana, cava,* for the other lexemes, thus trying to render the relational and differential play of synonyms in the scene. The choice of the matrix-word may have a performative value in the interpretation of directors and actors.

Finally we have textual criticism, which constitutes the very beginning or, rather, the very core of all translational work. Any translator has to deal as a philologist with quite a wide field of textual problems, the solution of which affects not only the language but also, on many occasions, the performance. I can here present a very scanty typology of cruces.

Let us start from a simple one, the different attribution of a speech that may change radically the meaning of a scene. In *Titus Andronicus*, 5.1.47–53, Aaron has been taken prisoner together with his child by Tamora, and Lucius, who wants them both hanged immediately, orders: "A halter, soldiers, hang him on this tree, / And by his side his fruit of bastardy." Aaron asks him not to touch his son: "Touch not the boy, he is of royal hand." Lucius does not bend: "Too like the sire for ever being good. / First hang the child, that he may see it sprawl— / A sight to vex the father's soul withal." At this point, in the early editions, Aaron intervenes in a desperate attempt to save his son: "Get me a ladder. Lucius, save the child." But both Pope and Capell attributed "Get me a ladder" to Lucius, leaving to Aaron "Lucius, save the child"; and

Capell added a stage direction that supported the emendation: "A ladder brought, which Aaron is made to ascend." The emendation substantially changes the action: in the early editions, Aaron takes the lead; in almost all the modern editions that accept the emendation, Aaron seems to be passively obliged to climb the ladder to the gallows. It seems to me that the early reading makes more sense: in order to save his child Aaron asks for a ladder and climbs it spontaneously to the gallows where he will recite his gospel of horrors. Here we can see how the translator's choice may affect the action itself. My translation followed the early reading.

Shakespeare's texts still keep many secrets. Translation may help to discover some of them. For instance it can disentangle confused original passages, and even recent conflations that lead to ridiculous results. Take for instance, in *Hamlet*, 4.2, the passage where he treats Rosencrantz and Guildenstern as sponges:

> *Rosencrantz*: Take you me for a sponge, my lord?
> *Hamlet*: Ay, sir, that soaks up the king's countenance, his rewards, his authorities. But such officers do the King best service in the end. **He keeps them,** *like an apple* in the corner of his jaw, [Q2 reading]—**he keeps them** *like an ape* **in the corner of his jaw** [F reading]—**he doth keep you** *as an Ape* **doth nuttes** [Q1 reading], first mouth'd to be last swallowed. When he needs what you have glean'd, it is but squeezing you, and, sponge, you shall be dry again.[10]

In this case only the usually reviled Q1 offers a satisfactory reading. The other two lack either the subject (Q2) or the object (F). Q1 offers the full meaning and a logical one, since it defines as nuts the food preserved by the ape in its mouth, something tasty and small enough to be taken in the corner of a jaw in order to grant the last savor. The compositors of Q2 certainly misunderstood the manuscript and comically ruined the sense, making the comparison disappear and incongruously putting a big object like an apple in the corner of the king's jaw. Not less comical was the interpretation of the compositors of F: they saved the ape but took out the food and so ruined the comparison, awkwardly obliging the king to open his mouth even more in order to lodge his officers, Gargantua-like, in one corner of it. Stubbornly sticking to their uncompromising contempt for Q1 as a degenerate offspring of the pure text, recent editors refuse any help from it: John F. Andrews follows Q2, Harold Jenkins and Philip Edward follow F, while G. R. Hibbard makes a bizarre conflation of Q2 and F ("He keeps them, like an ape an apple in the corner of his jaw"), and the same do Stephen Greenblatt and Susanne L. Wofford (who puts "an ape" inside square brackets). None of them want to acknowledge the fact that in this case it is Q1 that gives sense to the authoritative text, and not the reverse.

Finally, I will give an example of debatable emendation in one of the most difficult passages in the canon: *The Winter's Tale*, 1.2.136-44:

FOLIO READING
                      ... Can thy Dam, may't be
Affection? Thy Intention stabs the Center,
Thou do'st make possible things not so held,
Communicat'st with dreams (how can this be?)
With what's unreall: thou coactive art,
And fellow'st nothing. Then 'tis very credent,
Thou may'st co-joine with something, and thou do'st,
(And that beyond Commission) and I find it,
(And that to the infection of my Braines,
And hardning of my Browes.)[11]

ROWE'S EMENDATION
                      ... Can thy Dam? *may't be—
Imagination!* thou dost stab *to* th' Center.
Thou dost make possible things not be so held,
Communicat'st with Dreams—how can this be?
With what's unreal, thou coactive art,
And follow'st nothing. Then 'tis very credent,
Thou may'st co-join with something, and thou dost,
And that beyond commission, and I find it,
And that to the Infection of my Brains,
And hardning of my Brows.

The first editors, starting from Rowe, could make no sense out of the Folio reading and thought it better to emend the passage heavily. Pope and Johnson followed Rowe in breaking down the enjambment between the first and the second lines, and in substituting "imagination" for "affection," as well as the exclamation mark for the question mark. Moreover, in the fifth line Rowe substituted the comma for the colon of the Folio, thus linking "With what's unreal" to "thou coactive art." He was followed by Johnson, Warburton, Theobald, and then Malone, Collier, and Clark, these last three removing even the comma in the line in order to make the link absolutely clear. Warburton and Theobald still kept "imagination" in the place of "affection," but the later editors—with only the notable exception of Collier—starting from Steevens, returned to "affection," while keeping the exclamation mark and breaking down the enjambment from the previous line.

The reading of this difficult passage was thus established: in modern editions, apart from "imagination," Rowe's version, with all its extremely relevant changes in punctuation, and consequently in meaning, is still, with a few exceptions,[12] the accepted one.

How is this passage consequently interpreted? A critical line that goes from Capell to Kermode reads "affection" as the passion of jealousy that is beginning to shake Leontes. Another line (Steevens, Malone, etc.) reads "affection" as meaning "imagination," even though it rejects Rowe's emendation. Still another line, more faithful to the punctuation of the Folio, refers "affection" to Hermione ("thy dam") and interprets it as "lust," according to the meaning specified in the *OED* (s.v. "affection," II.3). Stephen Orgel (*The Oxford Shakespeare*) points out that "the referent of 'thy intention' is unclear, and upon this depends the meaning of the remainder of the speech"; but Jean Howard (*The Norton Shakespeare*) opts for Leontes's jealousy: "Passion (probably the passion of jealousy), your intensity ("intention") pierces my heart or to the core of my being."

To sum up, is Leontes referring here to Hermione's passion (love and lust) or to his passion (jealousy)? The Folio's reading is not that ambiguous: it is Hermione's passion. But are we sure that this passion is lust as it is conveyed by the word "affection" at the very beginning of the passage? In Greene's *Pandosto*, the source of the play, we find first "affected" and then "affection" twice at the beginning of the story, and while the narrator points out that it was a lawful, innocent feeling, he also ambiguously brings the reader to suspect that there is *more* than affection in this relationship.[13] A bit earlier in this same scene, when Leontes begins to feel suspicious, we read:

> Too hot, too hot!
> To mingle friendship far is mingling bloods.

> I have *tremor cordis* on me. My heart dances,
> But not for joy, not joy. This entertainment
> May a free face put on, derive a liberty
> From heartiness, from bounty, fertile bosom,
> And well become the agent. 'T may, I grant.
> But to be paddling palms and pinching fingers,
> As now they are, and making practised smiles
> As in a looking-glass; and then to sigh, as 'twere
> The mort o' th' deer—O, that is entertainment
> My bosom likes not, nor my brows.
>
> (ll. 108–19)

He is clearly questioning the nature of Hermione's *entertainment* of Polixenes: is it lawful or not? Is it just affection or something more? In the later passage, he seems to start meditating on the same point: may it be *only* affection? But immediately afterward he decides that it is too intense, too strong, to be only affection: it is lust, begotten by a preceding imaginary desire or fancy. I suppose that Shakespeare expanded the last statement quoted in Greene's narration, the hero abandoning the idea of a "honest affection" between his wife and his friend, and musing on the "disordinate fancy" of the former.

The whole passage shows the complex shifting significance of a meditation in progress, and therefore a dramatic energy that depends on ambiguous or rare words. Let us consider them.

"Affection" has eighty-three occurrences in the canon, and its meaning goes from emotion to feeling, to inclination, and passion.[14] Its ambiguous significance is best displayed in *The Merchant of Venice*, 4.1.50–52, where Shylock says:

> You'll ask me why I rather choose to have
> A weight of carrion flesh than to receive
> Three thousand ducats. I'll not answer that,
> But say it is my humour. Is it answered? ...
> Some men there are love not a gaping pig,
> Some that are mad if they behold a cat,
> And others when the bagpipe sings i' th' nose
> Cannot contain their urine; for *affection*,
> *Mistress of passion*, sways it to the mood
> Of what it likes or loathes.

Here "affection" appears to be hierarchically superior to "passion," and chronologically preceding it: it points to the condition of "being affected" by something very profound and impenetrable, almost a secret malady of the mind. If we follow the Folio's reading, we should then imagine that Leontes, soon after mentioning "affection" in the sense of friendly feeling, shifts to the other acceptation of passion or lust. This shifting should be seen in his immediate addressing himself to its dubious significance: "Thy intention." And "intention" is another complex word, meaning both aiming at something, like in the Latin *intendere* (to tend to, to aim at), and intensity. It is therefore both the subject Hermione is addressing her affection to, and the apparent intensity of its manifestation, which is frightening Leontes. This dangerous meaning of "affection" stabs the "centre": another rare word, which in Shakespeare means the center of the universe or of the earth or of man, and in this case his heart. But why is he using "centre" and not "heart"? In all probability because the flow of his thinking is here dismissing the idea of a more *superficial* affection than that of friendship, and concentrating on the extremity of passion, which is at the same time Hermione's lust and the effect it has on his very center of being (the two passions—lust and jealousy—being at this point closely interwoven).

Hermione's passion is now seen as limitless because it springs from the deepest layers of her mind: it was there *even before* finding the subject, Polixenes, on whom it now discharges itself. It lay hidden in her dreams, in what is *unreal* (another rare word in Shakespeare, since it occurs only twice, here and in *Macbeth*, 3.4.106, "unreal mock'ry, hence!"). According to the Folio's punctuation, the semicolon intervening here, "thou coactive art," is not linked with the previous phrase: *coactive* is an hapax and should mean here "coercive," "compulsory," as registered from 1605, and not necessarily "acting in concert," as stated by the *OED* with reference to this passage.[15]

If Hermione's passion has always been there, hidden in her most secret fantasies, it can very well *co-joine* (another hapax) with *something* real—with Polixenes at the moment—and being that *coactive*, once it has found its target, it knows no limits: it goes beyond "commission," another strange word in the context, which seems to mean beyond any lawful authorization of her conscience.

In a few lines of great dramatic intensity, "affection" has undergone a radical change, losing any shade of friendship and turning into passion (and lust). Furthermore it has shown Leontes its secret source in Hermione's unconscious, where it lay in the shape of imaginary desire and lust even before investing itself in a real lover. Woman is intrinsically a whore—as we can see in other passages in the canon: just think, for instance, of Posthumus's tirade on female innate lasciviousness—and her affection amounts to the *infection* of his brain, now working in its turn in the imaginary space within *nothing* and *something*, which is damnation.

Read in this key, the Folio needs no emendation. It is the task of the actor to make clear the elliptical shifting from the interrogation of "affection" to the answer it receives.

To conclude, the translator has to force his way into the original text with a greater indiscretion than that of the critic who may not lose the advantage of a distance in relation to his object. The translator is bound to enter the object, to investigate it, to palpate it in all of its connections and fissures. In a process that is at the same time interlinguistic and intratextual, he may sometimes discover hidden meanings that the native reader or critic is no longer capable to perceive, since certain phrases have been accepted in his language in slightly different ways, or because he is conditioned by a somewhat automatic comprehension. The translator's discoveries, in these cases, may come to revitalize, to regenerate the text, renewing its secret *energy*. From this point of view, translation can liberate forces that had remained hidden to native speakers and even to critics. The interlinguistic exchange may therefore provide surprising additions to textual hermeneutics.

Another aspect of translation concerns the amount of estrangement that it conveys into the target text. Estrangement being essential for any artistic invention, as has been shown for example by the theory of information, any disautomatization of the target language in the process of translation amounts to new expressive potentialities.

Notes

1. Among others, Suheyla Artemel, Manuel Conejero, Jean-Michel Déprats, Mladen Engelsfeld, Niels Hansen, Giorgio Melchiori, Kristian Smidt, Daniel Yang, Henryk Zbierski.

2. My translation: "Spiccate questa da questo se questo sta in altro modo."

3. My translation: "Essere così è nulla se non si è con sicurezza così."

4. My translation: "È un pugnale, questo, che vedo davanti a me, / l'impugnatura verso la mia mano? / Vieni, lasciati afferrare. Non ti prendo, ma ti vedo ancora. / Non sei percettibile al tatto, fatale visione, / come lo sei alla vista? O sei soltanto / un pugnale della mente, una falsa creazione / costruita dal cervello oppresso dalla febbre? / Ti vedo ancora, in forma palpabile / come questo che ora snudo. / Mi guidi nella direzione che stavo prendendo, / e uno strumento come questo stavo per usare. / I miei occhi sono diventati i buffoni degli altri sensi, / oppure valgono non più di tutti gli altri. / Ti vedo ancora, e sulla tua lama e sul manico / gocce di sangue, che prima non c'erano. / Non esiste questa cosa. È la faccenda sanguinaria / che così prende corpo ai miei occhi."

5. My translation: "Sebbene della morte del nostro caro fratello / Amleto la memoria sia ancora verde, / e a noi si convenga di recare cordoglio nel cuore, / e a tutto il nostro regno di star contratto / in un'unica fronte di dolore, / purtuttavia tanto ha il discernimento / combattuto con la natura che noi / con piú saggio dolore pensiamo a lui / ricordandoci al contempo di noi stessi. / Pertanto, la nostra un tempo sorella, / ora nostra regina, imperiale coerede / di questo stato guerriero, abbiamo noi, / per cosí dire, con gioia abbattuta, / con un occhio lieto e l'altro lacrimante, / con letizia nel funerale e lamentazione / nelle nozze, con uguale bilancia pesando / diletto e duolo, presa per moglie. / Né abbiamo, in ciò, escluso il vostro miglior senno, / che liberamente ha sostenuto tutto / questo affare. Per tutto, il nostro grazie."

6. My translation: "Guardati dall'attaccar briga, ma se ci sei dentro / comportati in modo che l'avversario debba guardarsi da te. / Concedi a tutti il tuo orecchio, ma a pochi la tua voce; / accetta l'opinione di ognuno, ma riservati il tuo giudizio."

7. My translation: "*Ric.*: Signora, voi non conoscete le regole della carità, / che rende bene per male, benedizioni per maledizioni. *An.*: Straccione, tu non conosci legge né divina né umana. / Nessuna bestia è così feroce da non conoscere un briciolo di pietà. / *Ric.*: Ma io non ne conosco affatto, e perciò non sono una bestia. / *An.*: Oh che meraviglia quando i diavoli dicono la verità! / *Ric.*: Oh maggior meraviglia quando gli angeli sono così infuriati. / Degnati, o divina perfezione di donna, / di darmi solo licenza che io mi scagioni / di questi supposti crimini, circostanziatamente. / *An.*: Degnati, o infetta peste d'uomo, / di darmi solo licenza che io accusi la tua maledetta persona / di questi ben noti delitti, circostanziatamente. / *Ric.*: O più bella di quanto la lingua possa dirti, concedimi / un po' di paziente ascolto perché io mi scusi. *An.*: O più lurido di quanto il cuore possa pensarti, / altra scusa non puoi avere se non quella di impiccarti. / *Ric.*: Una azione così disperata non farebbe che accusarmi. *An.*: E, in una azione così disperata, tu saresti scusato."

8. My translation: "*Caith.*: Fortifica al massimo il grande castello di Dunsinane. / C'è chi dice che è pazzo ... Ma è certo / che non riesce a stringere la sua causa malata / nella cintura del comando. *Ang.*: Ora egli sente che il suo titolo gli sta / troppo largo addosso, come la veste di un gigante / su un ladro nano. / *Ment.*: Chi può allora biasimare / i suoi sensi inceppati se recalcitrano e scartano, / quando tutto ciò che ha dentro si condanna / per il fatto di trovarcisi?"

9. My translation: "In breve, Ofelia, / non credere ai suoi voti, che sono

mezzani, / non del colore che mostrano i loro vestimenti, / ma meri procacciatori di cause profane / che suonano come impegni pii e santi / per meglio ingannare."

10. My translation: "*Rosen.*: Mi prendete per una spugna, mio signore? *Amleto*: Sissignore, che assorbe il favore del re, le sue ricompense, le sue influenze. Ma tali funzionari servono al re la miglior portata, alla fine. Egli se li tiene come fa la scimmia con le noccioline, in un angolo della mascella, i primi ad essere messi in bocca e gli ultimi ad essere ingoiati."

11. My translation: "Può la tua fattrice . . . / Può essere affetto? La tua intensità pugnala al centro. / Tu rendi possibili cose non credute tali, / comunichi con i sogni. Come può essere? / Con ciò che è irreale tu agisci di concerto / e ti accompagni al nulla. Allora è assai credibile / che tu possa congiungerti con qualcosa, / e lo fai, e lo fai oltre il lecito, e io lo scopro, / e questo mi infetta il cervello / e mi indurisce la fronte."

12. Orgel's edition in *The Oxford Shakespeare* maintains the Folio: "Can thy Dam, may't be / Affection? Thy" etc.).

13. "Bellaria, who in her time was the flower of courtesy, willing to shew how unfeignedly she loved her husband by his friend's entertainment, used him likewise so familiarly that her countenance bewrayed how her mind was affected towards him, oftentimes coming herself in his bed chamber to see that nothing should be amiss to mislike him.This honest familiarity increased daily more and more betwixt them . . . there grew such a secret uniting of their affections, that the one could not well be without the company of the other . . . He [Leontes] then began to measure all their actions, and [to] misconstrue of their private familiarity, judging that it was not for honest affection, but for disordinate fancy, so as he began to watch them more narrowly."

14. *OED*, s.v. "affection," II. Of the mind. 2.a. An affecting or moving of the mind in any way; a mental state brought about by any influence; an emotion or feeling. 3. Feeling as opposed to reason; passion, lust. Obsolete. Since 1300. 4. State of mind generally, mental tendency; disposition. Obsolete. 5. State of mind towards a thing; disposition towards, bent, inclination, penchant. Archaic. 6.a. Good disposition towards, goodwill, kind feeling, love, fondness, loving attachment. 10. An abnormal state of the body; malady, disease.

15. *OED*, s.v. "coactive," 1. Of the nature of force or compulsion; coercive, compulsory. Rare. 1605 T. Bell: The Pope hath no power coactive over any king. B. In passive sense. 1596: coactive fasting. 2. [co + active] Acting in concert. 1611: WT.

Bibliography

Aders, Ruth. 1987. "Mundart und Standardsprache auf Deutschschweizer Berufsbühnen: Stellungnahmen zur Praxis in jüngster Zeit." In *Mundart auf dem Berufstheater der deutschen Schweiz,* ed. Schweizerische Gesellschaft für Theaterkultur, 69–102. Willisau: Theaterkultur-Verlag.

Aers, Leslie, and Nigel Whealer, eds. 1991. *Shakespeare in the Changing Curriculum.* London: Methuen.

Amateur Theatre in Great Britain. 1989. London: Central Council for Amateur Theatre.

Anikst, Alexander. 1989. *Is Shakespeare Still Our Contemporary?* Ed. John Elsom. London: Routledge.

Ansúr, Alfredo. 1878. *Le Roi Traducteur ou Vive la République.* Lisbon: Tipografia Luso-Espanhola de Gumercindo de la Rosa.

Arany, János. 1962. "Zrínyi és Tasso." In *Arany János összes művei,* ed. Dezső Keresztury, vol. 10, *Prózai művek 1,* ed. Mária Keresztury, 330–439. Budapest: Akadémiai Kiadó.

———. 1966a. "A Cs. Kir. Tanhatósághoz." In *Arany János összes művei,* ed. Dezső Keresztury, vol. 13, *Hivatali iratok 1. Nagyszalonta—Nagykőrös—Budapest (1831–65),* ed. Endre Dánielisz, László Tőrös, and Pál Gergely, 102–3. Budapest: Akadémiai Kiadó.

———. 1966b. "Életrajzi pótlás." In *Arany János összes művei,* ed. Dezső Keresztury, vol. 13, *Hivatali iratok 1. Nagyszalonta—Nagykőrös—Budapest (1831–65),* ed. Endre Dánielisz, László Tőrös, and Pál Gergely, 104–6. Budapest: Akadémiai Kiadó.

———. 1968. "Fejes István költeményei." In *Arany János összes művei,* ed. Dezső Keresztury, vol. 11, *Prózai művek 2: 1860–1882,* ed. G. Béla Németh, 290–99. Budapest: Akadémiai Kiadó.

———. 1982. János Arany's letter to István Szilágyi, 9 March 1854. In *Arany János leveleskönyve,* ed. Györgyi Sáfrán, 226–28. Budapest: Gondolat.

[Araquistain, Luis]. 1916. "Cervantes y Shakespeare: Dos conmemoraciones." *España* 2, no. 55 (10 February): 13.

Armas y Cárdenas, José de. 1916. "Conversación de dos almas." In *A Book of Homage to Shakespeare,* ed. Israel Gollancz, 434. London: Oxford University Press.

———. 1916. "Inglaterra y Shakespeare." *España* 2, no. 67 (4 May): 11–12.

Arriaga, José. 1911. *Os Últimos 60 anos da Monarquia.* Lisbon: Livraria Editora.

Assmann, Aleida, and Dietrich Harth, eds. 1991a. *Mnemosyne, Formen und Funktionen der kulturellen Erinnerung.* Frankfurt: Fischer.

BIBLIOGRAPHY

———. 1991b. *Kultur als Lebenswelt und Monument*. Frankfurt: Fischer.

Assmann, Aleida, and Ute Frevert. 1999. *Geschichtsvergessenheit—Geschichtsversessenheit: Vom Umgang mit deutschen Vergangenheiten nach 1945*. Stuttgart: Deutsche Verlags-Anstalt.

Assmann, Jan, and Tonio Hölscher, eds. 1988. *Kultur und Gedächtnis*. Frankfurt: Suhrkamp.

Austin, John L. 1962. *How to Do Things with Words*. London: Oxford University Press.

Balan, Rada, Miruna Carianopol, Stefan Colibaba, Cornelia Coser, Veronica Focseneanu, Vanda Stan, and Rodica Vulcanescu. 1995. *English My Love*. Bucharest: Didactica si Pedagogica, R.A.

Banes, Sally. 1998. *Dancing Women: Female Bodies on Stage*. London: Routledge.

Bantas, Andrei, Petre Clontea, and Pia Brinzeu. 1993, 2000. *Manual de literatura engleza si americana*. Bucharest: Teora.

Barbu, Daniel. 1999. *Republica absenta*. Bucharest: Nemira.

Barrie, Sir James M. 1916. *Shakespeare's Legacy: A Farce*. London: Clement Shorter.

Bate, Jonathan. 1986. *Shakespeare and the English Romantic Imagination*. Oxford: Clarendon Press.

———. 1989. *Shakespearean Constitutions: Politics, Theatre, Criticism 1730–1830*. Oxford: Clarendon Press.

———. 1997. *The Genius of Shakespeare*. London: Picador.

———, ed. 1992. *The Romantics on Shakespeare*. Harmondsworth: Penguin.

Bauer, Roger, ed. 1988. *Das Shakespeare-Bild in Europa*. Berne: Francke.

Beckerman, Bernard. 1962. *Shakespeare at the Globe, 1599–1609*. New York: Macmillan.

Belgrad, Jürgen, ed. 1997. *TheaterSpiel: Aesthetik des Schul- und Amateurtheaters*. Hohengehren: Schneider Verlag.

Belsey, Catherine. 1991. "Making Histories Then and Now: Shakespeare from Richard II to Henry V." In *Uses of History: Marxism, Postmodernism and the Renaissance*, ed. Francis Barker, Peter Hulme, and Margret Iversen. Manchester: Manchester University Press.

Benjamin, Walter. 1968. "Theses on the Philosophy of History." In *Illuminations: Essays and Reflections*, ed. Hannah Arendt. New York: Schocken Books.

Bloom, Harold. 1994. *The Western Canon: The Books and the School of the Ages*. New York: Harcourt Brace.

———. 1999. *Shakespeare: The Invention of the Human*. London: Fourth Estate.

Bode, Christoph. 2000. "Azores High, Iceland Low: The Location and Dynamics of Shakespeare's Meaning and Value." In *Historicizing/Contemporizing Shakespeare: Essays in Honour of Rudolf Böhme*, ed. Christoph Bode and Wolfgang Kloos, 25–51. Trier: WVT.

Bohlmann, Joachim. 1988. "Two English Poets in East Europe: Shakespeare in the GDR." *Contemporary Review* 253: 154–55.

Böse, Maximilian, Norbert Lademann, and Jörg Siebold. 1987. *English for You VII*. Berlin: Volk und Wissen.

Bottoms, Janet. 1996. "Of *Tales* and *Tempests*: The Problematic Nature of Prose Re-tellings of Shakespeare's Plays." *Children's Literature in Education* 27: 73–86.

———. 2000. "Familiar Shakespeare." In *Where Texts and Children Meet*, ed. E. Bearne and V. Watson, 11–25. London: Routledge.

———. 2001. "Speech, Image, Action: Animating Tales from Shakespeare." *Children's Literature in Education* 32, no. 1: 3–15.

Bourdieu, Pierre. 1991. *Language and Symbolic Power*. Trans. Gino Raymond and Matthew Adamson. Ed. John B. Thompson. Cambridge: Polity Press, in association with Blackwell.

BRAE. 1916. *Boletín de la Real Academia Española*. 3: 245–47.

BRAE. 1917. *Boletín de la Real Academia Española*. 4: 261.

Braga, Teófilo. 1880. *História das Ideias Republicanas em Portugal*. Lisbon: Nova Livraria Internacional.

Bragança, D. Luís de, trans. 1956. *Hamlet—Drama em Cinco Actos*. Porto: Lello & Irmão.

Breitenberg, Mark. 1996. *Anxious Masculinity in Early Modern England*. Cambridge: Cambridge University Press.

Bristol, Michael. 1990. *Shakespeare's America, America's Shakespeare*. New York: Routledge.

Brontë, Charlotte. 1973. *Jane Eyre*. Ed. Margaret Smith. London: Oxford University Press.

Brook, Peter. 1991. Preface to *Shakespeare Our Contemporary*, by Jan Kott. London: Routledge.

Bunaciu, Doina, Veronica Focsaneanu, and Anca Tanasescu. 1995. *Limba engleza*. Bucharest: Editura didactica si pedagogica.

Burt, Ramsay. 1995. *The Male Dancer: Bodies, Spectacle, Sexualities*. London: Routledge.

Burt, Richard. 1998. *Unspeakable Shaxxxspeares: Queer Theory and American Kiddie Culture*. New York: St. Martin's Press.

Bütow, Wilfried, and Gottfried Wittig. 1986. *Unterrichtshilfen: Deutsch, Literatur, Klasse 9*. Berlin: Volk und Wissen.

Bütz, Michael R. 1997. *Chaos and Complexity*. Washington, D.C.: Taylor and Francis.

Campion, Thomas. 1909. *Works*. Ed. Percival Vivan. Oxford: Clarendon Press.

Cartelli, Thomas. 1999. "Shakespeare, 1916: *Caliban by the Yellow Sands* and the New Dramas of Democracy." In *Repositioning Shakespeare: National Formations, Postcolonial Appropriations*, 63–83. London: Routledge.

Catroga, Fernando. 2000. *O Republicanismo em Portugal*. Lisbon: Editorial Notícias.

Chaffurin, Louis, and Mark A. Delany, eds. 1929. Introduction to *Tales from Shakespeare*, by Charles and Mary Lamb. Paris: Croville-Morant.

Chapman, George. 1968. *All Fools*. Ed. Frank Manley. London: Edward Arnold.

Clermont, Charles. 1909. *Les Auteurs du Brevet Supérieur*. Paris: Hachette.

Colmer, Francis. 1916. *Shakespeare in Time of War: Excerpts from the Plays Arranged with Topical Allusion*. London: Smith, Elder & Co.

Crystal, David. 1998. "Verbing." *Around the Globe: The Magazine of the International Shakespeare Globe Centre* (summer): 20–21.

Cumber, John. 1979. *The Two Merry Milkmaids* (1620). Ed. G. Harold Metz. New York: Garland Publishing Inc.

Curtius, Ernst Robert. 1961. *Europäische Literatur und lateinisches Mittelalter*. 3d ed. Berne: Francke.

Cuvelier, Eliane. 1995. "Shakespeare, Voltaire, and French Taste." In *Shakespeare and France*, ed. Holger Klein and Jean-Marie Maguin, 25–47. Shakespeare Yearbook, vol. 5. Lewiston, N.Y.: Edwin Mellen.

Daileader, Celia. 1998. *Eroticism on the Renaissance Stage: Transcendence, Desire, and the Limits of the Visible*. Cambridge: Cambridge University Press.

Dávidházi, Péter. 1998. *The Romantic Cult of Shakespeare*. London: Macmillan.

Dekker, Thomas. 1953–68. *The Dramatic Works*. Ed. Fredson Bowers. Cambridge: Cambridge University Press.

Delabbastita, Dirk, and Lieven D'Hulst, eds. 1993. *European Shakespeares: Translating Shakespeare in the Romantic Age*. Amsterdam: John Benjamins.

Desmond, Jane. 1998. "Embodying Difference: Issues in Dance and Cultural Studies." In *The Routledge Dance Studies Reader*, ed. Alexandra Carter, 154–62. London: Routledge.

———, ed. 1997. *Meaning into Motion. New Cultural Studies of Dance*. Durham, N.C.: Duke University Press.

Dobson, Michael. 1992. *The Making of the National Poet: Shakespeare, Adaptation and Authorship, 1660–1769*. Oxford: Clarendon Press.

Downs, Harold, ed. 1934. *Theatre and Stage: A Modern Guide to the Performance of All Classes of Amateur Dramatic, Operatic, and Theatrical Work*. 2 vols. London: Pitman.

Durian, Hans. 1937. *Jocza Savits und die Münchener Shakespeare-Bühne (Die Schaubühne*, nr. 19). Emsdetten: Verlag H. & J. Lechte.

Edwards, Philip. 1989. "Notes." *The New Cambridge Shakespeare: Hamlet, Prince of Denmark*, ed. Philip Edwards, 74–243. Cambridge: Cambridge University Press.

Ellis-Fermor, Una. 1980. *Shakespeare's Drama*. Ed. Kenneth Muir. London: Methuen.

Engler, Balz. 1991. "Shakespeare in the Trenches." *Shakespeare Survey* 44: 105–11.

———. 1996. "Shakespeare's Passports." In *International Shakespeares: The Tragedies*. Edited by Patricia Kennan and Mariangela Tempera, 11–16. Bologna: Clueb.

Fenard, E. M. 1886. *Contes tirés de Shakespeare ou Pièces de Shakespeare Racontées en prose*. Paris: Garnier.

Fiedler, Leslie, and H. A. Baker, eds. 1979. *English Literature: Opening up the Canon*. Selected Papers from the English Institute. Baltimore: Johns Hopkins University Press.

Fineman, Joel. 1986. *Shakespeare's Perjured Eye: The Invention of Poetic Subjectivity in The Sonnets*. Berkeley and Los Angeles: University of California Press.

———. 1989. "Shakespeare's Ear." *Representations* 28: 6–13.

Fischer-Lichte, Erika, and Christoph Wulf, eds. 2001. *Theorien des Performativen. Paragrana* 10, no. 1.

Fischer-Lichte, Erika, and Harald Xander, eds. 1993. *Welttheater, Nationaltheater, Lokaltheater?—Europäisches Theater am Ende des 20. Jahrhunderts*. Tübingen: Francke Verlag.

Fitzmaurice-Kelly, James. 1916. *Cervantes and Shakespeare*. First Annual Master-Mind Lecture Henriette Hertz Trust, 16 May 1916. *Proceedings of the Bristish Academy* 8. London: Oxford University Press for the British Academy.

Florio, John. 1969. *His firste Fruites* (1578). Facsimile ed. Amsterdam: Da Capo Press.

Forgacs David. 1996. "Cultural Consumption, 1940s to 1990s." *Italian Cultural Studies. An Introduction*. Edited by David Forgacs and Robert Lumley. Oxford: Oxford University Press.

Foster, Susan L. 1996. *Choreography and Narrative: Ballet's Staging of Story and Desire*. Bloomington: Indiana University Press.

Fracci, Carla. 2001. "Vi racconto di quando fui la prima volta Giulietta." In *Romeo e Giulietta* (Theatre program, ballet choreographed by John Cranko), 19–26. Rome: Teatro dell'Opera di Roma.

Frye, Northrop. 1986. "Hamlet." In *Northrop Frye on Shakespeare*, ed. Robert Sandler, 82–100. New Haven: Yale University Press.

Gadamer, Hans-Georg. 1975. *Wahrheit und Methode: Grundzüge einer historischen Hermeneutik*. 4th ed. Tübingen: Mohr.

Garafola Lynn, ed. 1997. *Rethinking the Sylph: New Perspectives on the Romantic Ballet*. Middletown, Conn.: Wesleyan University Press.

Gardner, Howard. 1973. *The Arts and Human Development*. New York: Wiley.

———. 1982. *Art, Mind and Brain: A Cognitive Approach to Creativity*. New York: Basic Books.

———. 1983. *Frames of Mind: The Theory of Multiple Intelligences*. London: Fontana.

———. 1999. *Intelligence Reframed: Multiple Intelligences for the Twenty-first Century*. New York: Basic Books.

Gautier, Théophile. 1835. *Mlle. de Maupin*. Paris.

Gazzettino Sera. 1958 (26–27 July). Venice.

Gervinus, G. G. 1903. *Shakespeare Commentaries* (1849). Trans. F. E. Bunnètt. 6th ed. London: John Murray.

Gibińska, Marta. 1999. *Polish Poets Read Shakespeare: Refashioning of the Tradition*. Cracow: Tow. Nauk. Societas Vistulana.

Gillies, John. 1994. *Shakespeare and the Geography of Difference*. Cambridge: Cambridge University Press.

Glaap, Albert Rainer. 1997. "Muss es denn immer *Macbeth* sein?" *Der fremdsprachliche Unterricht* 31: 13–15.

Gocke, Rainer, and Angela Stock. 1999. *William Shakespeare: Macbeth. Teachers' Book*. Paderborn: Schöningh.

Goellner, Ellen, and Jacqueline Shea Murphy, eds. 1994. *Bodies of the Text: Dance as Theory, Literature as Dance*. New Brunswick, N.J.: Rutgers University Press.

Goethe, Johann Wolfgang von. 1963. "Shakespeare und kein Ende." In *Goethes Werke*. Hamburger Ausgabe. 5th ed. Hamburg: Christian Wegner.

———. 1986. *Essays on Art and Literature*. Ed. John Carey. Trans. Ellen von Nardroff. New York: Suhrkamp.

Gollancz, Israel, ed. 1916. *A Book of Homage to Shakespeare*. London: Oxford University Press.

Grau, Andrée, and Stephanie Jordan, eds. 2000. *Europe Dancing. Perspectives on Theatre Dance and Cultural Identity*. London: Routledge.

de Grazia, Margreta. 1991. *Shakespeare Verbatim*. Oxford: Clarendon Press.

Greenblatt, Stephen. 1984. *Renaissance Self-fashioning*. Chicago: University of Chicago Press.

———. 1988. *Shakespearean Negotiations: The Circulation of Social Energy in Renaissance England*. Oxford: Clarendon Press.

Gundle, Stephen. 1996. "Fame, Fashion, and Style: The Italian Star System." In *Italian Cultural Studies, an Introduction*, ed. David Forgacs and Robert Lumley, 309–26. Oxford: Oxford University Press.

Guntner, J. Lawrence. 1998. Introduction to *Redefining Shakespeare:. Literary Theory and Theater Practice in the German Democratic Republic*, ed. J. Lawrence Guntner and Andrew M. McLean, 29–57. Newark: University of Delaware Press.

Habicht, Werner. 1994a. "Romanticism, Antiromanticism, and the German Shakespeare Tradition." In *Shakespeare and Cultural Traditions*, ed. Tesuo Kishi, Roger Pringle, and Stanley Wells, 243–52. Newark: University of Delaware Press.

———. 1994b. *Shakespeare and the German Imagination*. International Shakespeare Association, Occasional Paper No. 5. Hertford: International Shakespeare Association.

———. 2001. "Shakespeare Celebrations in Times of War." *Shakespeare Quarterly* 52: 441–55.

Haines, C. M. 1925. *Shakespeare in France: Criticism from Voltaire to Victor Hugo*. London: Oxford University Press.

Halter, Ernst, Buschi Luginbühl, and Ernst Scagnet, eds. 2000. *Volkstheater in der Schweiz und im Fürstentum Liechtenstein*. Zurich: Offizin.

Hamburger, Maik. 1998. "Shakespeare on the Stage of the German Democratic Republic." In Wilhelm Hortmann, *Shakespeare on the German Stage: the Twentieth Century*, 369–434. Cambridge: Cambridge University Press.

Hanna, Judith Lynne. 1988. *Dance, Sex and Gender: Signs of Identity, Dominance, Defiance, and Desire*. Chicago: University of Chicago Press.

Harland, John et al., eds. 2000. *Arts Education in Secondary School: Effects*

and Effectiveness. Slough: National Foundation for Educational Research.
Harth, Dietrich. 1988. "Zerrissenheit: Der deutsche Idealismus und die Suche nach kultureller Identität." In *Kultur und Gedächtnis,* ed. Jan Assmann and Tonio Hölscher, 220–40. Frankfurt. a.M.: Suhrkamp.
Hattaway, Michael, Boika Sokolova, and Derek Roper, eds. 1994. *Shakespeare in the New Europe.* Sheffield: Sheffield Academic Press.
Hawkes, Terence. 1992. *Meaning by Shakespeare.* London: Routledge.
Hazlitt, William. 1924. *Lectures on the English Poets.* London: Oxford University Press.
Helgerson, Richard. 1992. *Forms of Nationhood: The Elizabethan Writing of England.* Chicago: University of Chicago Press.
Henning, Hans. 1980. "Rechenschaftsbericht 1978/1979." *Shakespeare Jahrbuch* 116: 176–91.
———. 1981. "Rechenschaftsbericht 1979/198." *Shakespeare Jahrbuch* 117: 207–14.
Hodgdon, Barbara. 1998. *The Shakespeare Trade: Performances and Appropriations.* Philadelphia: University of Pennsylvania Press.
Hoenselaars, A. J. 1994. "Mapping Shakespeare's Europe." In *Reclamations of Shakespeare,* ed. A. J. Hoenselaars, 223–48. Studies in Literature 15. Amsterdam: Rodopi.
Höfele, Andreas. 2001. "Millennial Shakespeare: Profile of a Cultural Megastar." *European Studies* 16: 183–205.
Hoffmann, Hans-Joachim. 1990. "Shakespeare und unsere Traditionen." *Shakespeare Jahrbuch* 126: 7–12.
Holderness, Graham, and Andrew Murphy. 1997. "Shakespeare's England: Britain's Shakespeare." In *Shakespeare and National Culture,* ed. John J. Joughin, 19–41. Manchester: Manchester University Press.
Homem, Rui Carvalho. 2001. "Of Negroes, Jews and Kings: On a Nineteenth-Century Royal Translator." *The Translator* 7 (April): 19–42.
Hortmann, Wilhelm, 1998. *Shakespeare on the German Stage: The Twentieth Century.* Cambridge: Cambridge University Press.
———. 2001. *Shakespeare und das deutsche Theater im XX. Jahrhundert.* Berlin: Henschel Verlag.
Ingarden, Roman. 1965. *Das literarische Kunstwerk. Mit einem Anhang von den Funktionen der Sprache im Theaterschauspiel.* Tübingen: Max Niemeyer Verlag.
Isaac, Megan Lynn. 2000. *Heirs to Shakespeare: Reinventing the Bard in Young Adult Literature.* Portsmouth, N.H.: Heinemann/Boynton-Cook.
Iser, Wolfgang. 1984. *Der Akt des Lesens.* Munich: Wilhelm Fink Verlag.
Jenkins, Harold, ed. 1982. *William Shakespeare: Hamlet.* London: Methuen.
Jeschke, Claudia. 1991. "From Ballet de Cour to Ballet en Action: The Transformation of Dance Aesthetics and Performance at the End of the Seventeenth and Beginning of the Eighteenth Centuries." *Theatre History Studies* 11: 107–22.
Jeudy, Raoul. 1885. *Contes tirés de Shakspeare: Contes choisis.* Paris: Jules Delalain et fils.

Johnson, Samuel. 1986. "Hamlet." *Selections from Johnson on Shakespeare*, ed. Bertrand H. Bronson and Jean M. O'Meara, 318–45. New Haven: Yale University Press.

Jones, A. H. 1916. *Shakespeare and Germany (Written during the Battle of Verdun)*. London: Chiswick Press.

Jonson, Ben. [1916] 1946. "To the memory of my beloued, The AVTHOR MR. WILLIAM SHAKESPEARE and what he hath left vs." In *Shakespeare Criticism: A Selection: 1623–1840*, ed. D. Nichol Smith, 3–5. London: Oxford University Press.

———. 1925–52. *Works*. Ed. C. H. Herford and P. and E. Simpson. Oxford: Clarendon Press.

Joughin, John J., ed. 1997a. *Shakespeare and National Culture*. Manchester: Manchester University Press.

———. 1997b. "Shakespeare, National Culture and the Lure of Transnationalism." In *Shakespeare and National Culture*, ed. John J. Joughin, 269–94. Manchester: Manchester University Press.

Juliá Martínez, Eduardo. 1918. *Shakespeare en España. Traducciones, imitaciones e influencia de las obras de Shakespeare en la literatura española*. Madrid: Tipografía de la Revista de Archivos, Bibliotecas y Museos.

Kahn, Coppélia. 2001. "Remembering Shakespeare Imperially: The 1916 Tercentenary." *Shakespeare Quarterly* 52: 456–78.

Kauffman, Stuart. 1996. *At Home in the Universe: The Search for Laws of Self-Organisation and Complexity*. Harmondsworth: Penguin.

Keegan, John. 1998. *The First World War*. London: Hutchinson.

Kelley, Catriona, and David Shepherd, eds. 1998. *Russian Cultural Studies, An Introduction*. Oxford: Oxford University Press.

Kennedy, Dennis, ed. 1993a. *Foreign Shakespeare: Contemporary Performance*. Cambridge: Cambridge University Press.

———. 1993b. *Looking at Shakespeare: A Visual History of Twentieth-Century Performance*. Cambridge: Cambridge University Press.

King, Rosalind. 1993. *The TUSCS Report: Theatres, Universities and Schools Conference on Shakespeare*. London: Times Supplements.

Klotz, Günther. 1980. "Die Shakespeare-Tage 1979." *Shakespeare Jahrbuch* 116: 182–91.

———. 1987. "Die Shakespeare-Tage 1986." *Shakespeare Jahrbuch* 123: 213–23.

———. 1990. "Die Shakespeare-Tage 1989." *Shakespeare Jahrbuch* 126: 229–37.

———. 1992. "Die Shakespeare-Tage 1991." *Shakespeare Jahrbuch* 128: 206–11.

Kott, Jan. 1991. *Shakespeare Our Contemporary*. Trans. Boleslaw Taborski. London: Routledge.

Kotte, Andreas. 1994. "Theater der Region, Theater Europas." In *Theater der Region, Theater Europas—2. Kongress der Gesellschaft für Theaterwissenschaft*, ed. Andreas Kotte, 11–24. Berne: Editions Theaterkultur Verlag.

Kozintsev, Grigori. 1977. *King Lear: The Space of Tragedy*. Trans. Mary Mackintosh. London: Heinemann Educational Books.

Küpper, Joachim. 1997. "Kanon als Historiographie: Überlegungen im Anschluss an Nietzsches *Unzeitgemässe Betrachtungen*, zweites Stück." In *Kanon und Theorie*, ed. Maria Moog-Grünewald, 41–64. Heidelberg: Winter.

Küpper, Reiner. 1982. *Shakespeare im Unterricht*. Würzburg: Königshausen und Neumann.

Lamb, Charles. 1842. *Le Mémorial de Shakespeare ou Contes shakespeariens*. Paris: Baudry.

———. 1914. *Les Contes de Shakespeare*. Trans. Téodor de Wyzewa. Paris: Laurens.

Lamb, Charles, and Mary Lamb. 1929. *Tales from Shakespeare*. Ed. Louis Chaffurin and Mark A. Delany. Paris: Croville-Morant.

———. *Letters of Charles and Mary Lamb*. 1935. Ed. E. V. Lucas. London: Dent.

Larson, K. E. 1989. "The Shakespeare Canon in France, Germany, and England, 1700–1776." *Michigan Germanic Studies* 15: 114–35.

Lecercle, J.-J. 1999. "The Münchausen Effect: (Why) Do We Need a Canon?" *European Journal of English Studies* 1: 86–100.

Ledebur, Ruth Freifrau von. 1974. *Deutsche Shakespeare-Rezeption seit 1945*. Frankfurt a.M.: Athenaion.

Levine, Linda. 1994. *Men in Women's Clothing. Anti-Theatricality and Effeminization, 1579–1642*. Cambridge: Cambridge University Press.

LeWinter, Oswald, ed. 1963. *Shakespeare in Europe*. Cleveland: Meridian.

Limon, Jerzy. 1985. *Gentlemen of a Company: English Players in Central and Eastern Europe*. Cambridge: Cambridge University Press.

Locatelli, Angela. 1999. "Shakespeare in Italian Romanticism: Literary Querelles, Translations, and Interpretations." In *Shakespeare and Italy*, ed. Holger Klein and Michele Marrapodi, 19–37. Shakespeare Yearbook, vol. 10. Lewiston, N.Y.: Edwin Mellen.

Lockyer, Margaret. 1989. "Shakespeare in Germany: Active Approaches." *Shakespeare and Schools* 10 (autumn): 6.

Loomba, Anja, and Martin Orkin, eds. 1998. *Post-Colonial Shakespeares*. London: Routledge.

Lubrich, Oliver. 2001. *Shakespeares Selbstdekonstruktion*. Würzburg: Königshausen & Neumann.

Mackail, J. W. 1916. *Shakespeare after Three Hundred Years*. The British Academy Annual Shakespeare Lecture 1916. London: Oxford University Press.

Mackintosh, Mary. 1977. Translator's introduction to *King Lear: The Space of Tragedy*, by Grigori Kozintsev. London: Heinemann Educational Books.

Madariaga, Salvador de. 1916. "El monólogo de Hamlet." *España* 2, no. 84: 6–7.

Margolies, David. 1992. *Monsters of the Deep: Social Dissolution in Shakespeare's Tragedies*. Manchester: Manchester University Press.

Marrapodi, Michele. 1993. *Shakespeare's Italy*. Manchester: Manchester University Press.

Marston, John. 1968. *The Dutch Courtesan.* Ed. Peter Davison. Edinburgh: Oliver and Boyd.

Martin, Mircea. 2001. "Harold Bloom—Canonizatorul si canonadele sale." *Caietele Echnox—Postcolonialism si Postcomunism.* Cluj: Dacia.

Martinelli, Alberto, Antonio M. Chiesi, and Sonia Stefanizzi. 1995. *Recent Social Trends in Italy, 1960–1995.* Montreal: McGill-Queen's University Press.

Massinger, Philip. 1976. *The Plays and Poems.* Ed. Philip Edwards and Colin Gibson. Oxford: Clarendon Press.

McLuskie, Kathleen. 1985. "The Patriarchal Bard: Feminist Criticism and Shakespeare: *King Lear* and *Measure for Measure.*" In *Political Shakespeare: New Essays in Cultural Materialism,* ed. Jonathan Dollimore and Alan Sinfield, 88–108. Manchester: Manchester University Press.

Melchiori, Giorgio. 1994. *Shakespeare, genesi e struttura delle opere.* Bari: Laterza, 1994.

Mesquita, Filomena. "Royal and Bourgeois Translators: Two Late-Nineteenth-Century Portuguese Readings of *The Merchant of Venice.*" In *Four Hundred Years of Shakespeare in Europe,* ed. A. Luis Pujante and Ton Hoenselaars, 145–60. Newark: University of Delaware Press, 2003.

Meyer, Meinert. 1990. "Macbeth oder McDonald's? Zur funktionalen Behandlung von Literatur und Ökonomie im weiterführenden Fremdsprachenunterricht." In *Kommunikativ-funktional orientierter Fremdsprachenunterricht: Dritte internationale Konferenz an der Martin-Luther-Universität Halle vom 21. bis 23. November 1990,* ed. Norbert Lademann and Gabriele Wendt, 554–59. Berlin: Aufbau.

Milanovič, Vujadin. 1996. "On Translating Shakespeare in the Balkans." Paper presented at the Twenty-Seventh International Shakespeare Conference, 18–23 August, Stratford-upon-Avon.

Mills, Sara. 1997. *Discourse.* London: Routledge.

Ministerium für Schule und Weiterbildung, Wissenschaft und Forschung des Landes Nordrhein-Westfalen, ed. 1999. *Richtlinien und Lehrpläne für die Sekundarstufe II—Gymnasium/Gesamtschule. Englisch.* Düsseldorf.

Ministerrat der Deutschen Demokratischen Republik. Ministerium für Volksbildung, ed. 1987. *Lehrplan für Deutsche Sprache und Literatur Klassen 8 bis 10.* Berlin: Volk und Wissen.

Miranda y Marrón, Manuel. 1904. *Cervantes y Shakespeare no murieron en el mismo día.* Mexico: El Tiempo.

Morozov, Mikhail. 1947. *Shakespeare on the Soviet Stage.* Trans. Daiv Magarshack. London: Soviet News.

Morse, Ruth. 1991. *Truth and Convention in the Middle Ages: Rhetoric, Reality, and Representation.* Cambridge: Cambridge University Press.

Mosner, Bärbel. 2000. *Das Leser-Tagebuch im Englischunterricht am Beispiel von Shakespeares Romeo and Juliet: Zum didaktischen Potential eines handlungsorientierten und hermeneutischen Lernverfahrens.* Frankfurt a.M.: Peter Lang.

Muir, Kenneth, and Samuel Schoenbaum, eds. 1971. *A New Companion to Shakespeare Studies.* Cambridge: Cambridge University Press.

Munday, Anthony. 1605. *The Triumphes of Re-United Britania*. London: W. Jaggard.

Németh, G. Béla. 1976. "A jozefinista illúzió fölvillanása 49 után: A Pesti Napló kezdeti szakasza." In *Létharc és nemzetiség: Irodalom- és művelődéstörténeti tanulmányok*, 414–44. Budapest: Magvető.

———. 1996. "Valahogy így volt." In *Emlékek, eszmék, emberek: Esszék*, 5–21. Budapest: Magyar Írószövetség és Belvárosi Könyvkiadó.

Nowottny, Winifred. 1962. *The Language Poets Use*. London: Athlone Press.

Oliveira, Lopes. 1947. *História da República Portuguesa. A Propaganda na Monarquia Constitucional*. Lisbon: Editorial Inquérito.

Orgel, Stephen. 1996. *Impersonations: The Performance of Gender in Shakespeare's England*. Cambridge: Cambridge University Press.

Ortega y Gasset, José. 1961. "Vieja y nueva política." In *Obras Completas*, vol. 1, 5th ed. Madrid: Revista de Occidente.

Ortigão, Ramalho. 1926. "'A situação política'—February 1877." In *As Farpas*. Lisbon: Empresa Literária Fulminense.

———. 1943–46. *Farpas Esquecidas*. Lisbon: Livraria Clássica.

Parker, Patricia. 1996. *Shakespeare from the Margin*. Chicago: Chicago University Press.

Pasternak, Boris. 1961. "Lyudi i polozheniya." *Novy mir* 1: 215.

Patterson, Annabel. 1996. "'All is True': Negotiating the Past in *Henry VIII*." In *Elizabethan Matter: Essays in Honour of S. Schoenbaum*, ed. R. B. Parker and S. P. Litner. Newark: University of Delaware Press.

Pêcheux, Michel. 1982. *Language, Semantics and Ideology*. Basingstoke: Macmillan.

Pereira, António Manuel. N.d. *Organização Política e administrativa de Portugal desde 1820*. Porto: Livraria Fernando Machado e Cª.

Perrin, J. B. 1783. *Contes Moraux, amusants et instructifs, à l'usage de la jeunesse tirés des Tragédies de Shakespeare*. London: by subscription.

Pfister, Manfred. 1988. *The Theory and Analysis of Drama*. Trans. John Halliday. Cambridge: Cambridge University Press.

———. 1992. "Hamlet und der deutsche Geist." *Shakespeare Jahrbuch (West)*: 13–38.

———. 1994. "Hamlets Made in Germany, East and West." In *Shakespeare in the New Europe*, ed. Michael Hattaway, Boika Sokolova, and Derek Roper, 76–91. Sheffield: Sheffield Academic Press.

———. 2001. "*Performance*/Performativität." In *Metzler Lexikon Literatur- und Kulturtheorie*, ed. Erika Fischer-Lichte and Christoph Wulf. 2d. ed.

Pinto, António José da Silva. 1882. "O *Hamlet* e a régia tradução." In *Combates e Críticas*. Porto: Tipografia António José Teixeira.

Poel, William. 1929. *Monthly Letters*. London: T.W. Laurie.

Price, Lawrence Marsden. 1953. *English Literature in Germany*. Berkeley and Los Angeles: University of California Press.

The Prince of Wales. 1991. *Shakespeare Birthday Lecture*. Birmingham: Birmingham University Press.

Prokofiev, Serjei. [1959?]. *Autobiography, Articles Reminiscences*. Compiled, edited and notes by S. Shlifstein. Translated by R. Prokofieva. Moscow: Foreign Languages Publishing House.

Pujante, A. Luis, and Ton Hoenselaars, eds. 2003. *Four Hundred Years of Shakespeare in Europe.* Newark: University of Delaware Press.

Puttnam, David. 2000. *All Our Futures: Creativity, Culture and Education: Report of the National Advisory Committee on Creative and Cultural Education.* London: Department for Education and Employment.

Real Decreto, 22 April 1914. *Gaceta de Madrid,* 23 April 1914. 175–76.

Real Decreto, 29 March 1915. *Gaceta de Madrid,* 30 March 1915. 936.

Real Decreto, 30 January 1916. *Gaceta de Madrid,* 31 January 1916. 234.

Redsell, Sandra. 1994. "Unser Shakespeare." *Shakespeare and Schools* 23 (spring): 6.

Rendle, Adrian. 1968. *Everyman and His Theatre: A Study of the Purpose and Function of the Amateur Theatre Today.* London: P. Hern.

Riehl, Joseph. 1980. *Charles Lamb's Children's Literature.* Salzburg: Institut für Anglistik.

Rosenberg, Marvin. 1961. *The Masks of Othello: The Search for the Identity of Othello, Iago and Desdemona by three Centuries of Actors and Critics.* Berkeley and Los Angeles: University of California Press.

———. 1972. *The Masks of King Lear.* Berkeley and Los Angeles: University of California Press.

———. 1978. *The Masks of Macbeth.* Berkeley and Los Angeles: University of California Press.

———. 1992. *The Masks of Hamlet.* Newark: University of Delaware Press.

Różewicz, Tadeusz. 1982. *Conversation with the Prince and Other Poems.* Introduced and translated by Adam Czerniawski. London: Anvil Press Poetry.

Ruppert y Ujaravi, Ricardo. 1920. *Shakespeare en España. Traducciones, imitaciones e influencia de las obras de Shakespeare en la literatura española.* Madrid: Tipografía de la Revista de Archivos, Bibliotecas y Museos.

Savits, Jocza. 1908. *Von der Absicht des Dramas: Dramaturgische Betrachtungen über die Reform der Szene, namentlich in Hinsicht auf die Shakespearebühne in München.* Munich: Etzold & Co.

———. 1917. *Shakespeare und die Bühne des Dramas: Erfahrungen und Betrachtungen von Jocza Savits.* Bonn: Verlag Friedrich Cohen.

Schabert, Ina, ed. 2000 *Shakespeare-Handbuch. Die Zeit—Der Mensch—Das Werk.* 4th ed. Stuttgart: Kröner.

Schläpfer, Beat. 1992. *Sprechtheater in der Schweiz.* Zurich: Pro Helvetia.

Schläpfer, Robert, Jürg Gutzwiler, and Beat Schmid. 1991. *Das Spannungsfeld zwischen Mundart und Standardsprache in der deutschen Schweiz.* Aarau: Sauerländer.

Schlegel. Friedrich von. 1859. *Lectures on the History of Literature, Ancient and Modern: From the German of Frederick Schlegel, Now First Completely Translated, and Accompanied by a General Index.* London: H. G. Bohn.

Schlösser, Anselm. 1984. "Über das Herangehen an *Hamlet.*" *Shakespeare Jahrbuch* 120: 103–12.

Schmid, Christian. 2000. "Von der Brauchbarkeit des Dialekts." In *Volks-*

theater in der Schweiz und im Fürstentum Liechtenstein, ed. Ernst Halter, Buschi Luginbühl, and Ernst Scagnet, 37–40. Zurich: Offizin.

Schrader, Willi. 1980. "Ergebnisse und neue Fragen." *Shakespeare Jahrbuch* 116: 69–74.

Sell, Roger D. 1992. "Teaching Shakespeare on Literary Pragmatic Principles." In *Literary Pedagogics after Deconstruction,* ed. Per Serrislev Petersen, 9–25. Aarhus: University Press.

Serpieri, Alessandro. 1980. *Amleto.* Milan: Feltrinelli (revised ed., 1997. Venice: Marsilio).

———. 1989. *Tito Andronico.* Milan: Garzanti.

———. 1997. *Il primo Amleto (Hamlet Q1).* Venice: Marsilio.

———. 2001. *Il racconto d'inverno,* in *I drammi romanzeschi.* Venice: Marsilio.

Serrão, Joaquim Veríssimo. 1995. *História de Portugal.* Lisbon: Editorial Verbo. IX.

Shakespeare, William. 1963. *A Midsummer Night's Dream.* Ed. Wolfgang Clemen. London: New English Library Ltd.

———. 1980. *Romeo and Juliet.* Ed. Brian Gibbons. London: Arden

———. 1986. *The Complete Works.* Ed. Stanley Wells and Gary Taylor. Oxford: Clarendon Press.

———. 1997. *The Norton Shakespeare.* Ed Stephen Greenblatt. New York: W.W. Norton and Company.

———. 1998. *Cymbeline.* Ed. Roger Warren. Oxford: Clarendon Press.

Shakespeare May Day 1916. 1916. London: Geo W. Jones.

Shakespeare Memorial. The Plea for a National Theatre. 1916. London: Daily Chronicle.

Shakespeare Tercentenary Observance in the Schools and Other Institutions. 1916. London: Geo W. Jones.

Simond, Charles. 1887. *Contes de Shakespeare Racontés aux Jeunes Gens.* Paris: H. Lecène et H. Oudin.

Soares, D. G. Nogueira. 1883. *Considerações sobre o Presente e o Futuro de Portugal.* Lisbon: Tipografia Universal.

Sohawon, Farzanah. 2001. "Les Tales from Shakespeare et la moralité: une étude historique et littéraire suivie d'une étude bibliographique et éditoriale portant sur les éditions françaises de cet ouvrage conservées par la Bibliothèque nationale de France." DEA dissertation, Université Paris 7.

Sokolova, Boika. 1994. "*The Merchant of Venice* in Bulgaria." in *Literature and Language in the Intercultural and Cultural Context: Proceedings of the Sixth International Conference on English and American Literature and Language, Kraków, 13–17 April 1993,* ed. Marta Gibińska and Zygmunt Mazur, 55–69. Kraków: Jagellonian University, Institute of English Philology.

Sorge, Thomas. 1992. "Vom Chaos des Spiels und der Ganzheitlichkeit." *Shakespeare Jahrbuch* 128: 147–56.

———. 1999. "The Sixties: Hamlet's Utopia Come True?" In *Redefining Shakespeare: Literary Theory and Theater Practice in the German Demo-*

cratic Republic, ed. J. Lawrence Guntner and Andrew M. McLean, 98–110. Newark: University of Delaware Press.

Spevack, Martin. 1973. *The Harvard Concordance to Shakespeare*. Hildesheim: Olms.

Squire, John. 1620. *Tes Irenes Trophaea*. London: Nicholas Okes.

Stříbrný, Zdeněk. 2000. *Shakespeare and Eastern Europe*. Oxford: Oxford University Press.

Taylor, Gary. 1989. *Reinventing Shakespeare: A Cultural History, from the Restoration to the Present*. New York: Weidenfeld and Nicolson.

Taylor, George. 1976. *A History of the Amateur Theatre*. London: Colin Venton.

Thadden, Rudolf von. 1991. "Aufbau nationaler Identität." In *Nationale und kulturelle Identität: Studien zur Entwicklung des kollektiven Bewulstseins in der Neuzeit*, ed. Bernhard Giesen. Frankfurt a.M.: Suhrkamp.

Thüringer Kultusministerium, ed. 1999. *Lehrplan für das Gymnasium: Englisch*. Erfurt.

The Troublesome Raigne of Iohn King of England. 1591. London: Sampson Clarke.

The True Tragedy of Richard III. 1594. London: Thomas Creede.

Turgenev, Ivan Sergeyevich. 1963. "Hamlet and Don Quijote: The Two Eternal Human Types." In *Shakespeare in Europe*, ed. Oswald LeWinter, 172–89. Cleveland: The World Publishing Company.

Ullrich, Allmut. 2000. "Ein Schulkommentar zu *Julius Caesar* im Spannungsfeld von Wissenschaftlichkeit und Kreativität. Zur innovativen Methode der *Cambridge School Shakespeare* Reihe." *Literatur in Wissenschaft und Unterricht* 33: 273–95.

Ulrici, Hermann. 1911. *Shakespeare's Dramatic Art: History and Character of Shakespeare's Plays* (1846). Trans. L. Dora Schmitz. 2 vols. London: G. Bell.

Vianu, Tudor. 1964. "Prefata." In *Shakespeare si Opera lui*. Bucharest: Editura pentru literatura universala.

Vickers, Brian, 1971. "Shakespeare's Use of Rhetoric." In *A New Companion to Shakespeare Studies*, ed. Kenneth Muir and Samuel Schoenbaum, 83–98. Cambridge: Cambridge University Press.

———. ed. 1974–81. *Shakespeare: The Critical Heritage*. 6 vols. London: Routledge & Kegan Paul.

Vilhena, Júlio. 1916. *Antes da República (Notas Autobiográficas)*. Coimbra: França e Arménio Editores.

Webster, John. 1995. *The Works*. Ed. David Gunby, David Carnegie, and Antony Hammond. Cambridge: Cambridge University Press.

Weimann, Robert. 1967. *Shakespeare und die Tradition des Volkstheaters*. Berlin: Henschelverlag.

———. 1992. "Shakespeare jenseits der Moderne. Zur Krise exemplarischen Erbens." *Shakespeare Jahrbuch* 128: 34–38.

———. 1997. "A Divided Heritage: Conflicting Appropriations of Shakespeare in (East) Germany." In *Shakespeare and National Culture*, ed. John Joughin. Manchester: Manchester University Press.

Williams, Simon. 1990. *Shakespeare on the German Stage*, vol. 1: 1586–1914. Cambridge: Cambridge University Press.

Wilson, Richard. 1992. "Introduction: Historicising New Historicism." In *New Historicism and Renaissance Drama*, ed. Richard Wilson and Richard Dutton. London: Longman.

Wittgenstein, Ludwig. 1997. *Philosophische Untersuchungen/Philosophical Investigations*. Trans. G. E. M. Anscombe. Oxford: Blackwell.

Wyler, Alfred. 1997. 5th rev. ed. *Dialekt und Hochsprache in der deutschsprachigen Schweiz*. Zurich: Pro Helvetia.

Yates, Frances. 1934. *John Florio: The Life of an Italian in Shakespeare's England*. Cambridge: Cambridge University Press.

Zadek, Peter. 1994. "Dialekt auf der Bühne." In *Peter Zadek. Das Wilde Ufer—Ein Theaterbuch*. Edited by Laszlo Kornitzer, 82–83. Cologne: Kiepenheuer & Witsch.

Contributors

HELENA AGAREZ MEDEIROS is a researcher at the department of English Studies of the University of Lisbon. She has just finished a master's thesis on the translation of Shakespeare's dramatic texts into Portuguese, with special focus on the nineteenth century. Her main field of interest is translation studies, especially translation history and the intersecting paths between literary translation and ideology.

LADINA BEZZOLA LAMBERT is a researcher and lecturer at the English department of the University of Basel, Switzerland. Her main areas of interest are Renaissance and seventeenth-century literature, rhetoric, and comparative studies, particularly the relation between literary and scientific writing. Most recently, she published a study on the poetics of early modern astronomy, *Imagining the Unimaginable* (2002). Her new project is concerned with theories of friendship and notions of identity in seventeenth-century literature.

CLARA CALVO is Reader at the University of Murcia, Spain. Her fields of interest are Shakespeare, linguistic approaches to literature, and reception studies. Her publications on Shakespeare and language (pronouns of address, politeness, and discourse analysis) include *Power Relations and Fool-Master Discourse in Shakespeare* (1991). She is also coauthor (with Jean Jacques Weber) of *The Literature Workbook* (1998) and has been responsible for the stylistics section in *The Year's Work in English Studies* since 1995.

PÉTER DÁVIDHÁZI is head of the department of Nineteenth-Century Literature at the Institute for Literary Studies of the Hungarian Academy and teaches English literature at Loránd Eötvös University, Budapest. His main research interest is the latent religious pattern of literary cults and foremost among his books is *The Romantic Cult of Shake-*

speare: Literary Reception in Anthropological Perspective (1998). He coedited two international collections of studies, *Literature and Its Cults: An Anthropological Approach* (1994) and *Shakespeare and Hungary* (1996), and published two monographs and a volume of his studies in Hungarian.

LLOYD DAVIS teaches in the School of English at the University of Queensland in Brisbane, Australia. He has written essays and books on cultural studies, Victorian and early modern literature, as well as *Guise and Disguise: Rhetoric and Characterization in the English Renaissance* (1993). He is also the editor of *Sexuality and Gender in the English Renaissance: An Annotated Edition of Contemporary Documents* (1998) and *Shakespeare Matters: History, Teaching, Performance* (2003). He currently edits *AUMLA*, the journal of the Australasian Universities' Languages and Literature Association.

MICHAEL DOBSON is professor of Renaissance Drama at the University of Surrey Roehampton, in London, and theater reviewer for *Shakespeare Survey*. His most recent publications include *The Oxford Companion to Shakespeare* (2001, with Stanley Wells as associate general editor) and *England's Elizabeth: An Afterlife in Fame and Fantasy* (2002, cowritten with Nicola Watson). He is currently working on a history of the amateur performance of Shakespeare.

BALZ ENGLER, professor of English at the University of Basel, Switzerland, has published a critical edition of *Othello* (1976), including a German prose translation, and a book on translation (*Rudolf Alexander Schröders Uebersetzungen von Shakespeares Dramen*, 1974). He is also the author of *Reading and Listening* (1982) and *Poetry and Community* (1990). He has edited volumes on community drama (*Das Festspiel*, with Georg Kreis, 1988), *Writing & Culture* (1992), and *European English Studies: Contributions towards the History of a Discipline* (with Renate Haas, 2000).

PETER HOLLAND is McMeel Family Professor of Shakespeare Studies in the department of Film, Television, and Theatre at the University of Notre Dame. From 1997 to 2002 he was director of the Shakespeare Institute, Stratford-upon-Avon, and professor of Shakespeare Studies at the University of Birmingham. His most recent book is *English Shakespeares*

(1997). He is general editor, with Stanley Wells, of the Oxford Shakespeare Topics series.

NANCY ISENBERG is a member of the department of Comparative Literature at the University of Rome III. Her interests are early modern theater, literature and ballet, and eighteenth-century Anglo-Italian connections. She has published on ballets of *Romeo and Juliet, Taming of the Shrew, Cinderella, Orlando*, and *Dracula*. Most recently she has edited *Mio caro Memmo, lettere d'amore di Giustiniana Wynne a Andrea Memmo, a Venezia 1758–60* (2003), and coedited (with Viola Papetti) *Eroine sulla scena elisabettiana* (2003).

RUSSELL JACKSON is professor of Shakespeare Studies and director of the Shakespeare Institute at the University of Birmingham. His recent publications include a translation of Theodor Fontane's reports on London Shakespeare productions in the 1850s and a study of stagings of *Romeo and Juliet* since 1947 in the New Arden series "Shakespeare at Stratford." He edited *The Cambridge Companion to Shakespeare on Film* (2000) and coedited (with Jonathan Bate) *The Oxford Illustrated History of Shakespeare on Stage* (2nd ed., 2001).

ROS KING is a senior lecturer in English at Queen Mary, University of London. She is also a theater director, dramaturg, and a musician. She combines that practical experience with research in history and textual bibliography, and in education. She is the editor of *The Works of Richard Edwards: Politics, Poetry, and Performance in Sixteenth-Century England* (2001). She is completing a book entitled *Cymbeline: Constructions of Britain*.

RUTH FREIFRAU VON LEDEBUR teaches at the University of Siegen, Germany. Her fields of interest are Shakespeare's work and Shakespeare's reception in Germany, the history of the German Shakespeare Society in the context of research, theater representation and politics, the teaching of literature, and teaching methodology. She has written numerous articles on these topics in scholarly journals. Her major publications are: *Deutsche Shakespeare-Rezeption seit 1945* (1974) and *Der Mythos vom deutschen Shakespeare: Die Deutsche Shakespeare-Gesellschaft zwischen Politik und Wissenschaft 1918–1945* (2002).

DAVID MARGOLIES is a reader in the department of English and Comparative Literature of Goldsmiths College, University of London, and lectures on Shakespeare, Renaissance literature, and popular culture. He wrote *Novel and Society in Elizabethan England* (1985) and *Monsters of the Deep: Social Dissolution in Shakespeare's Tragedies* (1992) and has published extensively on Marxist approaches to literature.

RUTH MORSE teaches Renaissance and postcolonial literature at the University of Paris–VII. She was trained as a medievalist. Among her books are *Truth and Convention in the Middle Ages: Rhetoric, Representation, and Reality* (1996) and *A. D. Hope: Selected Poems*. She has published numerous articles on Shakespeare and is currently working on the reception of Shakespeare in France.

MADALINA NICOLAESCU is full professor in the English department of the University of Bucharest, where she teaches Shakespeare as well as feminist theory. Her latest books on Shakespeare are *Meanings of Violence in Shakespeare's Plays* (2002) and *Eccentric Mappings of the English Renaissance* (1997). She has also written on earlier Protestant drama: *Reform and Propaganda in Sixteenth-Century Germany and England* (1995). Her studies on postcommunist gender identities have been collected in *Fashioning Global Identities— Romanian Women in the Post-Socialist Transition* (2001).

MANFRED PFISTER holds the chair of English Literature at the Freie Universität Berlin. He has published widely on drama and theater in general (*Das Drama*, 1977; English translation: *The Theory and Analysis of Drama*, 1988) and on Shakespeare in particular, on the English and European fin-de-siècle (*Die Nineties*, 1983; *Oscar Wilde: "The Picture of Dorian Gray,"* 1986), on travel writing (*The Fatal Gift of Beauty: The Italies of English Travellers*, 1996; *Venetian Views, Venetian Blinds*, 1999) and on literary and cultural theory (*Intertextualität*, 1985). His two most recent books are *Laurence Sterne* (2001) and *A History of English Laughter* (2002).

ALESSANDRO SERPIERI teaches English literature at the University of Florence. His main fields of interest are romantic and modern poetry, theory of drama, translation studies, and, most of all, Shakespeare. He has edited and translated many plays by Shakespeare as well as the *Sonnets,* and written essays on Shakespeare. His main publications are *T. S. Eliot: le strutture profonde* (1973), *Shakespeare: I sonetti dell'immortalità* (1975), *Otello: l'Eros negato* (1978), *Retorica e immaginario* (1986), *Nel laboratorio di Shakespeare* (1988), *On the Language of Drama* (1989), and *Polifonia shakespeariana* (2002).

ALEXANDER SHURBANOV is professor of English literature at the University of Sofia, Bulgaria, where he teaches English Renaissance literature, literary stylistics, and translation. His publications include *Renaissance Humanism and Shakespeare's Lyrical Poetry* (1980), *Between Pathos and Irony: Christopher Marlowe and the Genesis of Renaissance Drama* (1992), *The Translation of English Literature in Bulgaria* (with Vladimir Trendafilov, 2000), *Painting Shakespeare Red: An East-European Appropriation* (with Boika Sokolova, 2001), and *Poetics of the English Renaissance* (2002). He has translated into Bulgarian verse Chaucer's *The Canterbury Tales* and Milton's *Paradise Lost.*

SYLVIA ZYSSET is a doctoral student in the English Department of the University of Basel, Switzerland. She is currently finishing her bilingual (English-German) critical edition of Shakespeare's *The Two Gentlemen of Verona.* Her main fields of interest are theater and performance studies in general and, more particularly, actor-audience relationships, questions concerning gender and performance, including use of language and word games in Shakespeare's plays and the Elizabethan theater. She has written essays and articles on Shakespeare and the theater in newspapers and journals.

Index

Abusch, Alexander, 174, 176
Aders, Ruth, 155, 159, 163
Aers, Leslie, 179
Alba, Jacobo FitzJames Stuart y Falco, 17th Duke of (1878–1953), 79, 93 n. 5
Albania, 256
Alexander, Nigel, 271
Alfred the Great, King of Wessex (871–899), 45
Alighieri, Dante, 54
Allen, William, 76 n. 16
Althusser, Louis, 186
Andrews, John F., 275
Anikst, Alexander, 233, 237, 238
Ansúr, Alfredo, 68, 71–73, 75 n. 7, 76 n. 24
Arany, János, 98–107
Araquistain, Luis, 91
Arden, Mary, 40
Ariosto, Ludovico, 39
Aristotle, 259
Armas y Cárdenas, José de, 88
Arthur, Legendary King of England, 120
Assmann, Aleida, 62 n. 1, 178
Assmann, Jan, 62 n. 1
Attenborough, Michael, 119
Austen, Jane, 202
Austin, J.L., 259
Austria, 56, 155
Ávila e Bolama, Antonio José, Marques and Duke of (1806–1881), 69–70

Bader, Emil, 158, 161
Badger, Richard, 86
Baker, H. A., 53
Balan, Rada, 185
Bale, John, 190
Banes, Sally, 139 n. 7

Bantas, Andrei, 184
Barbu, Daniel, 191
Bardot, Brigitte, 132
Barisi, Mario, 159
Barker, Howard, 232
Barnet, Sylvan, 31
Barrie, J. M., 86, 88
Barton, John, 119
Bate, Jonathan, 18 n. 2, 37, 80
Bauer, Roger, 62 n. 4
Beaumont, Francis, 220, 223, 226
Beckerman, Bernard, 31
Belgium, 39
Belsey, Catherine, 191
Benjamin, Walter, 190
Benn, Gottfried, 110
Berlioz, Hector, 61
Berriman, John, 124
Blair, Tony, 40
Bloom, Harold, 12, 51–52, 188
Boccaccio, Giovanni, 36
Bode, Christoph, 59
Bogdanov, Michael, 119
Bohlmann, Joachim, 170
Bolingbroke, Henry Saint John, Lord (1688–1766), 224
Bond, Edward, 232
Booth, Edwin, 98
Borck, Caspar Wilhelm von, 49
Borghers, Alphonse, 198, 199
Böse, Maximilian, 168, 169
Bottoms, Janet, 203
Bowdler, Thomas, 196
Boyd, Michael, 119
Bradley, A. C., 86
Brando, Marlon, 132
Brecht, Bertold, 125, 170, 260
Brinzeu, Pia, 184
Bristol, Michael, 220
Britain. *See* Great Britain
Brontë, Charlotte, 195

302

INDEX

Brook, Peter, 116, 139 n. 4, 152, 195, 230–36, 237, 256
Bucius, Johannes, 24
Bulgaria, 18, 246–47, 250, 252–56
Bunaciu, Doina, 184
Burt, Richard, 53
Bütow, Wilfried, 170
Bütz, Michael R., 211

Calvo, Clara, 15
Campion, Thomas, 21–23
Capell, Edward, 273–74, 276
Car, Robert, Earl of Somerset, 21
Carl Alexander, Grand-Duke of Sachsen-Weimar-Eisenach (1818–1901), 141
Carvalho, Maria Amália Vaz de, 72, 76 n. 20
Castilho, António Feliciano de, 75 n. 1
Catherine the Great, Tsarina of Russia (1762–1796), 61
Cazamian, Louis, 184
Ceausescu, Nicolae, 191
Cervantes, Miguel de, 15, 54, 78–94
Chaffurin, Louis, 193, 202
Chagall, Marc, 139 n. 5
Chagas, Pinheiro, 75 n. 5, 76 n. 16
Chapman, George, 25
Charity, Charity, 127 n. 2
Charles V of Spain (1519–1558), 24
Charles, Prince of Wales (*1948), 167, 168, 172
Chasles, Philarète, 198
Chateaubriand, François-René de, 222
Chiesi, Antonio, 133
Christie, Agatha, 121
Clark, W.C., 276
Clarke, Thomas J., 93 n. 9
Clément, Nicolas, 223
Clontea, Petre, 184
Coleridge, Samuel Taylor, 226
Collier, Jeremy, 276
Colmer, Francis, 91
Conti, Antonio, 49
Cranko, John, 16, 129–39
Croatia, 56, 256
Crystal, David, 163
Cumber, John, 25
Curtius, Ernst, 47

Cuvelier, Eliane, 223, 224
Czechoslovakia, 130

D'Hulst, Lieven, 223
Daiches, David, 184
Dávidházi, Péter, 16, 50
Davis, Lloyd, 16–17
Day, Martin, 184
Dearing, Sir Ron, 207
de Grazia, Margareta, 11
Dekker, Thomas, 26, 254
Delany, Mark A., 193, 202
Denmark, 29, 55–57
Derungs, Ursicin G.G., 163
Dingelstedt, Franz, 50, 140, 148, 150
Dobson, Michael, 15, 122, 224
Donne, John, 269
Drake, Nathan, 223
Dresen, Adolf, 174
Dryden, John, 221, 222, 224
Ducis, Jean-François, 67, 197
Durian, Hans, 140, 148, 149, 150

East Germany, 169, 170, 173–77, 186
Edward I, King of England (1272–1307), 104
Edwards, Philip, 104, 275
Ekberg, Anita, 132
Elizabeth I, Queen of England (1558–1603), 24
Ellis-Fermor, Una, 249
Eminescu, Mihai, 182–83, 186
Empson, William, 239
England, 12, 15, 17, 22, 23, 26, 27–28, 29, 30, 32–34, 36, 37, 39–40, 41, 50, 56, 57, 58, 60, 61, 68, 78–94, 113–28, 134, 142, 224, 226, 230, 231, 239
Engler, Balz, 13, 81
Erasmus of Rotterdam, 57
Eschenburg, Johann Joachim, 49

Federal Republic of Germany. *See* West Germany
Feiligrath, Ferdinand, 90
Ferry, Jules, 201
Fiedler, Leslie, 53
Fineman, Joel, 221, 229
Fischer-Lichte, Erika, 62 n. 3
Fitzmaurice-Kelly, James, 79
Fletcher, John, 213, 220
Florio, John, 34, 58

Focsaneanu, Veronica, 184
Forgacs, David, 132
Forman, Simon, 33
Foster, Susan, 137
Foxe, John, 190
Fracci, Carla, 129, 133
France, 12, 15–16, 17, 27, 28, 29, 32, 35, 36, 39, 50, 55, 59, 79, 193, 194, 197, 199, 204, 222, 223, 224
Franz Josef, Emperor of Austria (1848–1916), 104
Freiligrath, Ferdinand, 173
Freud, Sigmund, 226
Frevert, Ute, 178
Friel, Brian, 36
Frye, Northrop, 97
Furnivall, F. J., 144

Gadamer, Hans-Georg, 58, 63 n. 6
Garafola, Lynn, 137
Gardner, Howard, 209, 210, 215
Garrick, David, 41
Gautier, Théophile, 202
Genée, Rudolph, 141, 149
German Democratic Republic. *See* East Germany
Germany, 17, 41–45, 50–51, 55–56, 79, 80–81, 84, 90, 140–51, 155, 164, 167, 168, 172, 174, 177, 179, 180, 222, 225
Gervinus, Georg Gottfried, 144, 222, 227, 228
Gianotti, Gian, 163
Gibbs, Hazel, 127
Gibson, Rex, 179, 180, 206
Gillies, John, 23
Glaap, Albert Rainer, 172
Gocke, Rainer, 172
Godwin, Mary, 196, 197, 204
Godwin, William, 196, 197, 204
Goethe, Johann Wolfgang von, 51, 54, 61–62, 80, 150, 170, 225, 226, 227
Gollancz, Sir Israel, 79, 82–83, 86, 88, 91, 93 nn. 5, 10, and 11, 94 n. 18
Gombrich, Ernst, 40
Goslicius, Laurentius, 110
Gounod, Charles, 204
Grammaticus, Saxo, 55
Granville-Barker, Harley, 140
Great Britain, 12, 13, 15, 16, 23, 25, 32–36, 55, 57, 59, 80–81, 82, 83–84, 113–28, 143, 194, 197, 205

Greece, 256
Green, Michael, 121
Greenblatt, Stephen, 54, 60, 163, 191, 275
Greene, Robert, 54, 276–77
Gundle, Stephen, 132
Guntner, J. Lawrence, 174
Gurr, Andrew, 31

Habicht, Werner, 81, 92 n. 1, 93 n. 10, 170, 177, 181, 223, 225
Haines, C.M., 224
Hall, Edward, 119, 190
Hall, Peter, 119, 234
Hamburger, Maik, 173, 174
Hanna, Judith Lynne, 137
Harland, John, 210 n. 1
Harth, Dietrich, 62 n. 1, 168
Hattaway, Mick, 18 nn. 3 and 4, 63 n. 4, 123
Hawkes, Terrence, 36, 186, 213
Hazlitt, William, 226, 227
Hegel, Georg Wilhelm Friedrich, 225
Heilbronn, Lilah, 216
Heine, Heinrich, 170
Helgerson, Richard, 57
Henning, Hans, 175, 181
Herder, Johann Gottfried, 223
Herford, Charles, 22
Hibbard, G. R., 275
Hobsbawm, Eric, 168
Hodgdon, Barbara, 53
Hoenselaars, Ton, 18 n. 3, 24
Höfele, Andreas, 127 n. 1
Hoffmann, Hans-Joachim, 177
Holderness, Graham, 84, 179
Holinshead, Raphael, 190
Holland, 32, 36
Holland, Peter, 13
Holliday, Sir Leonard, 25
Hölscher, Tonio, 62 n. 1
Homem, Rui Carvalho, 76 n. 25
Horace, 47
Hortmann, Wilhelm, 140
Howard, Jean, 276
Howard, Lady Frances, 21
Hugo, François-Victor, 197
Hugo, Victor, 197
Hungary, 16, 39, 50, 95–110, 140

INDEX

Hyde, Douglas, 93n.10
Hytner, Nicholas, 127

Ibsen, Henrik, 155
Ingarden, Roman, 99–100
Ireland, 84, 113
Isaac, Megan Lynn, 203
Isenberg, Nancy, 16
Iser, Wolfgang, 99–100
Italy, 16, 24, 32, 36, 49, 58–59, 79, 129–39, 227

Jackson, Barry, 124
Jackson, Russell, 17
James I, King of England (1603–1625), 33–34, 36, 120
Jenkins, Harold, 275
John Lackland, King of England (1199–1216), 197
Johnson, Samuel, 97, 223, 275–76
Jones, Henry Arthur, 81, 90
Jones, Sir Francis, 21
Jonson, Ben, 22, 25, 37, 54, 55, 185, 220, 223, 224, 249, 254
Joughin, John, 63n.4, 168, 179
Jowett, John, 39
Juliá Martínez, Eduardo, 93n.4
Juvenal, 55

Kahn, Coppélia, 82, 92n.1, 93nn.6 and 11, 94n.18
Karamzin, Nikolaj, 49
Kaufman, Stuart, 212
Kean, Charles, 141
Keegan, John, 83
Kennedy, Dennis, 18n.3, 140
Kermode, Frank, 276
King, Ros(alind), 15, 207
Klotz, Günther, 174–76
Knight, Wilson, 176
Knolles, Richard, 22
Köhler, Wolfgang, 100
Kohlund, Franziska, 159
Komisarjevsky, Fyodor Fyodorovich, 116
Kott, Jan, 175, 231, 234
Kozintsev, Grigori, 16, 230, 233–37
Küpper, Joachim, 63n.6, 170
Kyd, Thomas, 185

Lademann, Norbert, 168, 169
Lamb, Charles, 15, 193–204

Lamb, Mary, 15, 193–204
Larson, K. E., 62n.4
Lautenschläger, Karl, 141–42
Lavrovsky, Leonid, 130
Lecercle, J.-J., 54
Ledebur, Ruth Freifrau von, 15
Lee, Sir Sidney, 142–43
Legouis, Emile, 184
Lessing, Gotthold Ephraim, 150, 170, 223, 225
Le Tourneur, Pierre Félicien, 224
LeWinter, Oswald, 222, 224, 225, 228, 229
Limon, Jerzy, 60
Locatelli, Angela, 227
Lockeyer, Margaret, 180
Lodge, Thomas, 39
Loomba, Anja, 53
Loren, Sofia, 132
Lubrich, Oliver, 62
Lucena, Valentina de (Maria Amália Vaz de Carvalho), 72
Luís I, King of Portugal (1861–1889), 67–77
Luther, Martin, 57
Luxembourg, 39

Machiavelli, Nicoló, 57
Mackail, J. W., 81
Mackintosh, Mary, 230
Macmillan, Sir Kenneth, 136
Madariaga, Salvador de, 90
Mäde, Hans-Dieter, 174, 176
Major, John, 205
Malone, Edmund, 223, 226, 276
Margolies, David, 16
Marlowe, Christopher, 54, 56, 60, 185
Marowitz, Charles, 176
Marrapodi, Michele, 32
Marrón, Miranda y, 92n.2
Marston, John, 26
Marti, Markus, 63n.5
Martin, Mircea, 188
Martinelli, Alberto, 133
Massinger, Philip, 22, 223
Mastroianni, Marcello, 132
Maura, Antonio, 94n.18
Maxwell, J. C., 269
McDonagh, Thomas, 93n.9
McLuskie, Kathleen, 53, 123
Medeiros, Helena Agarez, 18

Melchiori, Giorgio, 134
Melo, Fontes Pereira de, 69
Mendelssohn, Felix, 147
Merry del Val, Alfonso, 94 n. 18
Mesquita, Filomena, 76 n. 25
Middleton, Thomas, 37, 38–39
Milanovic, Vujadin, 256
Milev, Geo, 247–48
Mills, Sara, 79–80
Milton, John, 91, 224
Modugno, Domenico, 132
Molière, 147
Montaigne, Michel de, 34, 55, 57
Moore, Stephen, 128 n. 2
Morin, Henri, 195
Morocco, 29
Morozov, Mikhail, 139 n. 3
Morris, William, 93 n. 5
Morse, Ruth, 16, 198
Mosner, Bärbel, 178
Muenster, Sebastian, 24
Müller, Heiner, 174, 176, 237
Munday, Anthony, 25
Müntzer, Thomas, 177
Murphy, Andrew, 84, 179
Murray, Arthur, 225
Myers, Bruce, 152, 157

Naef, Louis, 157, 163
Nashe, Thomas, 117
Németh, G. Béla, 106–7
Nicolaescu, Madalina, 17
Nicolai, Otto, 61
Nikolov, Spas, 252
Noble, Adrian, 119
Norway, 55
Nowottny, Winifred, 239, 240
Nunn, Trevor, 116, 128 n. 2
Nureyev, Rudolf, 136

Ognyanov, Lyubomir, 246, 253, 254
Ohnesorg, Benno, 44
Olivier, Sir Laurence, 116, 234
Onís, Federico de, 88
Orgel, Stephen, 22, 38, 276
Orkin, Martin, 53
Ortega y Gasset, José, 88, 94 n. 19
Ortigão, Ramalho, 76 nn. 17 and 21
Ovid, 47

Palacio Valdés, Armando, 94 n. 18
Parker, Patricia, 190

Pasternak, Boris, 233, 237, 239
Pato, Bulhão, 75 n. 6
Patten, John, 216
Patterson, 190
Pearse, Patrick H., 93 n. 9
Pêcheux, Michel, 79
Peele, John, 54
Pennington, Michael, 119
Perfall, Carl Baron von, 141–43
Pericles, 196
Perrin, J.B., 197, 200, 203
Petőfi, Sándor, 102
Petrarca, Francesco, 60
Petrov, Valeri, 241–42, 245, 248, 252–56
Pfister, Manfred, 14, 51, 61, 62 n. 3, 174, 186, 249
Pichot Amédée, 198
Pimlott, Stephen, 119
Pinero, A. W., 86–87
Pinto, Silva, 73, 76 n. 19
Piotrovsky, Andrei, 130
Pirandello, Luigi, 259
Pistoni, Mario, 138
Plancius, Petrus, 24
Plautus, 57
Plutarch, 57
Poel, William, 140, 142–43, 150
Poland, 50, 56
Ponte, Carlo, 132
Pope, Alexander, 273, 275
Popov, Alexy, 139 n. 3
Portugal, 18, 67–77
Possart, Ernst, 149–150
Presley, Elvis, 132
Price, Lawrence Marsden, 60
Prokofiev, Serjei, 129–31, 133–34, 137, 139 n. 2
Pujante, Angel Luis, 18 n. 3
Puttnam, David, 210

Racine, Jean, 54, 60, 220, 221
Radlov, Serjei, 130, 139 n. 2
Redsell, Sandra, 180
Rendle, Adrian, 128 n. 3
Riehl, Joseph, 204
Romania, 17, 50, 182, 183, 185, 186, 187, 188, 189, 191, 192
Ronsard, Pierre de, 199
Roper, Derek, 63 n. 4
Rosenberg, Marvin, 18 n. 1
Rossi, Ernesto, 67

INDEX

Rossini, Gioachino, 61
Rowe, Nicholas, 195, 275
Różewicz, Tadeusz, 109–10
Russia, 16, 17, 49, 50, 129–31

Salvini, Tommaso, 67
Savits, Jocza, 17, 140–51
Schabert, Ina, 50, 62
Scharl, Luise, 141
Schiller, Friedrich, 51, 80, 145, 170, 228
Schläpfer, Beat, 155, 163
Schlegel, August Wilhelm von, 80, 150
Schlegel, Friedrich von, 80, 226
Schlegel-Tieck (transl), 170, 237
Schlösser, Anselm, 175, 176, 181
Schmid, Christian, 163
Schneider, Hansjörg, 159
Schrader, Willi, 175
Schuhmann, Kuno, 43
Scofield, Paul, 232
Scotland, 28, 29, 34, 84, 113
Sell, Roger D., 179
Sellers, Charles, 75 n. 14, 76 n. 23
Seneca, 57
Serbia, 256
Serpieri, Alessandro, 18
Shakespeare, William:
  Plays:
    All Is True (Henry VIII), 118; *All's Well that Ends Well*, 116, 128 n. 2, 227; *Antony and Cleopatra*, 31, 104–5, 197; *As You Like It*, 39–40, 122, 202, 207, 240, 250; *Comedy of Errors*, 30, 116, 163; *Coriolanus*, 31, 62, 116, 197; *Cymbeline*, 13, 28, 30, 32–37, 197; *Hamlet*, 11, 18, 29, 38, 45, 50, 54, 55–57, 67–77, 94 n. 16, 95–110, 148, 151, 158, 163, 170, 173–76, 197, 230, 233, 234, 237, 241, 243, 244, 247–51, 262, 264–65, 266, 268, 269, 271, 272; *Henry IV*, 27, 119, 150, 197, 250; *Henry V*, 11, 18, 27, 62, 83, 84, 119, 173, 189, 190, 191, 197, 239, 254; *Henry VI*, 27–28, 150; *Julius Caesar*, 48–49, 151, 170, 172, 184, 197, 201, 207, 208, 224, 225, 240, 243, 244, 248; *King John*, 28, 33, 46; *King Lear*, 11, 16, 25, 33, 75 n. 2,
    142, 147, 148, 150, 172, 197, 208, 212–14, 230, 231, 233, 235, 236, 240, 241, 243, 244, 250, 251; *Love's Labor's Lost*, 28, 149, 240, 242, 251; *Macbeth*, 31, 38, 75 n. 2, 170, 172, 175, 178, 197, 244, 247, 250, 256, 262, 263–64, 270–71, 278; *Measure for Measure*, 38–39, 158, 163; *Merchant of Venice, The*, 29, 38, 62, 75 n. 3, 115, 124, 149, 173, 203, 251, 254, 277; *Merry Wives of Winsor, The*, 61, 163; *Midsummer Night's Dream, A*, 75 n. 1, 116, 124, 140, 147, 158, 159, 160, 163, 172, 207, 208, 251; *Much Ado About Nothing*, 27, 163, 164; *Othello*, 22, 75 nn. 1, 2, and 3, 115, 172, 197, 208, 225, 227, 250, 266; *Pericles*, 149; *Richard II*, 83, 119, 150, 197, 250, 268; *Richard III*, 37, 75 n. 3, 116, 150, 173, 197, 208, 266–67; *Romeo and Juliet*, 16, 38, 75 nn. 2 and 3, 129–39, 156, 158, 160, 161, 163, 175, 185, 207, 208, 225, 227, 228, 242, 244, 253–54, 268; *Taming of the Shrew, The*, 75 n. 3, 105–6, 161, 163, 213; *Tempest, The*, 28, 54, 62, 158, 163, 193, 201, 208; *Timon of Athens*, 197; *Titus Andronichus*, 269–70, 272, 273; *Twelfth Night*, 37, 56, 159–61, 163, 269; *Winter's Tale, The*, 28, 37, 56, 83, 121, 123, 124–27, 275–79
  The Histories: 50, 115–16, 118, 119–20
  Other works:
    The Sonnets, 46–47, 49; sonnet no. 18, 46; sonnet no. 55, 47; *Rape of Lucrece, The*, 75 n. 3; *Venus and Adonis*, 75 n. 3
Shaw, George Bernard, 32, 87
Sher, Sir Antony, 116, 126
Shurbanov, Alexander, 18
Siebold, Jörg, 168, 169
Simond, Charles, 199
Simpson, Percy, 22
Sohawan, Farzanah, 200, 201
Sokolova, Boika, 63 n. 4, 203
Sorge, Thomas, 173, 175
Soromenho, Augusto, 76 n. 18
Soviet Union, 14, 130–131, 230

Spain, 22, 24, 29, 32, 36, 50, 78–94
Spevack, Martin, 45
Squire, John, 21
Stalin, Josef, 130
Stanescu, Nichita, 182
Steevens, George, 276
Stefanizzi, Sonia, 133
Steinmann, Paul, 160, 163, 164
Stock, Angela, 172
Stoppard, Tom, 176
Stříbrný, Zdeněk, 61, 63 n. 4, 237
Switzerland, 13, 14, 56, 152

Taylor, Gary, 38, 51, 219
Taylor, George, 128 n. 3
Taylor, Pamela, 42
Tebbit, Norman, 206
Tennyson, Alfred Lord, 91
Thadden, Rudolf von, 168
Thatcher, Margaret, 206
Theobald, Lewis, 276
Tieck, Ludwig, 140, 146
Tipley, Francis, 21
Tolstoy, Leo, 228, 229
Torriano, Giovanni, 59
Tree, Herbert Beerbohm, 151
Turgenev, Ivan, 102

Ulanova, Galina, 130
Ullrich, Allmut, 179
Ulrici Hermann, 227, 228
United Kingdom. *See* Great Britain

Valera, Collaut, 84, 87
Verdi, Giuseppe, 43, 61, 204

Vianu, Tudor, 187–88
Vickers, Brian, 222, 223, 266
Visscher, Nicolas, 23
Voltaire, 197, 220, 221, 223, 224–26

Wagner, Richard, 145
Wales, 34, 36–37, 84, 113
Warburton, William, 276
Warren, Roger, 34, 35
Watson, Liz, 126
Webster, John, 26
Wehrli, Richard, 161
Weimann, Robert, 60, 158, 174, 186, 187
Wells, Stanley, 180, 181, 258
West Germany, 169, 176
Whealer, Nigel, 179
Wilder, Thornton, 118
Williams, Simon, 140
Wittgenstein, Ludwig, 100–101
Witting, Gottfried, 170
Wofford, Susanne L., 275
Wolfit, Donald, 125
Wulf, Christoph, 62 n. 3
Wyler, Alfred, 163
Wyzewa, Téodor de, 195, 199

Yates, Frances, 63 n. 7
Yeats, William Butler, 83
Yugoslavia, 14

Zapatero, Martínez, 84, 87
Zysset, Sylvia, 14